Vietnamese Evangelicals and Pentecostalism

Global Pentecostal and Charismatic Studies

Edited by

VOLUME 29

The titles published in this series are listed at *brill.com/gpcs*

Vietnamese Evangelicals and Pentecostalism

The Politics of Divine Intervention

By

Vince Le

BRILL

LEIDEN | BOSTON

Cover illustration: A young girl looking at a stream during the flood season in the Northern Highlands of Vietnam, 2013. Photo by Hachi8 (Ngô Huy Hòa).

Library of Congress Cataloging-in-Publication Data

Names: Le, Vince, author.
Title: Vietnamese Evangelicals and Pentecostalism : the politics of divine
intervention / by Vince Le.
Description: Boston : Brill, 2018. | Series: Global Pentecostal and charismatic studies,
ISSN 1876-2247 ; volume 29 | Includes bibliographical references.
Identifiers: LCCN 2018039993 | ISBN 9789004383821
Subjects: LCSH: Christianity–Vietnam. | Evangelicalism–Vietnam. | Pentecostalism–Vietnam.
Classification: LCC BR1187 .L4 2018 | DDC 275.97/082–dc23
LC record available at https://lccn.loc.gov/2018039993

Typeface for the Latin, Greek, and Cyrillic scripts: "Brill". See and download: brill.com/brill-typeface.

ISSN 1876-2247
ISBN 978-90-04-38382-1 (paper back)
ISBN 978-90-04-38383-8 (e-book)

This book is printed on acid-free paper and produced in a sustainable manner.

For
Uyên-Thư

∵

Contents

Abbreviations

C&MA	Christian and Missionary Alliance
CPV	Communist Party of Vietnam
ECVN	Evangelical Church of Vietnam
HCMC	Hồ Chí Minh City

Foreword

It is a very great pleasure to write this 'Foreword' for Vince Le. I first met Vince when I visited Regent University School of Divinity in 2013 and he provided some research support because I was taking study leave from the University of Birmingham at the time. Subsequently, when I accepted a post at Regent University, he became my Graduate Assistant (2015–2016) and I got to know him better. During his final year at Regent University, I was appointed to his dissertation committee and found myself reading his work in detail for the first time. I enjoyed reading his dissertation, as well as the lively engagement we had during his oral examination! We kept in contact after his return to Vietnam and I was pleased to learn of his interest in submitting his dissertation for publication in the *Global Pentecostal and Charismatic Studies* (GPCS) series. After seeing the manuscript find its way through the peer review process, I am delighted to be able to commend Vince's work in this Foreword.

The GPCS series is interested in charting the boundaries of Pentecostal and Charismatic movements in different parts of the world. It is especially interested in studies that break new ground by being the first to discuss a particular trajectory or manifestation. While there have been earlier studies of Evangelicalism in Vietnam, to my knowledge, this is the first sustained piece of research on Vietnamese Evangelicalism as it has been impacted by Pentecostal spiritual commitments and practices. This is significant because it changes the way in which Evangelicalism should be discussed, especially in Vietnam and quite possibly in Asia. It is popular among some academic accounts of Pentecostalism to define it over and against Evangelicalism, and this is an understandable reaction given the Reformed influence on Evangelicalism that has played out in many contexts. It has led, for example, to the cessationist debate. This Reformed influence was particularly acute in the Fundamentalist reaction to Pentecostalism in the 1920s and 1930s. As a counter, the pietistic roots of Evangelicalism are often stressed as mediated via a Wesleyan tradition and there are good reasons for such a response even today. But what this kind of study provides is a window into a different Evangelical reality. It is one that is rooted in a non-western context, which is negotiating its own theological identity and cultural relevance. This negotiation is not primarily with reference to western issues and debates, although there are clearly ongoing influences and important interactions, but with regard to its own social, economic and political context. This is really important for the study of Pentecostalism and its relationship with Evangelicalism because it shows that there is no single, universal narrative regarding Pentecostalism that can be told straightforwardly at all times and in all places. There are certain key characteristics for sure and the one that this book highlights is *divine intervention*, signalling the idea that the Holy Spirit is active as an agent empowering individuals in their everyday lives and the church's mission in the world.

This is a book that also highlights important themes in the study of the 'pentecostalization' of Evangelicalism. Fundamentally, it illuminates the relationship between the church and the world, and in particular how Evangelicalism in Vietnam negotiates its relationship between the state, the wider Vietnamese culture, as well as the global and globalizing forces of Pentecostalism. The church is always embedded in a given society and it wrestles with its ministry and mission in its own locale, even as it belongs to broader Christianity. In this study, we see all these tensions at play and the different forces of 'push and pull' are being managed by means of a Pentecostal apocalypticism that embodies a critical approach to the powers. In Vince's account, he acknowledges all of these tensions and uses an approach that highlights insights from the grassroots of the movement. This means paying attention to the role that marginalized, rural communities play, especially the role of women, where justice is pursued by means of prayer for deliverance. It means considering the quest for self-betterment among marginalized ethnic communities and the role that culture plays in the hegemony of the communist state. It means being attentive to the agency of the poor as they have adopted the prosperity gospel as a survival strategy in order to procure basic needs, which are expressed in practices associated with the informal economy. Amid all of these political, cultural and economic forces, Vietnamese Evangelicalism addresses the condition of being underprivileged by means of a theology of blessing and a spirituality of empowerment. Thus we discover the impact that Pentecostalism makes on Evangelicalism in an Asian context, which changes the boundary of knowledge in the field and makes an original academic contribution.

Finally, it is important to encourage younger scholars from Vietnam and other Asian countries to disseminate their work with academic publishers like Brill. It is never easy to obtain a publishing contract and to see the book project through to completion. The process to publication is a rigorous one, which is as it should be. So, this publication should serve as a signal that there is a desire to facilitate Pentecostal and Charismatic scholarship emerging from Asia and around the world. I am delighted that this book is published with Brill and it stands as a testament to the quality of Asian Pentecostal scholars. I look forward to reading many more books and articles by Vince Le, as well as those published by others like him, and I am very pleased he decided to start his publishing journey with the GPCS series.

Mark J. Cartledge
Co-Editor
Global Pentecostal and Charismatic Studies series
Regent University School of Divinity, USA

Preface

The development of pentecostalism among contemporary Vietnamese evangelicals, in spite of being a grassroots phenomenon in a remote corner of the earth, belongs to the vast trans-national evangelical-pentecostal network. This development itself is an example of how the global and the local, the spiritual and the material, the past and the present interact multi-directionally in a single process of identity negotiation and cultural exchange. Precisely in the enthusiastic beliefs and practices of its practitioners, the pentecostal movement possesses a grassroots knowledge that is generally left out of academic study and a particular theological perspective that, nevertheless, has the potential to enrich the overall theological discourse, at least in the case of the Vietnamese evangelical tradition.

This book evolved from my doctoral research on the contemporary development of pentecostalism within Vietnamese evangelicalism. The original study brought about an awareness of the necessity to open a more adequate dialogue on the overall Vietnamese evangelical approach to the many social and political upheavals created by colonial malaise and contesting visions for modernity during the last century. The goal of this work consists in generating a proper living context for appreciating the emerging pentecostalism among contemporary Vietnamese evangelicals. By using pentecostal spirituality and its evangelical shell to enhance life, several underprivileged Vietnamese evangelicals at the grassroots level have married the deeply local-based *meaning* dictated by the particularity of living context and the profoundly universal *truth claims* made by a religion aspiring to reach all four corners of the earth.

In the following pages I shall also seek to explicate the major guiding concepts that Vietnamese evangelicals have used in their social interaction. My approach will show a calculated attempt to include underprivileged (read: pentecostal) perspectives that are often elided in the scholarly evangelical discourse in Vietnam and elsewhere, and my purpose is to propose a paradigm shift in Vietnamese evangelical thinking. When in the future the Vietnamese evangelical tradition seeks to renew its role and mission in Vietnam, I hope my analysis will enrich that discussion; and further, I hope that my work will inspire others to offer their contributions to the revision of the Vietnamese evangelical manifesto for increasing the tradition's commitment to human solidarity and flourishing. Since I intend this book to encourage further conversation among contemporary Vietnamese evangelicals, I have included a generous number of references in the footnotes.

In the process of writing of this book, I have been appreciative of the comments, criticism, and well wishes I have received from those who have read parts or all of the manuscript at various stages of its preparation, including Professors Mark J. Cartledge, Néstor Medina, Reg Reimer, Jonathan Tran, Amos Yong, and the soon to be Dr. Enoch Charles. Special thanks are due to Danielle Stoia, Ph.D., for her superb developmental editing, and to Connie Gundry Tappy for her excellent copy-editing services.

During my years of theological formation at Regent University School of Divinity, Professors Amos Yong and Néstor Medina helped me to develop both a more critical approach toward my personal theological formation and a deeper appreciation of my own faith tradition, especially its grassroots manifestation. They and Professor Mark J. Cartledge went beyond the call of duty to offer me valuable academic guidance and helpful advice on matters related to my scholarly and professional development. Divinity professors Kimberly E. Alexander, Diane J. Chandler, Dale M. Coulter, Vinson Synan, Graham Twelftree, and Wolfgang Vondey also offered inspiration and criticism for which I am greatly indebted, while the University's library provided excellent research assistance to me.

A grant from Langham Partnership funded my study at Regent. I am grateful for the care I received from Drs. Frederick Gale, Ian Shaw, and Elaine Vaden. Dr. Donald Dawson, who recently retired from his directorships of the World Mission Initiative and the New Wilmington Mission Conference, was instrumental in my becoming a Langham Scholar.

At the Vietnamese School of Theology (Union University of California, Westminster, CA), my thanks go to Drs. Đoàn Hưng Linh, Ngô Kim Liên, Nguyễn Xuân Sơn, and Trương Văn Thiên Tư for their support of my study. Engaging with the scholarly works of Drs. Lê Thiện Dũng, Nguyễn Hữu Cương, Nguyễn Lê Quỳnh Hoa, and Trương Văn Thiên Tư has played an important role in the present study; I am grateful for the collegiality of these scholars.

Mr. Nguyễn Cao Trí and Dr. Trần Văn Thanh shared with me an important archive on Vietnamese evangelicalism developed on the centenary of the inaugural work of pioneer C&MA missionaries in Vietnam in 2011. In addition to this archive, the conversations I had with Rev. Dương Thị Thảo, Mr. Lê Đình Tuấn, Mrs. Lê Thị Hồng Ân, the late Rev. Dr. Nguyễn Xuân Đức, and Dr. Reg Reimer have been critical to my understanding and interpretation of the Vietnamese evangelical tradition. Naturally, all errors of fact and interpretation represented in this work are my own.

Friends in the Doctor of Philosophy program at Regent University School of Divinity and in the US Langham Scholars Program provided valued friendship, support, and feedback. Conferences, seminars, and consultations organized by the Lutheran Theological Seminary at Philadelphia (the 2012 Asian Theological Summer Institute), the Society for Pentecostal Studies (the 2014 annual meeting), Harvard Divinity School (the 2014 Ways of Knowing conference), Regent University School of Divinity (the Summer 2015 Ph.D. research seminar), and Langham Partnership (the 2011–2015 scholars consultations) offered opportunities for me to test hypotheses, exchange ideas, and receive helpful feedback.

The family of Mr. Lê Quang Huy and Mrs. Lê Thị Hòa welcomed me to their home during my time in Virginia. My family, relatives, and friends living in Đà Lạt, Hà Nội, and HCMC (in Vietnam), and in Florida, California, Texas, Pennsylvania, and Oregon (in the United States) provided support that sustained me and my scholarly endeavors, and for that support I am deeply grateful.

Hà Nội, Eastertide 2018

Introduction

This is a book about the politics of pentecostalism at work among contemporary Vietnamese evangelicals. It tells the story of how a segment of Vietnamese evangelicalism uses pentecostalism in an attempt to (re)organize communal and individual life in both the Vietnamese evangelical community and wider Vietnamese society. At the heart of the pentecostalism at work among contemporary Vietnamese evangelicals is the belief in *divine intervention*, an enthusiastic belief that God, through the work of the Spirit, will act for the benefit of believers even in the most mundane moments of everyday life. Granted, the pentecostal belief in *divine intervention* is built on the long-held Vietnamese evangelical conviction that God does act to change the course of human affairs at God's will; but pentecostal belief holds a higher degree of openness to and expectation of extraordinary events than does Vietnamese evangelicalism—and does so with a particular focus on the outward manifestation of the work of the Spirit of God in the world.

In today's Vietnam, evangelical Christianity is the fastest growing religion. Reg Reimer, a longtime Canadian expert on Vietnamese evangelicalism, reported that the Vietnamese evangelical population grew from 1 million to 2.25 million between the end of the Second Indochina War (the so-called Vietnam War) in 1975 and the year 2010.[1] Research published on the website of the Government Committee for Religious Affairs of the State of Vietnam also observed that, while the national population doubled from 1975 to 2005, the evangelical population multiplied at least sixfold.[2] Notably, in both cases the growth was tremendous, given the decline in the total number of religious people as reported in the official State censuses in 1999 and 2009.[3]

The Vietnamese evangelical tradition subscribes to the so-called "quadrilateral hallmarks" of the evangelical ethos described by David Bebbington a few

---

1 Reg Reimer, *Vietnam's Christians: A Century of Growth in Adversity* (Pasadena: William Carey Library, 2011), 1. See also Jason Mandryk, *Operation World: The Definitive Prayer Guide to Every Nation*, 7th ed. (Colorado Springs: Biblica, 2010), 882–86.

2 Nguyễn Cao Thanh, "Đạo Tin Lành ở Việt Nam từ 1975 đến nay, tư liệu và một số đánh giá ban đầu" ["Evangelicalism in Vietnam, from 1975 to present: sources and initial comments"], The Government Committee for Religious Affairs, 2013, accessed April 4, 2017, http://btgcp.gov.vn/Plus.aspx/vi/News/38/0/240/0/2737/.

3 General Statistic Office of Vietnam, *2009 Vietnam Population and Housing Census* (Hà Nội: Tổng Cục Thống Kê, 2009); General Statistic Office of Vietnam, *1999 Vietnam Population and Housing Census* (Hà Nội: Tổng Cục Thống Kê, 1999).

 | DOI:10.1163/9789004383838_002

decades ago: the prominence of the salvific death of Jesus, the authority of the Bible, the necessity of being "born again," and the importance of evangelism.[4] Added to the list are the emphases on eschatological thinking about the end times and the need to lead a holy life—emphases that show the influence of pioneer Christian and Missionary Alliance (C&MA) missionaries on Vietnamese evangelicalism.

Vietnamese pentecostal evangelicals inhabit the same evangelical ethos described above, but they place additional emphasis on personal, direct, and miraculous encounter with God, which they believe can be mediated through practices including but not limited to participatory worship, speaking in tongues, fasting, and prayer for healing and deliverance.[5] Some of these beliefs and practices are considered "new"; in fact, however, they have a long history in Vietnamese evangelicalism. As the pentecostal movement gains in number of adherents, it is arguable that the ideas being increasingly adopted by the people in the pews are growing in popularity because they work in ways that are meaningful to those who believe.[6] As of today, about one-third to one-half of Vietnamese evangelicals (and counting) associate themselves with pentecostalism.[7]

A closer look at the contemporary Vietnamese evangelical demographic also reveals an important fact: evangelicalism grows mainly among the country's ethnic minorities. Such minorities make up 14 percent of the Vietnamese population, yet they account for three-quarters of all the evangelicals in the country. The average Vietnamese evangelical is a person belonging to an ethnic

4 David Bebbington, *Evangelicalism in Modern Britain: A History from the 1730s to the 1980s* (London: Unwin Hyman, 1989), 2–17.

5 On the beliefs and practices of contemporary pentecostalism, organized under the category of pentecostal spirituality, see Steven J. Land, *Pentecostal Spirituality: A Passion for the Kingdom* (Sheffield, UK: Sheffield Academic, 1993), and Mark J. Cartledge, *Encountering the Spirit: The Charismatic Tradition*, Traditions of Christian Spirituality (Maryknoll, NY: Orbis, 2007). See also, Daniel E. Albrecht and Evan B. Howard, "Pentecostal Spirituality," in *The Cambridge Companion to Pentecostalism*, ed. Cecil M. Robeck Jr. and Amos Yong (New York: Cambridge University Press, 2014), 235–53).

6 For a similar argument, see Graham Ward, *Unbelievable: Why We Believe and Why We Don't* (London: I. B. Tauris, 2014).

7 For further information, see Vince Le, "The Pentecostal Movement in Vietnam," in *Global Renewal Christianity: Spirit-Empowered Movements Past, Present, and Future*, vol.1: *Asia and Oceania*, ed. Vinson Synan and Amos Yong (Lake Mary, FL: Charisma House, 2015), 181–95. See also Jason Mandryk, *Operation World: The Definitive Prayer Guide to Every Nation*, 882–86; Nguyễn Cao Thanh, "Đạo Tin Lành ở Việt Nam từ 1975 đến nay, tư liệu và một số đánh giá ban đầu" ["Evangelicalism in Vietnam, from 1975 to present: sources and initial comments"]; and Thái Phước Trường, *Hội Thánh Tin Lành Việt Nam: 100 năm hình thành và phát triển* [*The Evangelical Church of Vietnam: 100 Years of Forming and Development*] (HCMC: Hội Thánh Tin Lành Việt Nam Miền Nam, 2011), 202.

minority group living in the highlands, centered in provinces indicated by the World Bank as having the highest poverty headcount in the country and far away from its commercial hubs.[8] This typical contemporary Vietnamese evangelical is usually a woman who speaks her native language.[9] She may or may not be able to communicate in Vietnamese, the language of the *Việt* people and the official language of the State. Also, by virtue of living in one of the country's poorest provinces, she has less economic power and less access to economic development opportunities than the average Vietnamese individual does.

At the same time, in the effort to recruit new members among the ethnic majority *Việt* people, urban evangelical churches have realized greater success among young migrant workers who have left their villages to find work in the cities than among the urbanites themselves. Thus migrant workers, who contribute significantly to the economic growth of Vietnam but benefit little from it, have become yet another new face of Vietnamese evangelicalism.[10]

Twentieth-century Vietnam, the social-historical context of the present study, constitutes a society that underwent (and is still undergoing) crucial transformation due to colonialism, warfare, and communist rule and ambition. In very broad strokes, contemporary Vietnam can be considered a post-colonial, post-war, communist society. The country has a century-long history of experiencing French colonialism before the Vietnamese Revolution in 1945 and endured warfare from 1945 to 1975. Vietnam has been led solely by the Communist Party of Vietnam (CPV) since 1975. While the early-communist Vietnam of the 1980s was primarily a closed-door society,[11] the late-communist Vietnam since the 1990s to the present day pursues an "open-door" policy that brings remarkable economic growth to the country.

Post-1990s, late-communist Vietnam presents the Vietnamese people in general with several old and new problems. Most notable is the state-party's insistence on ideological attachment, which protects and expands the

8 On poverty headcounts by province in Vietnam, consult the World Bank publication "mapVIETNAM," accessed April 4, 2017, http://www.worldbank.org/mapvietnam/.

9 The issue of women's making up a majority in Vietnamese evangelicalism is similar to the issue in Chinese Protestantism. For further information, consult Chen-yang Kao, "Church as 'Women's Community': The Feminization of Protestantism in Contemporary China," *Journal of Archaeology and Anthropology* 78, no. 1 (2013): 107–40.

10 See Nguyễn Đức Lộc, ed., *Tình cảnh sống của người công nhân: Thân phận, rủi ro và chiến lược sống* [*Living Conditions of Workers: Life, Risk, and Coping Strategy*] (Hà Nội: Tri Thức, 2015); and Nguyễn Đức Lộc, ed., *Những người thiểu số ở đô thị: Lựa chọn, trở thành, khác biệt* [*Urban Minority Groups: Choosing, Becoming, Differentiating*] (Hà Nội: Tri Thức, 2016).

11 For background information, consult Đặng Phong, *Tư duy kinh tế Việt Nam 1975–1989* [*Economic Thinking in Vietnam 1975–1989*], 2nd ed. (HCMC: Tri Thức, 2014).

privileges of the powerful, and its use of capitalism to grow the economy, thus building the CPV's legitimacy to rule while indulging the hedonistic consumerism of rent-seekers as a display of national prosperity. Rapid urbanization has facilitated economic growth since the 1990s, but the ineffective use of land (turning arable land into industrial zones), labor (turning young peasants into cheap manufacturing labor), and capital (providing subsidies, such as tax reduction and investing in infrastructure, by offering credits to attract investments that share little profit with the host community) has had negative results: increased dispossession and inequality, decreased health and morale of the masses, and unfavorable conditions for both cultural and national flourishing.[12] Economic growth among the *Việt* ethnic majority inhabiting the coastal lowlands stands in sharp contrast to the worsening conditions of ethnic minorities inhabiting the highlands or living along the border of Cambodia and Vietnam, thus deepening the groups' longstanding ethnic tension due to land disputes, ideological disagreements, and the colonial-like belittlement of the ethnic "others." Further, the State's ethnic policies have been manipulated in pursuit of the economic interests of those who hold political and economic power instead of the ethnic groups those policies were meant to benefit[13]—hence an interesting link between the rapid evangelicalization among these ethnic minorities and their "deteriorating positions" in contemporary Vietnam.[14] It is within this Vietnam—a future-oriented society on a rough path in search of development and progress while haunted by a specter of past colonialism and warfare—that this book discusses Vietnamese evangelicalism and the key ideas that shape its social engagement, reveal its principal social concerns, and help explain its embracing of pentecostalism.

Because the present study seeks to discuss Vietnamese evangelicals in their local social context in order to identify challenges that may have given rise to

12 On dispossession and urbanization in contemporary Vietnam, see Erik Harms, *Luxury and Rubble: Civility and Dispossession in the New Saigon* (Berkeley: University of California Press, 2016). On issues pertaining to the CPV's presiding over a neoliberal economy in relation to property rights, see Hue-Tam Ho Tai and Mark Sidel, eds., *State, Society and the Market in Contemporary Vietnam: Property, Power and Values* (New York: Routledge, 2013).

13 So argues Ito Masako in *Politics of Ethnic Classification in Vietnam*, trans. Minako Sato, Kyoto Area Studies on Asia (Melbourne: Trans Pacific, 2013).

14 See, most recently, Benjamin Dwayne et al., "Growth with Equity: Income Inequality in Vietnam, 2002–14," *The Journal of Economic Inequality* 15, no. 1 (March 2017): 25–46; and Saurabh Singhal and Ulrik Beck, "Ethnic Disadvantage: Evidence Using Panel Data," in *Growth, Structural Transformation, and Rural Change in Viet Nam: A Rising Dragon on the Move*, ed. Finn Tarp (New York: Oxford University Press, 2017), 256–75.

their adoption of pentecostalism, I have opted not to focus on the encounter between Western missionaries and native Vietnamese converts, nor do I engage in a critical assessment of the historical colonialism interwoven with the modern Western missionary movement. While it is true that focusing on those aspects would surely identify elements which show native Vietnamese evangelicals as having issues with the paternal practices of Western missionaries, the overall attitude of Vietnamese evangelicals is not one of resistance to the impact of the Western missionary movement. In fact, the native Vietnamese welcome foreign teachings, practices, and resources as long as they believe these "imports" can help them cope with the challenges of life they encounter in their own society. Thus, while this study will mention the missionary-native dynamics here and there, the emphasis will concentrate on investigating how Western-centric knowledge and a Western way of life continue to shape the way Vietnamese evangelicals and their Vietnamese interlocutors examine the issues that are important to their contemporary lives, even though Vietnam is no longer a colony of any Western power. As Christianity moves southward, the struggle of evangelicals who, while living in former colonies, navigate life at the juncture of nation-building and globalization in Global South societies presents a major source of theological reflection that the global evangelical theological enterprise cannot ignore.[15] For example, the concern for the poor requires a careful analysis of discourses on development that still favors Western knowledge over local knowledge of the best means for reducing global poverty.[16] Such analysis is made more complex by continuing colonialism in the

15 The approach of this study thus complements the work of Kay Higuera Smith, Jayachitra Lalitha, and L. Daniel Hawk, eds., *Evangelical Postcolonial Conversations: Global Awakenings in Theology and Praxis* (Downers Grove, IL: IVP Academic, 2014), a ground-breaking volume that seeks to "decolonize the established colonial remnants of Western hegemony" (p. 25). The editors of *Evangelical Postcolonial Conversations* at the same time remind readers of the problem of native elites that "mimic colonial models in their own mission strategies" (p. 26). This assertion may be the case in several incidents, but it is also important to note that the mimicry of the missionaries by the natives, does, on the one hand, constitute a resistance to missionary practices by way of quiet alterations to those practices; on the other hand, the mimicry also simply represents a pragmatic decision to "get things done" rather than constituting dependency of thought. For an example of this subtle understanding, see Angela Tarango, *Choosing the Jesus Way: American Indian Pentecostals and the Fight for the Indigenous Principle* (Chapel Hill, NC: The University of North Carolina Press, 2014), chapter 3.

16 Christine Sylvester, "Development Studies and Postcolonial Studies: Disparate Tales of the 'Third World,'" *Third World Quarterly* 20, no. 4 (1999): 703–21: 703. See also Bill Ashcroft et al., *Post-Colonial Studies: The Key Concepts*, 3rd ed. (London: Routledge, 2013), vii; and Ilan Kapoor, *The Postcolonial Politics of Development* (New York: Routledge, 2008).

form of the endemic phenomenon of marginalization of specific social groups by dominant groups (based on differences in class, caste, ethnicity, and religion) in the newly independent states in the Global South after the end of the historical European colonial period.[17]

Given the above considerations, to situate Vietnamese evangelicals in the context of contemporary Vietnam for the purpose of academic study thus engenders an investigation into at least several cross-related issues, which this book examines: *Evangelically*, the issue of the agency of pioneer Western missionaries and early Vietnamese converts in defining the terms of interaction between evangelicalism and Vietnamese society—a defining process that arose in Vietnam's colonial context in the early twentieth century and that continues to provide a foundation for Vietnamese evangelical thinking in early twenty-first century Vietnam; *Politically*, the struggle of the evangelical Christians to understand and respond to the State's relentless pursuit of cultural hegemony and national economic development—a struggle defined by assimilation measurements undertaken by the State toward a minority religious group based not only on ideological differences but also on ethnic differences, while ethnic minorities have now become the majority in the evangelical demographic of contemporary Vietnam; *Academically*, the examination of discourses, ideas, and concepts at the intersection of a threefold dynamic—that between Western and Vietnamese evangelicals in the ownership and censorship of evangelical theological discourses, between evangelical and communist Vietnamese in the construction of Vietnamese political discourses, and between the evangelical West and the secular West in a struggle for social influence through the development and promotion of ideas at home and abroad. It is precisely from within this web of connections that the development of pentecostalism has emerged among contemporary Vietnamese evangelicals.

Since contemporary Vietnam is a one-party state, it goes without saying that any critical analysis which uses contemporary Vietnam as a social context for studying will inevitably discuss the ruling CPV and the state it has crafted. Although the state-party may interpret critical engagement with its ideology and platform as an act that seeks to undermine state authority, the present book contends that the subversion of any regime (and the intellectual tradition it represents) is less likely to be the result of a deliberate act of opposition, and more likely to be the direct consequence of a failure of the ruling party

17 On continuing colonialism, see Pramod K. Nayar, *Postcolonial Literature: An Introduction* (New Delhi: Pearson, 2008), 99–100.

to deliver what it promised, even on its own terms,[18] or of an escalation of intra-elite group conflicts.[19] The analysis presented in this book is only political in the sense that it considers how structural power, which includes cultural-psychological, social, economic, and political arrangements, has been used to organize contemporary Vietnam.[20] Moving beyond the ultimate concern of the powers that be about the longevity of their regime, this book does not endorse or reject any particular political party platform but, instead, seeks to focus on how key concepts and ideas, emerging from different scholarly and grassroots perspectives, have facilitated the social engagement of Vietnamese evangelicals.

In a nutshell, this study shall make the case for a general interpretation that the pentecostal belief in *divine intervention* grows as it offers meaning to an underprivileged segment within contemporary Vietnamese evangelicalism. The claim, however, is far from being straightforward, since the long-held evangelical ethos that gives rise to this focus on *divine intervention* also and at the same time shows itself at an impasse—one that questions its ability to engage and respond efficiently to the inevitable challenges of modernity in a communist society.

In the first chapter of this book, my narrative of the Vietnamese evangelical tradition begins with a summary of the overarching concept that governs Vietnamese evangelical thinking, namely, the concept of *the world*, and the pentecostal perspective on how *divine intervention* happens in *the world*. The next three chapters engage three other major socio-political concerns of Vietnamese evangelicals; each chapter will serve as a proper context in which to illustrate an essential aspect of the pentecostal emphasis on *divine intervention*. The three socio-political concerns to be discussed are those of *justice*, *culture*, and *development*. The last chapter coordinates the arguments of the previous four chapters and illustrates their interrelatedness. This concluding chapter contends that the focus on *divine intervention* constitutes a legitimate grassroots understanding that should be registered in the overall pentecostal discourse about God's way in contemporary Vietnam—and perhaps in other

18 This conclusion may be deduced from the theoretical work of political ethicist Alasdair MacIntyre in his *After Virtue: A Study in Moral Theory* (Notre Dame: University of Notre Dame Press, 1981), chapter 6.

19 This position is argued similarly by Martin Gainsborough in *Vietnam: Rethinking the State* (London: Zed Books, 2010), 21–23.

20 On "being political" as providing analysis and criticism of the use of structural power, see Peter Scott and William Cavanaugh, eds., *The Blackwell Companion to Political Theology* (Oxford: Blackwell, 2004), 2.

areas of the Global South as well. Such grassroots perspective is intertwined with the way Vietnamese evangelicals use the concept of *the world*. At the turn of the twentieth century, *the world* concept functioned at the core of the evangelical ethos, as the motivation for the message of salvation for the Vietnamese people during turbulent social conditions. Today, the concept is undergoing a foreseen change with the times.

CHAPTER 1

The World

1.1 Zeitgeist

The year was 1927 when Vietnamese evangelicals held their first national and constitutional conference, followed by their adoption of the official name Evangelical Church of French Indochina in the group's Church Constitution a year later. Back then, Vietnam was known to the world as belonging to Indochina, a constructed French colony that included modern-day Vietnam, Laos, and Cambodia. The Vietnamese regions of French Indochina, all using Vietnamese as the primary vernacular, included Cochinchina (southern Vietnam), Annam (central Vietnam), and Tonkin (northern Vietnam). While Cochinchina was ruled directly by the French, Annam and Tonkin were French protectorates ruled nominally by the Vietnamese Imperial Court.[1] Although several ethnic groups had been, since former times, and still were inhabiting Vietnam, the Evangelical Church of French Indochina mainly represented the *Việt* ethnic group living in the populated lowlands of the Vietnamese regions of French Indochina.

The birth and development of the native evangelical church was mainly the result of the missionary work of the America-based C&MA in French Indochina in 1911, even though some evangelistic efforts by French Protestants and the British and Foreign Bible Society certainly pre-dated 1911.[2] When the pioneer C&MA missionaries first set foot on Vietnamese land, they quickly learned that the coastal, populated lowland region of Vietnam was essentially a society founded on Sinitic learning—a society that over the centuries had masterfully navigated the asymmetric yet stable relationship with China.[3] The missionary Grace Hazenberg Cadman, in her fund-raising book *Pen Pictures of Annam and Its People*, rendered "Annam" (a former name of Vietnam that also referred to the central region of Vietnam) as "Peaceful Southland."[4] Little did she know

1 On the French administration of Indochina, see K. W. Taylor, *A History of the Vietnamese* (Cambridge: Cambridge University Press, 2013), chapter 10, esp. pp. 477–83.

2 Đặng Ngọc Phúc, *Những người Tin Lành ở Việt Nam trước năm 1911* [*Protestants in Vietnam Prior to 1911*] (San Diego: Self-published, 2011).

3 See also Brantly Womack, *China and Vietnam: The Politics of Asymmetry* (New York: Cambridge University Press, 2006), and *China among Unequals: Asymmetric Foreign Relations in Asia* (Singapore: World Scientific, 2010).

4 Grace Hazenberg Cadman, *Pen Pictures of Annam and Its People* (New York: The Christian Alliance Publishing, 1920). (http://reader.library.cornell.edu/docviewer/digital?id=sea:029#page/16/mode/2up.) See also the common understanding of Vietnam as a peaceful

 | DOI:10.1163/9789004383838_003

that the irenic Southland of her first impression was, in fact, a society on the verge of turbulent change, perplexed as it was by the military power, technological advance, and brutal exploitation of the adventurous French colonists at a time when the "Middle Kingdom" as a center of power was declining. Old guards of the so-called Vietnamese tradition continued to use the Chinese language in their writings and upheld their own version of Confucianism in an effort to preserve the moral authority of tradition and erase colonial malaise. At the same time, Vietnamese youth, especially in southern Vietnam, preferred to use the French language (not Vietnamese or Chinese) and ideas rooted in the Western humanist tradition to debate the problems and opportunities presented by the French rule of Indochina. These young people, being more preoccupied with "change," were eager to sacrifice identity for modernity; they stood in contrast to conservatives, who wished to uphold "tradition" as a supreme mark of national and spiritual identity.[5] The Romanized Vietnamese writing system, created by Roman Catholic missionaries for evangelistic purposes in the seventeenth century, also began to gain traction a few decades ago, thus resulting in an increased rate of literacy. This development allowed more Vietnamese to engage in the debate over the fate of Vietnam, a country caught in the tension between decreasing Sinitic influence and growing French influence. Especially for the Vietnamese youth who were born after the French had firmly established their rule over Vietnam and who had more access to different Western perspectives on colonialism and *mission civilisatrice*, the existential struggle was rather multifaceted. It included a determination to resolve colonialism, a quest for national modernity, and an aspiration for Western-style individual freedom—vital needs the inherited Vietnamese tradition appeared unable to meet.

By the 1920s, it became clear that Vietnam's social movements were now organized and populated by Vietnamese youth, with the two "faces" of the anticolonialist movement of the previous generation withdrawing from the stage of history: Phan Châu Trinh passed away in 1926, and Phan Bội Châu was detained in Huế in 1925 until his death in 1940.[6] The young leaders and their mass

---

French colony in the 1910s in Truong Buu Lam, *Colonialism Experienced: Vietnamese Writings on Colonialism, 1900–1931* (Ann Arbor: University of Michigan Press, 2000), 1.

5 For further information, consult Hue-Tam Ho Tai, *Radicalism and the Origins of the Vietnamese Revolution* (Cambridge: Harvard University Press, 1996), 6.

6 On Phan Châu Trinh, consult Vĩnh Sính, ed., *Phan Châu Trinh and His Political Writings* (Ithaca, NY: Cornell University Press, 2009). On Phan Bội Châu, see Phan Bội Châu, *Overturned Chariot: The Autobiography of Phan Bội Châu*, trans. Vĩnh Sính and Nicholas Wickenden (Honolulu: University of Hawaii Press, 1999).

followers of the 1920s were rather iconoclastic, most obviously in their attack-by-distortion on the Confucian foundation of Vietnamese society. They asserted that such a foundation was useless in bringing about personal freedom, national independence, and social advancement in the face of colonialism. The counter-strike of those who wished to uphold the Confucian legacy functioned at the same level of distortion in its portrayal of the tradition.[7] It was in the context of this sentiment-charged complexity that Nguyễn An Ninh, a celebrated youth leader of his generation, gave his famous "The Ideal of Annamite Youth" speech in 1923. While condemning what he saw as the unquenchable greediness of the French and demanding more freedom and human dignity for the young people of Vietnam, he also mercilessly attacked the Confucian traditional mentality and thinking among his contemporary Vietnamese.[8]

The emergence of Vietnamese evangelicals as a social group corresponded well with the radical spirit of the 1920s. More than anything else, the evangelical tenet of rejecting ancestor worship as a logically flawed practice constituted a daring dismissal of this Vietnamese tradition, which had for different reasons reached popular consensus on the importance of filial piety. Converts to evangelicalism also saw the missionaries and their way of life as representatives of modernity but without the ruthless colonialist agenda they saw in the French. At the same time, the evangelical preaching of the forgiveness of sin created a sense of newly found individual freedom in those who would believe, and the emphasis on love and moral holiness fed the common hope that more converts meant more chances for social betterment.

At the onset of the 1930s, ideological currents complicated the radicalism of Vietnamese youth by fueling the idea that the problem of colonialism could be solved only by violent means. The *Yên Bái* mutiny in February 1930, led by the Vietnamese Nationalist Party, and the *Nghệ Tĩnh* uprising in March 1930, started by the Vietnamese communists, were two chief examples of the masses' being mobilized by revolutionaries radicalized along the path of violence. As revolution became in vogue, the concern for personal freedom understandably deferred to party discipline.

Within the political and cultural milieu of the late 1920s and the early 1930s, Vietnamese evangelicals clearly stated in their 1928 Church Constitution that

---

7 On this issue, see Tai, *Radicalism and the Origins of the Vietnamese Revolution*, chapter 1.

8 Nguyễn An Ninh, "The Ideal of Annamite Youth," a speech given on October 15, 1923, reprinted in Mai Quốc Liên and Nguyễn Sơn, eds., *Nguyễn An Ninh—tác phẩm* [*Nguyễn An Ninh—Collected Works*] (HCMC: Văn Học, 2009), 57–78. See also Nguyễn An Ninh, "France in Indochina (1925)," in *Colonialism Experienced: Vietnamese Writings on Colonialism, 1900–1931*, ed. Truong Buu Lam (Ann Arbor: University of Michigan Press, 2000), 190–207.

they did not wish to pursue party politics or violent revolution. Instead, they continued to uphold the radical spirit of the 1920s (with its emphasis on the positive aspects of modernity, for instance) in the monthly publication of *Thánh Kinh Báo* [*Bible Magazine*], which featured not only moral and spiritual guidance but also basic knowledge of healthcare, science, and a modern way of life.

The religious self-understanding of these evangelicals was thus rather ambiguous. On the one hand, converting to evangelicalism was considered a religious conversion proper, for converts had to relinquish their former religious affiliations. On the other hand, the faith grew not through the establishment of an elaborate system of institutions, doctrines, and rituals, but rather through a broad claim, accompanied by simple reasoning, on how evangelicalism offered a workable solution to the disenchantment with traditional values and the malaise created by *mission civilisatrice*. Throughout the development of Vietnamese evangelicalism, its adherents were more preoccupied with popular ancestor worship as a basic tenet of the Vietnamese tradition—a tenet they rejected as an excessive duty that had lost its original meaning—than with any institutionalized religion of the land.

On second thought, the direct duel between evangelicalism and the cult of the ancestors further demonstrated the ambiguous status of both systems as religions proper. The cult of the ancestors was ambiguous in its dual appeal to (1) the popular religious belief in the continued connection between dead and living members of the same family, and (2) the Confucian-founded filial piety that sustained the perpetuation of ancestor worship as a civil ceremony to uphold what was considered the ultimate value of a Confucian-based society. In this context, rejection of the cult of the ancestors, or any radical revision of it, represented a rejection of the orthodoxy of the so-called Vietnamese tradition. The evangelical approach to the cult of the ancestors was simply to reject it outright—an insensitive move but nevertheless a move in line with the radical and iconoclastic mood of the time. The issue thus framed—namely, whether one should worship only the ancestors one knows or only God as one's ultimate ancestor—was purposefully crafted as a philosophical question intended to generate the rethinking of a particular practice (and move people from worshiping the immediate ancestors to worshiping the one true God) more than to provide an opportunity to elaborate the religiosity that sought to connect the worlds of the dead and the living.

It was within this world of French Indochina in the early twentieth century—a world of wrestling with colonialist exploitation, disenchantment with tradition, aspiration for personal freedom and national modernity, and influential revolutionist currents—that Vietnamese evangelicals emerged as a social group. As a one that resonated with the iconoclasm of the Vietnamese youth but not with their radical bent toward revolution, both the foreign missionaries and the early native converts found the concept of *the world*, in its evangelical sense, convenient to convey their message to Vietnamese society: *the world* was full of suffering and tragedy caused by the brutal exploitation of colonialism and the cruel violence of revolutionism; yet *the world* could be better if more people, French and Vietnamese alike, would only turn to Jesus and begin to live according to the Christian moral code and a modern way of life, not according to now-ineffective Vietnamese tradition and the French civilizing mission. The message was simple, but it struck a chord with many Vietnamese individuals on several aspects.

1.2 The World

When the C&MA first opened an evangelistic station in central Vietnam in 1911, *the world* was a core concept of its spiritual message to the native people: salvation from *the world* to be part of a heavenly kingdom was possible through believing in Jesus Christ. Twenty years later, in 1931, *the world* as a powerful evangelical concept was showcased in print for the first time in a monthly magazine, *Thánh Kinh Báo* [*Bible Magazine*], a joint endeavor under the patronage of foreign missionaries and native church leaders.[9] The second issue of the magazine showcased the concept with the exhortation, "Do not love the world," from 1 John 2:15, thus making this concept second only to the *Fourfold Gospel*—the C&MA's signature set of beliefs in Jesus as Savior, Sanctifier, Healer, and Coming King—featured in the very first issue of the magazine.[10]

It is noteworthy that the *Yên Bái* mutiny and the *Nghệ Tĩnh* uprising, in February and March 1930, respectively, were events that dramatically disrupted the entire colony. They marked the rise of violent revolution in French Indochina

9 On the political culture in which *Thánh Kinh Báo* was published, see Philippe Peycam, *The Birth of Vietnamese Political Journalism: Saigon, 1916–1930* (New York: Columbia University Press, 2012). The production of *Thánh Kinh Báo* by pioneer C&MA missionaries and early native evangelicals involved their possession of a modern printing machine and the operation of a printing house. The importance of the early twentieth-century printing culture to "the making of modern Vietnam," as Shawn Frederick McHale observed in his *Print and Power: Confucianism, Communism, and Buddhism in the Making of Modern Vietnam* (Honolulu: University of Hawaii Press, 2008), also invites further research on evangelicals' interactions with wider Vietnamese society and evangelicals' self-understanding of their social role in colonial Vietnam.

10 *Thánh Kinh Báo*, no. 1 (January 1931) and no. 2 (February 1931).

and provided the social background for evangelicals to write about *the world* in terms of chaos, rebellion, and disruption with rumors of war in their early-1931 issue of *Thánh Kinh Báo*. As the evangelical discourse went, the root cause of the societal problem lay in the fact that *the world* was comprised of sinful individuals, who could not help but disrupt human relations and create "sinful" social structures.[11] Sinful people, however, had the potential to be redeemed if they accepted Jesus as Savior, who then reconciled them with God. As more individuals would turn to Jesus, morally corrupt society would improve and become a better place for all—though only temporarily, for human society was still destined for complete destruction. In this regard, positive changes in the life of the converts (and how those changes positively affected people around them) were showcased as the best illustrations of the potential for the moral and social impact of the evangelical faith in the temporal world.

The world concept was also understood as having a spiritual dimension. Here *the world* represented the totality of the material world influenced by destructive, supernatural, evil forces. The understanding of *the world* in Vietnamese evangelical thinking was rather ambiguous and covered a broad spectrum, ranging from *the world* as created-by-God-yet-fallen (thus inherently good and deserving of redemptive action) to *the world* as being demonic (thus deserving condemnation, not redemption). Additionally, Satan was the ontologically evil being that controlled *the world*. Christians were expected to resist Satan and Satan's legions, with different evangelical circles emphasizing different practices of resistance, ranging from holiness (i.e., maintaining a holy Christian life in order not to fall under the control of evil) to spiritual warfare (i.e., engaging in spiritual struggle to undermine the power of evil in *the world*).

In retrospect, Vietnamese evangelicals usually viewed other religions and traditional Vietnamese cultural-religious practices as belonging to *the world*. Thus the evangelical attitude toward other religions and traditional beliefs and practices also sits somewhere along the redeemable-condemnable spectrum, depending on the level of the adherent's commitment to the exclusive soteriology of evangelical Christianity. This attitude has always constituted a subtext of the evangelical discourse about *the world*, but the idea lacks substance and has been used less frequently in the official evangelical public argument. The reason for the underdevelopment of an evangelical understanding of religion and culture in Vietnamese evangelicalism is due to the fact that evangelicals see themselves as offering a "God solution" to moral and societal problems that

11 Information is taken from "Gieo gì gặt nấy" ["Reap What You Sow"] and "Kinh Thánh và xã hội" ["The Bible and Society"], featured front-page articles in *Thánh Kinh Báo*, no. 2 (February 1931) and no. 3 (March 1931).

have a spiritual root cause, hence the vehement call by both missionaries and native believers that evangelicalism is *not* a religion *per se*.

The belief in *the world* as a turbulent and chaotic place reached new heights in and after the 1945 Vietnamese Revolution, when the country began to undergo thirty years of warfare and division. During this period, the Vietnamese became involved in two major wars: the First Indochina War (or the Anti-French Resistance War, as it is known in contemporary Vietnam, from 1945–1954), and the Second Indochina War (commonly known worldwide as the Vietnam War, between North and South Vietnam, from 1955–1975).

In 1944, at the dawn of the First Indochina War, a Vietnamese evangelical preacher in Central Vietnam even predicted that *the rapture*—the event through which, according to many evangelicals, both dead and living believers will be caught up in the clouds to meet Jesus at his second coming—would happen very soon, on a particular date of the same year.[12] After the preacher's prediction failed to come true, he made a second attempt (unsurprisingly with the same result) in 1945—the year when the Second World War caused the brief involvement of the Japanese in Vietnam and the year of the Great Vietnamese Famine, the greatest famine in the history of modern Vietnam.[13] What was astonishing was that the evangelical apocalyptic thinking attracted a considerable number of Vietnamese evangelicals in Central Vietnam, even the superintendent of a large evangelical district. The *apocalyptic* thinking, however, was not monopolized by the evangelicals; it also spread widely through the rapid growth of two millennial religions, *Cao Đài* and *Hòa Hảo*, in the southern part of the country. These emerging religions went even further by quickly turning into major armed struggles against the French colonial forces.[14] This sequence of events around the middle of the twentieth century illustrated how famine, rumors of war, and apocalyptic thinking reinforced one another and

12 This prediction is recounted in Lê Văn Thái, *Bốn mươi sáu năm trong chức vụ* [*Forty-Six Years in Ministry*] (Sài Gòn: Tin Lành, 1970), 183–90.

13 On the Great Famine, see Geoffrey Gunn, *Rice Wars in Colonial Vietnam: The Great Famine and the Viet Minh Road to Power* (Lanham, MD: Rowman & Littlefield, 2014); Văn Tạo and Furuta Moto, *Nạn đói năm 1945 ở Việt Nam: Những chứng tích lịch sử* [*The 1945 Famine in Vietnam: Historical Evidences*] (Hà Nội: Tri Thức, 2011).

14 On the politics of the religion of *Cao Đài*, see Jayne S. Werner, *Peasant Politics and Religious Sectarianism: Peasant and Priest in the Cao Dai in Viet Nam* (New Haven: Yale University Press, 1981). On the religion of *Hòa Hảo*, see Hue-Tam Ho Tai, *Millenarianism and Peasant Politics in Vietnam* (Cambridge: Harvard University Press, 1983). On the Vietnamese Catholic struggle during colonial times, see Charles Keith, *Catholic Vietnam: A Church from Empire to Nation* (Berkeley: University of California Press, 2012). On Buddhist, communist, and nationalist struggles related to an emerging printing culture, consult McHale, *Print and Power*.

confirmed the earlier Vietnamese evangelical thinking about *the world*, namely, that the physical world was indeed chaotic, full of tragedy, and destined soon to be destroyed.

During the Vietnam War, Vietnam was an increasingly polarized society, violently divided along a "communist-versus-free-world" ideological line. This division resulted in the establishment of North Vietnam and South Vietnam. The League for the Independence of Vietnam, and thereafter the CPV, assumed political power in the North, which it ran as a socialist state named the Democratic Republic of Vietnam. Concurrently, non-communist political leaders formed another government in the South, formally known as the Republic of Vietnam.

As the Vietnam War escalated, Vietnamese evangelicals, most of them now residing in South Vietnam, were caught in a dilemma. On the one hand, the cruel reality of war confirmed and prolonged their belief in *the world* as it had been narrated since colonial times, namely, that *the world* was chaotic and full of tragedy. On the other hand, several factors prompted Vietnamese evangelicals to focus on providing charity and war relief: (1) the urgent need to help those afflicted by the war, (2) their feeling of commonality with their Vietnamese compatriots in struggling with the war, and (3) the ability of Vietnamese evangelicals to access more Western aid (because of the United States' increasing involvement in the Vietnam War beginning in the 1950s). But this war-prompted refocusing by Vietnamese evangelicals left them no time to reflect on how their charitable and relief activities would be compatible with the original evangelical mission of saving souls from *the world*.[15] Hence during wartime the evangelicals struggled internally between doing relief work (to respond to the immediate wounds caused by warfare) and evangelism (to ensure that people were saved spiritually)—a tension not fully resolved by the evangelical leaders of the day. As a result, evangelicals' original understanding of *the world* as corrupt remained intact, but evangelical thinking about *the world* was now colored with an existential struggle of being Vietnamese in wartime.[16]

15 See, for example, their access to the support of World Vision in Ruth Goforth Jeffrey, *Amazing Grace: A Brief Account of My Life in China and Vietnam* (Stouffville, ON: D.I. Jeffrey, 1975), 56–57; and Tường Vi, "7 năm truyền Tin Lành và hoạt động xã hội trên toàn cõi Việt Nam" ["Seven Years of Evangelism and Social Action in Vietnam"], *Thánh Kinh Báo*, no. 391 (December 1971): I–VIII.

16 See Khang Lĩnh, "Thế đứng của người thanh niên Cơ Đốc trong giai đoạn hiện tại" ["The Social Position of the Christian Youth at the Present Time"], *Thánh Kinh Báo*, no. 374 (April 1970): 5–9; and Khang Lĩnh, "Một bông hồng cho quê hương" ["A Rose for My Country"], *Thánh Kinh Báo*, no. 380 (November 1970): 8–12.

The contemporary period in Vietnam began in 1975. It is marked historically by the end of the Vietnam War and the institutionalization of the CPV as the sole political power. Most religious groups are marginalized and viewed as organized social groups that may unnecessarily trouble the state-party's right to rule. In recent years, the country's economic growth and increasing wealth caused the state to become more religious-like in its public rituals and ceremonies, thus creating greater ambiguity as to what may be counted as sacred and what constitutes the secular. In this setting, the original evangelical belief that *the world* is a corrupt social structure has been deepened by several factors: (1) the national struggle to (re)establish a moral foundation, which the national communist leadership fails to provide, (2) the perception of economic development as the root of indulgent hedonism, and (3) the observation that national development policies often benefit greedy rent-seekers more than the socially disadvantaged. Thus in contemporary Vietnam, evangelicals continue to foster *the world* discourse by asserting that there is a "God solution" for immoral and corrupt societies.

Although the above perspective of *the world* has everything to do with the political regime in charge, the evangelical discourse would insist that politics has never belonged to the purview of the evangelical Christian faith, for evangelical leaders either genuinely believe that theirs is a purely spiritual business of saving souls, or they simply do not want to jeopardize the growth of evangelicalism in Vietnam by contesting any political power, be it the past French rule of Indochina or the current CPV. As a result, the positive changes in the lives of converts are often showcased in the moral-social evangelical discourse as the most defensible line of argument for the *raison d'être* of evangelicalism in Vietnam.

The evangelicals' voluntary non-participation in party politics in contemporary Vietnam has also been interpreted as a sign of contempt for the power of a state-party that subordinates the religious others.[17] As the argument goes among evangelicals, however, when *the world* is perceived as a dangerous place, to remain uninvolved is, in fact, a good option for resisting oppression. At the same time, remaining uninvolved conveniently creates an alternative ideological space in which to live outside a problematic world.[18] This

17 Quynh-Hoa Nguyen, "Tin Lành: The Bible and the Construction of an Evangelical Vietnamese Christian Identity (1975–2007)" (Ph.D. diss., Claremont Graduate University, 2013), 166.

18 James C. Scott, *Domination and the Arts of Resistance: Hidden Transcripts* (New Haven: Yale University Press, 1990). See also Richard A. Horsley, ed., *Hidden Transcripts and the Arts of Resistance: Applying the Work of James C. Scott to Jesus and Paul* (Atlanta: Society of

understanding partly explains why some Vietnamese house-church leaders decide not to register their churches as legal entities. From their perspective, they are simply refusing to be part of a structure that gives them more restrictions than freedoms. For example, if they do not register, they can (relatively speaking) conduct any church activity that they want to conduct. When they register with the state, they must ask local authorities for permission before gathering people for church activities or taking a mission trip.

A shortcoming of this discourse on *the world* consists in its using evangelical language that, perhaps understandably, seeks to spiritualize reality—language that thereby hampers adequately articulating the potential for the evangelical faith to make a significant moral and social impact in the temporal world. For example, while the Vietnamese evangelical approach to Vietnamese society can rightly be understood as a critique of that society, what constitutes that critique is underdeveloped in the Vietnamese evangelical *corpus*. To rediscover the social critique of Vietnamese evangelicals will require a kind of Foucauldian archaeology—an excavation of historical materials to decipher the hidden, social meanings of the spiritual writings developed by early Vietnamese evangelicals.[19] This shortcoming not only prevents contemporary evangelical scholars from clarifying the social manifesto of the Vietnamese evangelical tradition from a historical perspective but also prompts them to adopt readily the idea of *transformation* as a wholly positive approach to contemporary Vietnamese society.

1.3 Transformation

Since the 1990s, the concept of *transformation*, understood as active social engagement to effect positive change, has been promoted by several Vietnamese evangelical scholars as a desirable Vietnamese evangelical approach to bettering society.[20] In their writings, these scholars have also adopted *culture* as a more intelligible, academically compatible term to replace *the world*; but the change has created further ambiguity, for while *the world* is to be rejected,

Biblical Literature, 2004), and James C. Scott, *The Art of Not Being Governed: An Anarchist History of Upland Southeast Asia* (New Haven: Yale University Press, 2010).

19 See Michel Foucault, *The Archaeology of Knowledge* (New York: Pantheon, 1972).

20 Most notable is Dung Le, "The Bamboo Cross: Toward a Vietnamese Theology and Christian Educational Ministry in Vietnam" (D.Min. diss., Claremont School of Theology, 1994). See also Tu Truong, "Mệnh Trời: Toward a Vietnamese Theology of Mission" (Ph.D. diss., Graduate Theological Union, 2009); and Quynh-Hoa Nguyen, "Tin Lành."

culture, especially Vietnamese culture, is to be appreciated and improved by transformative actions.

It is noteworthy that most, if not all, of the academic writings by Vietnamese evangelicals about the idea of *transformation* emerged from within the theological academy in the United States, where, under the shadow of H. Richard Niebuhr's *Christ and Culture*, the concept of *culture*, and the accompanying idea of *transforming culture*, has enjoyed popularity.[21] Concurrently, in the West's theological academy, the development of critical assessments of the missionary movement and its connection with historical European colonial expansion also encouraged Vietnamese evangelical authors to investigate deeply rooted cultural tensions between Western missionaries and the native people.[22] Within this particular academic incubator, Vietnamese evangelical authors have increasingly advanced the discussion on faith and society by putting special emphasis on the cultural aspects of Vietnamese society and taking a critical approach to the Western missionary movement.

In general, these Vietnamese evangelical authors criticized Western missionaries for introducing thoughts and practices that alienated Vietnamese evangelicals from their own culture during the colonial period.[23] Most notably, criticism was directed at the missionaries' ignorance concerning the natives' celebration of the death anniversary of deceased family members. An author cited approvingly the perspective of Đào Duy Anh, a prominent Vietnamese historian and cultural anthropologist, that the genuine meaning of celebrating death anniversaries consisted in presenting an occasion for a family reunion that presented opportunities to educate younger members of the extended family on filial piety.[24] The missionaries were also criticized for seeking conversions mainly among the poorer Vietnamese and disapproving the natives' pursuit of higher education, thus resulting in a negative public image of Vietnamese evangelicalism as a faith of the poor and less educated.

In another account, early missionaries were criticized for having a culturally imperialist attitude toward the Vietnamese. One Vietnamese evangelical scholar recounts that, in the writing of the early missionaries, the Vietnamese people were represented as "savage," "spiritually dead," and "morally

21 H. Richard Niebuhr, *Christ and Culture* (New York: Harper & Row, 1951).

22 See, for example, R. S. Sugirtharajah, *The Bible and the Third World: Precolonial, Colonial and Postcolonial Encounters* (New York: Cambridge University Press, 2001).

23 Tu Truong, "Mệnh Trời," 59; Phu Le, "A Short History of the Evangelical Church of Viet Nam (1911–1965)" (Ph.D. diss., New York University, 1972), 162; Cuong Nguyen, "The Growth of Certain Protestant Churches in Saigon under the Vietnamese Communist Government" (D.Min. diss., San Francisco Theological Seminary, 1995), 23.

24 Tu Truong, "Mệnh Trời," 63.

degraded."[25] Utilizing a kind of textual analysis that followed what Edward Said did in his seminal work *Orientalism*,[26] the same author also stated that the Christian Bible was imposed on the natives as the ultimate authority, with Western missionaries functioning as the right interpreters, thus effectively enhancing Western imperialism.[27] This perspective claimed the missionaries came to Vietnam not only with a religion but also with an imperialist spirit that assumed the superiority of the West over other peoples and cultures, thus causing native believers to become foreigners in and to their own homeland.

While the writings of Vietnamese evangelical scholars offer a helpful perspective on the Western evangelical missionary movement, they offer a limited critical assessment of the views of well-known Vietnamese intellectuals, such as the previously mentioned Đào Duy Anh and fellow leading scholars Phạm Quỳnh and Trần Quốc Vượng by treating these scholars as authorities without questioning their cultural and political biases. Thus the discussion shows a paradigm shift in Vietnamese evangelicals' academic thinking from the colonial to the postcolonial period. During colonial times, early Vietnamese evangelicals thought they were engaging with and addressing a problematic world, while postcolonial Vietnamese evangelical authors, because of their treatment of Vietnamese culture as non-problematic, see the evangelicals, not the outside world, as having problems. This paradigm shift raises Vietnamese academic evangelicals' capacity for self-criticism, but their limited efforts to develop an equally informed cultural criticism fail to create a framework for evaluating whether the evangelical self-criticism is reasonable. Moreover, the attention given to foreign missionaries inadvertently continues to overlook the agency of early native believers in forming the Vietnamese evangelical approach to their own society and their use of the concept of *the world*, not *culture*, in constructing the evangelical manifesto. As a result, early native believers continue to be voiceless in these discussions.

With attention shifting to the concept of *culture*, Dung Le, one of the most systematic and theologically oriented Vietnamese evangelical authors, suggests that the evangelical church has a two-step transforming mission in Vietnam: to inculturate (the evangelical version of) the gospel in the Vietnamese culture and to let the gospel purify Vietnamese culture.[28] In the first step, the

25 Quynh-Hoa Nguyen, "Tin Lành," 78.

26 Edward Said, *Orientalism* (New York: Vintage, 1979), translated into Vietnamese as *Đông phương luận* by Lưu Đoàn Huynh, Phạm Xuân Ri, Trần Văn Tụy (Hà Nội: Tri Thức, 2014).

27 Quynh-Hoa Nguyen, "Tin Lành," 81–82. This thesis is, however, underdeveloped. It may be assumed on the basis of other works, such as R. S. Sugirtharajah's *The Bible and the Third World*, but scholars will need to make such arguments.

28 Dung Le, "The Bamboo Cross," 26, 137, 165.

gospel needs to become incarnate through the use of local cultural materials to represent it to the native Vietnamese—a move inspired by the work of Taiwanese theologian C. S. Song.[29] In the second step, once the gospel is inculturated, it will transform the negative aspects of Vietnamese culture. For example, if Vietnamese evangelicals can embrace the transforming practice of ordaining women who are called to the ministry, they will successfully counterbalance one aspect of the traditional patriarchal culture that minimizes the social presence and agency of women. In this and other ways, the idea of *transformation* includes the promotion of corrective actions that can improve culture.

Another line of transformational thinking proposes the inclusion of charity and humanitarian aid as valid components of the evangelical mission—a proposal resulting from the belief that missionaries have placed too much emphasis on evangelism and the establishment of churches and thus shortchanged social involvement.[30] The suggested solution is that Vietnamese evangelicals pay adequate attention to both tasks, those of sharing the Good News and of providing charity and humanitarian aid to the needy, thus bringing about healing, liberation, and human flourishing to Vietnamese society.[31] Furthering this line of thought, the praxis of *transformation* is also conceived as involvement in community development work, such as looking after the elderly, caring for orphans, and providing medical care to the sick, as illustrated through the work of the Socio-Medical Committee of the Evangelical Church of Vietnam–South (ECVN-South).[32]

The proposed transformational thinking, however, presents both practical and theoretical challenges when it reaches Vietnamese evangelicals at the grassroots level. In practice, *transformation* has taken an unexpected turn as a result of being imbued with a power-driven, politically-fascinated imagination. Several Vietnamese evangelicals believe political power can be used to implement Christian values in *the world* so *the world* can be transformed into a better place for all. The desire to change *the world* through politics is evidenced in countless prayers that political leaders will become God-fearers, lead the nation with integrity, and treat Christians with dignity. Among pentecostal evangelicals, transformational expectation is even higher; because they give special

---

29 See C. S. Song, *Theology from the Womb of Asia* (Maryknoll, NY: Orbis, 1986).

30 Tu Truong, "Mệnh Trời," 67. See also Cuong Nguyen, "The Growth of Certain Protestant Churches," 18; Phạm Xuân Tín, "Lược sử Giáo Hội Tin Lành Việt Nam" ["A Short History of the Evangelical Church of Vietnam"] (unpublished manuscript, 1991).

31 Tu Truong, "Mệnh Trời," vi, 287.

32 See also the emphasis on community development as a worthy evangelical work to bring about social transformation in D. A. Carson, *Christ and Culture Revisited* (Grand Rapids: Eerdmans, 2008), 202.

attention to the belief in God's empowerment and miraculous intervention in worldly events, they expect to see the faithful appointed to political offices and then honor God by doing good deeds for the whole nation. Granted, the political impact of Vietnamese pentecostal evangelicals happens on a much smaller scale as compared to other global contexts in which pentecostal Christians represent a larger segment of the population and therefore hold considerable political power. But following a rising trend in the Global South,[33] the dream of transforming *the world* through political power exists and is growing among Vietnamese pentecostal evangelicals.

The power-driven imagination of *transformation* is also demonstrated in Vietnamese evangelicals' enthusiastic reception of *dominion theology*, the teaching that society must be governed and directed by Christian principles. In Vietnam, *dominion theology* is popularized through the teaching that Christians have a "mandate" to "dominate" the seven public spheres of business, government, media, arts and entertainment, education, the family, and religion in order to transform society.[34] This perspective becomes problematic when the belief in God's empowerment is fused with the belief that Christians must subdue and rule over the earth, thus producing a triumphant attitude that is prone to the misuse of power whenever power is granted.[35]

Political power also fascinates Vietnamese evangelicals when it is conceived as a convenient means to end religious persecution. Although persecution and martyrdom are perceived as means through which Christianity grows, persecuted evangelicals may not see persecution as a blessing; if at all possible, they would rather find a different way to win converts.[36] In fact, persecuted

33 For further information on this trend, see the two essays in the section "Pentecostalism and Politics" in Donald E. Miller et al., eds., *Spirit and Power: The Growth and Global Impact of Pentecostalism* (New York: Oxford University Press, 2013), 101–41.

34 "7culturalmountains.org," accessed February 30, 2017, http://www.7culturalmountains.org/. See also C. Peter Wagner, *Dominion!: How Kingdom Action Can Change the World* (Grand Rapids: Chosen Books, 2008). For a recent examination of pentecostal growth and the use of *dominion theology* (in Brazil), see Rudolf von Sinner, "Pentecostalism and Citizenship in Brazil: Between Escapism and Dominance," *International Journal of Public Theology* 6, no. 1 (2012): 99–117.

35 On pentecostal triumphalism, see David J. Courey, *What Has Wittenberg to Do with Azusa?: Luther's Theology of the Cross and Pentecostal Triumphalism* (London: T&T Clark, 2015). See also Jung Young Lee's call for the resistance of triumphalist desire among marginalized people in his *Marginality: The Key to Multicultural Theology* (Minneapolis: Fortress, 1995).

36 Argued similarly in Gerald Schlabach, "Deuteronomic or Constantinian: What is the Most Basic Problem for Christian Social Ethics?" in *The Wisdom of the Cross: Essays in Honor of John Howard Yoder*, ed. Stanley Hauerwas et al. (Grand Rapids: Eerdmans, 1999), 449–71, esp. 451–56.

churches are more likely to pray for the cessation of persecution, and even for the realization of some similar, peaceful version of Christendom in which Christianity would not only be legalized but also receive political favor. For the most part, this perspective sees the Christendom arrangement as a blessing and foretaste of the coming reign of God. Although it has been noted that abuse of power did emerge through the first "experiment" of Christendom due to the lack of experience on the part of Emperor Constantine and the fourth-century Christians in Europe and East Africa,[37] there is hope that, by learning from the mistakes of the past, the next Constantines and the next churches living in the contemporary Global South may get Christendom right.[38] Since this perspective on Christendom views political power as a means of *transformation*, it has less relevance to Vietnamese pentecostal evangelicals in their current socio-political setting, for these people have limited access to political power in general. Christendom thus remains a desire more than an actual mode of engagement with *the world* that Vietnamese evangelicals can practice.

In addition to the above practical challenges, transformational thinking also presents theoretical problems for Vietnamese evangelicals. Here problems emerge in their uncritical use of Niebuhr's *Christ and Culture* by treating Niebuhr's proposal of *Christ transforming culture* as intrinsically good and, presumably, without theological limits.[39] In a quick summary of Niebuhr,

37 John Howard Yoder, "The Constantinian Sources of Western Social Ethics," in *The Priestly Kingdom: Social Ethics as Gospel* (Notre Dame: University of Notre Dame Press, 1985), 135–47.

38 William T. Cavanaugh, "What Constantine Has to Teach Us," in *Constantine Revisited: Leithart, Yoder, and the Constantinian Debate*, ed. John D. Roth (Eugene, OR: Wipf & Stock, 2013), 83–99; Peter J. Leithart, "Afterword," in *Constantine Revisited*, 184–87. See also Peter J. Leithart, *Defending Constantine: The Twilight of an Empire and the Dawn of Christendom* (Downers Grove, IL: IVP Academic, 2010); and J. Alexander Sider, "Constantinianism before and after Nicea: Issues in Restitutionist Historiography," in *A Mind Patient and Untamed: Assessing John Howard Yoder's Contributions to Theology, Ethics, and Peacemaking*, ed. Ben C. Ollenburger and Gayle Gerber Koontz (Telford, PA: Cascadia, 2004), 126–44.

39 For a criticism of the notion of *transformation*, see John Howard Yoder, *The Politics of Jesus: Vicit Agnus Noster* (2nd ed., Grand Rapids: Eerdmans, 1994), 240, 246–47. As of today, the Vietnamese evangelical scholarly discussion has not engaged Yoder or the wider Yoderian scholarship. Yoder's sexual misconduct can also stain his theological legacy. On Yoder's sexual abuse, see Rachel Waltner Goossen, " 'Defanging the Beast': Mennonite Responses to John Howard Yoder's Sexual Abuse," *Mennonite Quarterly Review* 89 (January 2015): 7–80. On how to (re)appropriate Yoder's theology in the light of his misconduct, see David Cramer et al., "Scandalizing John Howard Yoder," *The Other Journal*, July 17, 2014, accessed February 1, 2017, http://theotherjournal.com/2014/07/07/scandalizing-john-howard-yoder/.

Christ, in broad terms, encompasses the Christian Messiah, the Jesus of the New Testament, the Christian church, and Christians in general. *Culture,* also in broad terms, represents *the world,* the wider public, and all spheres of life. Niebuhr's typology offers five options to how the Christian church can relate to culture: against culture, accommodated to culture, in paradoxical relation to culture, above culture, and transforming culture. Niebuhr maintains that a Christian community is faithful as long as it aligns itself with one of these particular positions since each has support from the Christian scriptures. Niebuhr, however, favors the idea of *Christ transforming culture* and is more critical of the idea of *Christ against culture.*

The use of Niebuhr directs Vietnamese evangelical thinking about *the world* toward an investigation of the level of compatibility between *faith* and *culture,* and Vietnamese evangelical scholars often identify with Niebuhr's category of *Christ against culture.* Here Vietnamese evangelicals are pictured as a sectarian group that holds a nihilistic stance against the outside world. Furthermore, Niebuhr's typology quickly offers Vietnamese authors a solution to the problem of being *against culture,* namely, embarking on a mission of *transforming culture,* which includes charity and performing corrective actions that can improve culture.

It is, however, noteworthy that the Niebuhrian proposal of *transforming culture* has no viable link to the Jesus of the New Testament. The late Anabaptist ethicist John Howard Yoder correctly points out the tension that, for Niebuhr, Christ is "the Lord both over nature and all human history by virtue of his resurrection and ascension," while Jesus, on the other hand, is a "radical monotheist" whose chief concern is to " 'point away' both from the world and from himself to his Father who alone is worthy of loyalty."[40] When Niebuhr juxtaposes Christ and Jesus in this manner, Jesus is rendered inadequate to provide serious guidance for Christian engagement with *the world.* In contrast to Niebuhr, Yoder thinks the critical Christian idea is *Jesus against the world,* not *Christ transforming culture.* Jesus, for Yoder, comes to *the world* not to transform it but to proclaim the Jubilee message of forgiveness, reconciliation, and liberation of God's kingdom in a nonviolent manner and to endure hardships patiently if *the world* violently protests the message.[41] For evangelicals in contemporary Vietnam, or for that matter evangelicals in other Global

40 John Howard Yoder, "How H. Richard Niebuhr Reasoned: A Critique of Christ and Culture," in *Authentic Transformation: A New Vision of Christ and Culture; with a Previously Unpublished Essay by H. Richard Niebuhr,* by Glen Stassen et al. (Nashville: Abingdon, 1996), 31–89: 59–60.

41 So goes the major thesis of Yoder's *The Politics of Jesus.*

South settings, this question of where the emphasis lies is of the utmost concern, because evangelicals are inclined to derive normative actions from the New Testament teachings of Jesus more than from those of any other figure. In Vietnamese evangelical theology, therefore, a major challenge in using the category of *transformation* consists in interpreting how the Jesus of the New Testament, and not the Christ constructed by theologians, is an archetype of Christian social engagement.[42]

One can certainly follow Yoder one step further by suggesting that the Christian life does not need to be socially passive or irresponsible while embracing a stance against *the world*. The people of God should always "seek the welfare of the city," as the prophet Jeremiah exhorts diasporic Jews of the sixth century BCE.[43] Like these Jews, the contemporary Christian church for Yoder is also a diasporic community-one living in exile in *the world*. Yoder suggests the church can settle in and serve the entire world through secular professions that benefit *the world*. While the idea of "seeking the welfare of the city" is positive, it creates an inconsistency in Yoder's own theological ethics. Although Yoder's theology begins with Jesus, who came to proclaim a message of Jubilee, it ends with Jeremiah as offering norms of Christian social ethics. Is this inconsistency a result of Yoder's inability to find a New Testament Jesus who teaches his disciples to seek society's common good?

In retrospect, Yoder's proposal of "seeking the peace of the city" is an attempt to prove that his ethical prescription is responsible, effective, and has transformative results—values that his contemporary American public may approve. Such approval gives evidence that Yoder's earlier, more radical-Jesus politics has been co-opted into mainstream American pragmatist thinking about *transformation* as Yoder envisioned the concept during his lifetime.[44] Likewise, Vietnamese evangelicals find transformational thinking attractive because they believe that works of *transformation* can demonstrate their Vietnamese identity and commitment, thus revealing their desire to be treated

42 For an initial Christological development in this direction, see Glen Stassen, "Concrete Christological Norms for Transformation," in Stassen et al., *Authentic Transformation*, 127–90. See also Darío López Rodriguez, *The Liberating Mission of Jesus: The Message of the Gospel of Luke*, trans. Stefanie E. Israel and Richard E. Waldrop (Eugene, OR: Wipf & Stock, 2012).

43 John Howard Yoder, *For the Nations: Essays Evangelical and Public* (Grand Rapids: Eerdmans, 1997), 51–53, 71. See also Richard Bourne, *Seek the Peace of the City: Christian Political Criticism as Public, Realist, and Transformative* (Eugene, OR: Cascade, 2009).

44 For Yoder's rejection of efficacy and achievement of the good cause in the 1970s, see Yoder, *The Politics of Jesus*, 240, 246–47. For his later return to "social effectivity" in the 1990s, see Yoder, *For the Nations*, 2.

with more respect by mainstream Vietnamese and to be validated in their faith. There is, therefore, a shared sentiment among Vietnamese evangelical scholars, a "grief for the church that is not working for the good of all people," that propels the idea of *transformation* as a worthy endeavor.[45] In societies that are more hostile to evangelicals, this psychological factor is even more apparent, and it needs to be examined in order for others to understand how it contributes to the preference for *transformation* in evangelicals' writings in Vietnam and elsewhere.

To summarize, as Vietnamese evangelical authors continue to consider the meaning of *transformation*, the concept needs further consideration in at least three aspects: its theological rationale of Jesus as authoritative for the agenda of social change; its usefulness as a political-theological category, given the general situation of the powerlessness of Vietnamese evangelicals; and its compatibility relative to the evangelical tension of being "in *the world* but not of *the world*." Apparently, the tension as to whether Christians should separate from *the world* or seek to transform *the world* is here to stay. Thus, those who wish to advance transformational thinking in Vietnamese evangelicalism bear the burden of wrestling with the complexity that the late ethicist Jean Bethke Elshtain eloquently expressed about a decade ago:

> As a stand-alone posture, against too often turns into brittle condemnation, a stance of haughty (presumed) moral superiority, wagons circled. Transform on its own may degenerate into naïve idealism and utopianism ... Avoiding these extremes, we must see Christ against and for, agonistic and affirming, arguing and embracing. This is complex but, then, Christianity is no stranger to complexity.[46]

1.4 Apocalypse Now!

Within the context of the pentecostal emphasis on *divine intervention*, the idea of *apocalypse* is viewed as the often-preferred way God uses to engage *the world*. Because underprivileged Vietnamese evangelicals at the grassroots level perceive *the world* (understood as contemporary Vietnamese society) as full of injustice, hedonism, corruption, and hostility, *the world* deserves an *apocalypse*. But contrary to popular belief about *apocalypse* as bringing closure,

45 Quynh-Hoa Nguyen, "Tin Lành," 217.

46 Jean Bethke Elshtain, "With or Against Culture?" *Books & Culture* 12, no. 5 (September-October 2006): 28–30: 30, as quoted in D. A. Carson, *Christ and Culture Revisited*, 227.

the *apocalypse* informed by the New Testament Book of Revelation includes both a destruction of the old world and an inauguration of a new world. In the language of Revelation 21, "a new heaven and a new earth" emerge at the end of the *apocalypse* following the nullification of the old world. As Jesus came to *the world* with an apocalyptic mission to proclaim the subversion of the *status quo* of *the world* and unveil new realities, Jesus continues to send his disciples into *the world* to do likewise at the present time. The message is that Jesus is the Lord, who assumes sovereignty, challenges the *status quo*, unveils new realities, and anticipates the healing of *the world*.[47] While the popular apocalyptic literature treats *apocalypse* as a closing event, this perspective maintains that *apocalypse* is an inauguration of a new reality.[48] In this grassroots perspective of the pentecostalism prevalent among the contemporary Vietnamese evangelicals, God often intervenes in *the world* through a rather disruptive, *apocalypse*-like event more than through a long process of gradual *transformation*.

In a nutshell, pentecostalism's emphasis on the belief that God will intervene in human affairs in an apocalyptic manner offers two relevant values to the underprivileged in contemporary Vietnam: the *apocalypse* of *the world* is essentially a call for the subversion of the unfavorable social *status quo*, as well as an invitation to imagine a new, improved condition of life. For Vietnamese evangelicals, who represent a marginalized group within Vietnamese society, *apocalypse* is first and foremost a proclamation that the social conditions of marginalization due to ideological and other differences do not need to continue as they are. To the wider Vietnamese public, *apocalypse* represents a Christian missional mentality by proclaiming that contemporary Vietnamese society does not need to continue as it is. The proposed concept of *apocalypse* asks first for a disruption, since transformative engagement, when initiated by the less powerful in an asymmetric relationship of power, often leads to the co-opting of the less powerful into the existing power structure and the maintenance of the *status quo* of that structure, thus hindering the unveiling of newness. Here *apocalypse* is also a necessarily disruptive intervention into a

47 For further information, see Nathan Kerr, *Christ, History and Apocalyptic: The Politics of Christian Mission* (Eugene, OR: Cascade, 2008).

48 On the *apocalypse* as the unveiling of newness, see Amos Yong, *In the Days of Caesar: Pentecostalism and Political Theology*, Sacra Doctrina: Christian Theology for a Postmodern Age Series (Grand Rapids: Eerdmans, 2010), chapter 8. Also, on the *novum* at the center of the emergence of the pentecostal phenomenon, see Nimi Wariboko, *The Pentecostal Principle: Ethical Methodology in New Spirit*, The Pentecostal Manifestos Series (Grand Rapids: Eerdmans, 2011), 203.

society so comfortable with the current configuration of power relations that its collective imagination is no longer able to envision alternative social constructions.[49]

On the other hand, the apocalyptic proclamation of subverting the *status quo* in search of new realities should not be promoted as a constant mode of engaging *the world*. Divine interruption, from a historical perspective, is an all-consuming period that is supposed to last for a certain length of time.[50] The taxing nature of engagement in constantly proclaiming subversion makes doing so unrealistic; therefore, the apocalyptic proclamation of subversion is to find its balance in outward disruption (to seek the destruction of the old world) and inward construction (to refine the imagination of a new world).

The helpful insights of feminist theologian Sarah Coakley define the apocalyptic imagination of a better world as "the opening up of space and a non-coercive power that is enacted in vulnerability."[51] The marvels of imagination reveal the possibility that, even in a state of inequality, new patterns of life can be imagined, new connections developed, and new ways of being made possible. For the powerless evangelicals and other marginalized, wrongfully treated people in contemporary Vietnam, the invitation to participate in such imagination is relevant because it is an invitation to create new relationships and new networks of hope and trust, even amid oppressive power structures. Such emphasis on the imagination of newness is a major factor in explaining the attraction of the evangelical message at the grassroots level. An anthropological account of the significance of conversion for a major evangelical ethnic group in Vietnam, therefore, is rightly titled *The New Way*.[52] Its insistence on the positive imagination of life is similar to the psychological language of Holocaust survivor Viktor Frankl that life has meaning under all circumstances,

49 Similar criticism concerning the lack of collective imagination, directed at the configuration of material life in many African societies, can be found in Nimi Wariboko, *Economics in Spirit and Truth: A Moral Philosophy of Finance* (New York: Palgrave, 2014), 115, 134.

50 So argues Cecil M. Robeck Jr. in *The Azusa Street Mission and Revival* (Nashville: Thomas Nelson, 2006), 313–26.

51 Sarah Coakley, "*Kenosis* and Subversion: On the Repression of 'Vulnerability' in Christian Feminist Writing," in *Swallowing a Fishbone?*, ed. Daphne Hampson (London: SPCK, 1996), 82–111, as quoted in Mark G. Brett, "Diaspora and Kenosis as Postcolonial Themes," in *Decolonizing the Body of Christ: Theology and Theory after Empire?*, ed. David Joy and Joseph Duggan (New York: Palgrave Macmillan, 2012), 127–40: 129. See also the discussion on kenosis in the section titled "Postcolonial Theology and Ethics," in Mark G. Brett, *Decolonizing God: The Bible in the Tides of Empire* (Sheffield: Sheffield Phoenix, 2009), 178–204.

52 Tam T. T. Ngo, *The New Way: Protestantism and the Hmong in Vietnam* (Seattle: University of Washington Press, 2016).

and human beings, even in situations of unavoidable suffering, still have the freedom to find meaning.[53]

It is understandable that society will *not* change exactly in the way the evangelicals imagine. Sometimes society does improve and reflect the evangelical imagination of what should be, sometimes not—hence the wisdom from the Augustinian perspective that Christians are to remember their engagement with *the world* is simply *iconic* at best.[54] Such understanding is a welcome component of apocalyptic thinking in recognition of the shortcomings of human powers of imagination. While imagination differentiates humankind from other animals,[55] the faculty of imagination is a rather new addition to the human brain. This faculty can point toward a positive future but is most likely to create an inaccurate picture of what will actually become reality.[56]

It can also be said that the suggested apocalyptic imagination of newness has a kenotic quality in its inviting new thinking. While its proclaiming the subversion of the *status quo* may sometimes give the impression of being reactionary (by promoting the turning of the power structure upside down so the powerless become powerful and *vice versa*), kenotic imagination invites new thinking about relationships of power in non-hierarchical and non-dualistic terms. As the term kenosis denotes, it is an invitation to rethink from *outside* the existing form of the current structures, in contradistinction to *transformation,* which implies preservation of the existing form. In kenotic imagination, it is not that the current power structure is reversed (thus suggesting its preservation), but that the power structure is reimagined differently. The kenosis aspect helps the apocalyptic mission move beyond the subversion of existing power structures in order to ignite an imagination of power in non-hierarchical terms.

53 Viktor Frankl, *Man's Search for Meaning* (1946. Boston: Beacon, 2006). See also Robert C. Leslie, *Jesus and Logotherapy: The Ministry of Jesus as Interpreted through the Psychotherapy of Viktor Frankl* (New York: Abingdon, 1965).

54 See Charles T. Mathewes, *The Republic of Grace: Augustinian Thoughts for Dark Times* (Grand Rapids: Eerdmans, 2010). See also Gerald Schlabach, "The Christian Witness in the Earthly City: John H. Yoder as Augustinian Interlocutor," in *A Mind Patient and Untamed: Assessing John Howard Yoder's Contribution to Theology, Ethics, and Peacemaking*, ed. Ben C. Ollenburger and Gayle Gerber Koontz (Telford, PA: Cascadia, 2004), 221–44; Peter Burnell, *The Augustinian Person* (Washington, DC: The Catholic University of America Press, 2005).

55 See, for example, the argument in Yuval Noah Harari, *Sapiens: A Brief History of Humankind* (London: Harvill Secker, 2014).

56 On the foibles of imagination, discussed in laypeople's terms, see Daniel Gilbert, *Stumbling on Happiness* (New York: Alfred A. Knopf, 2006).

What kenotic imagination is *not* is an invitation to embrace self-emptying and self-abnegation, although this thinking is inspired by the Christology of Philippians 2:1–11, which sees Christ Jesus as setting an example of Christian humility and self-emptying. For Vietnamese evangelicals, this thinking is unhelpful because it induces the powerless to practice self-abnegation rather than self-assertion, and because it relies on the goodwill of the powerful "other" to determine whether or not to allow space for the powerless. It is only in the context of redistributing power to the powerless that the idea of self-emptying can be constructive, in that it can help these newly empowered persons to resist the temptation of "lording" over others—a latent problem in even the most marginalized communities, since they also have the potential to create internal, abusive power structures. It is in the context of this ongoing challenge concerning the abuse of power that the apocalyptic mission has relevance, for it calls for subverting each new system of abuse that becomes the *status quo*. Here the need for constant awareness of the potential for power abuse to re-emerge constitutes an affirmation of feminist theologian Kwok Pui-lan's passionate call for "*more* analysis" (emphasis original) of cultural, socio-economic, and political conditions in theological constructions.[57] The apocalyptic mission expects that Christians will eventually find their place in *the world*, but they must develop a consciousness that identifies and rejects emerging abuses of power when newly founded institutions or transformed existing structures "default back to sovereign power."[58]

In the context of dispossessing ethnic minorities of land and resources,[59] many of the dispossessed are evangelicals; and in the context of increasing

57 As quoted in George E. Tinker, *American Indian Liberation: A Theology of Sovereignty* (Maryknoll, NY: Orbis, 2008), 35.

58 Roger Haydon Mitchell and Julie Tomlin Arram, eds., *Discovering Kenarchy: Contemporary Resources for the Politics of Love* (Eugene, OR: Cascade, 2014), 13. See also Roger Haydon Mitchell, *Church, Gospel, and Empire: How the Politics of Sovereignty Impregnated the West* (Eugene, OR: Wipf & Stock, 2011); and Roger Haydon Mitchell, *The Fall of the Church* (Eugene, OR: Wipf & Stock, 2013).

59 On the problem of material dispossession, see the special issue on contests over land in rural Vietnam, *Journal of Vietnamese Studies* 9, no. 3 (Summer 2014). The issue of land grabbing in contemporary Vietnam is also well-reported in the media. See, for example, the section on Vietnam in Radio Free Asia's video report "Asia's Great Land Grab: A Special RFA Report," April 2015, accessed April 30, 2015, http://www.rfa.org/english/news/special/landgrab/home.html, and "Out of sight: Continuing grinding poverty in Vietnam's minority regions is a liability for the Communist Party," *The Economist*, April 4, 2015, accessed April 30, 2015, http://www.economist.com/news/asia/21647653-continuing-grinding-poverty-vietnams-minority-regions-liability-communist-party-out. For a theological resource on the intersection of dreaming (the imagination) and land (the material space of life) in the thinking of aboriginal peoples, see Hans-Georg Ziebertz

consumerism and hedonism in late-communist Vietnam, the kenotic aspect of the apocalyptic imagination also has particular material implications—it represents the rejection of hoarding natural resources, land, sources of energy, and materials. Thus the call to "preserve space" for the powerless does not refer merely to space for discussing ideas and opinions; more importantly, it refers to space in which to live and to adequate material resources for furthering life, including restitution for wrongful dispossession in the past and promotion the stewardship of resources. From this perspective, the kenotic imagination and other Christian principles of restitution and stewardship also have the potential to comprise a helpful theological category in the Vietnamese public square.

Also in the context of the dispossession of land, it becomes difficult to advocate *exile* as a normal stage of life, although the metaphor of *exile* has been widely used to refer to Christians as a spiritual people longing for a heavenly home.[60] A desirable social norm for Vietnamese evangelicals should be a settled life, imagined as a life rooted in a relatively peaceful, undisputed land, with a just social structure and good social and economic conditions to support human flourishing, assuming that the faithful remain conscious of potentially emerging abuses of power in their midst as living conditions improve. Moreover, the concept of *exile* has been intellectualized in the writings of authors working in the academia of the Global North, increasingly viewed as a helpful stage in the development of the mind to become critical and unattached to ideologies of exclusion, thus less attention has been given to the material dimension of the dispossession and "landlessness" of people in the Global South.[61] That said, as an ethical norm the imagination of a settled life, in which people enter a "promised land," is preferred to *exile* for stimulating Vietnamese evangelical thinking about how they should rebuild life in a world characterized by

---

and Friedrich Schweitzer, eds., *Dreaming the Land: Theologies of Resistance and Hope*, International Practical Theology (Berlin: Lit-Verlag, 2007). On dispossession, see also Judith Butler and Athena Athanasiou, *Dispossession: The Performative in the Political* (Malden, MA: Polity, 2013).

60 See Gerald Schlabach, "Deuteronomic or Constantinian"; Walter Brueggemann, *The Land: Place as Gift, Promise, and Challenge in Biblical Faith*, 2nd ed., Overtures to Biblical Theology (Minneapolis: Augsburg Fortress, 2003). In contrast, on *exile* as a normal stage of Christian life, see Yoder, "See How They Go with Their Face to the Sun," in *For the Nations: Essays Evangelical and Public*, 51–78.

61 Compare, for example, Edward Said, *Representations of the Intellectual: The 1993 Reith Lectures* (New York: Pantheon, 1994), chapter 3, and his *Power, Politics, and Culture* (New York: Vintage, 2002), 53–68, esp. 56.

corruption and dispossession. This approach bears a general resemblance to the use of the Exodus story in the early days of liberation theology as it developed in Latin America.[62] The ethical requirement that people in exile or diaspora have the opportunity to return "home" is thus to show an "exilic consciousness" in order to prevent exclusivity between peoples and territories.[63]

In retrospect, apocalyptic thinking, in its imagination of how life should be in a new world, is helpful in creating an enhanced framework of thought—one that includes both a radical rejection of *the world* which creates suffering among evangelicals, and an initial sanctioning of the pursuit of transformative social actions by evangelicals, who may do so as a form of anticipatory participation in the unveiling of the new world promised by Jesus. This enhanced framework, therefore, does not insist on excluding *transformation* as a mode of engaging *the world*; rather, it asks how social engagement can resist the tendency to be co-opted into existing power structures.

The limitation of the apocalyptic viewpoint, of course, is its lack of emphasis on understanding the church as an alternative *polis* to *the world*—a *polis* in which the primary mission of the church should be the building of Christian identity through Christian discipleship embodied in liturgy and narrative, not the ongoing, outward proclamation of the apocalyptic message to the outside world. While a balanced theological construction of Christian mission may wish to include *apocalypse* and discipleship together, both elements can serve as equally good starting points. Regarding Vietnamese evangelicals, it is simply convenient to begin with *apocalypse* in large part due to its popularity within their grassroots thinking about *the world* and the way God intervenes in *the world*.[64]

---

62 Gustavo Gutierrez, *A Theology of Liberation: History, Politics, and Salvation* (New York: Orbis, 1973), 155–56.

63 Argued Alain Epp Weaver in his *States of Exile: Visions of Diaspora, Witness, and Return* (Scottdale, PA: Herald Press, 2008), and *Mapping Exile and Return: Palestinian Dispossession and a Political Theology for a Shared Future* (Minneapolis: Fortress Press, 2014).

64 On how the emphasis on the apocalyptic mission results in a rather vague understanding of the church, see Nathan Kerr's abstract vision of the church as a "non-place" in *the world* in his "*Communio Missionis*: Certeau, Yoder, and the Missionary Space of the Church," in *The New Yoder*, ed. Peter Dula and Chris K. Huebner (Eugene, OR: Cascade, 2010), 317–35. See also Stanley Hauerwas's section "Mission after Christendom: A Response to Kerr," in his *War and the American Difference: Theological Reflections on Violence and National Identity* (Grand Rapids: Baker Academic, 2011), 174–79.

1.5 Conclusion

As has been noted, the concept of *the world* is fundamental to the evangelical message in Vietnam and has been rather consistently used in close relation to the moral and social conditions of twentieth-century Vietnam; in this usage, *the world* has carried negative connotations concerning Vietnamese society, Vietnamese culture, the Vietnamese state, and other Vietnamese social institutions. Accordingly, *the world* concept describes more accurately than the concept of *culture* the total reality that Vietnamese evangelicals are engaging. As a result, the scholarly discussion on Vietnamese evangelicalism may find *the world* to be the most important umbrella term for facilitating thinking about how best to engage Vietnamese society.[65]

In contemporary Vietnamese evangelical thinking, *the world* is essentially a morally corrupt society, full of injustice and hedonism, in which Vietnamese evangelicals experience powerlessness, marginalization, and hostility due to their being religious and ethnically different from their compatriots. The idea of transforming society, regardless of how positive it may appear, needs to undergo further development in at least three different aspects: reflection on the compatibility of the idea of *transformation* with the evangelical conviction of being "not of this world"; examination of the usefulness of *transformation* as a political-theological category given the general situation of powerlessness on the part of Vietnamese evangelicals; and theological construction of a "Jesus-ology," not a "Christ-ology," that brings about transformative social action.

Within the development of pentecostalism among contemporary Vietnamese evangelicals, the idea that God intervenes in *the world* in an apocalyptic manner gains traction because it offers relevant meaning to believers, who feel they are in an underprivileged position in Vietnamese society. Apocalyptic thinking not only gives the faithful a language for proclaiming an end to the unfavorable conditions of their life but also encourages their imagination of a new life in terms of securing both material and spiritual well-being after the *divine intervention* occurs. This apocalyptic thinking has three advantages over transformational thinking. First, by proclaiming the subversion of the *status quo*, the notion of *apocalypse* charges *the world* with constructing hierarchical structures of power that need to be challenged, not transformed; thus

65 For an example of the use of *the world* concept to facilitate the social engagement of Christian evangelicals, see The Third Lausanne Congress, *The Cape Town Commitment: A Confession of Faith and a Call to Action* (Peabody, MA: Hendrickson, 2011). See also Thomas Schirrmacher, ed.,"The Whole World." Special issue, *Evangelical Review of Theology* 34, no. 3 (2010).

the notion of *apocalypse* has relevance to the lived experience of Vietnamese evangelicals and resonates with their conviction of being "not of this world." Second, through the provision of kenotic space to reimagine power relations and the nature of power, apocalyptic thinking makes itself relevant to the powerless condition of Vietnamese evangelicals. It is also noteworthy that this kenotic space for imagining new power relations, or the settling of evangelicals in an improved society, has both ideological and material dimensions, so it can resist the tendency to spiritualize the political significance of *apocalypse* and ground it more in the material struggle of the underprivileged in contemporary Vietnam. Additionally, the theology of *apocalypse,* centered on the conviction of *Jesus against the world,* is more Jesus-oriented than the high-Christological transformational thinking and can therefore accommodate any socially transforming actions through its pursuit of newness. Thus the (re) emerging understanding that, in Jesus, God carries out God's *divine intervention* in an *apocalypse*-like manner is an important perspective rooted in the vernacular of pentecostalism among contemporary Vietnamese evangelicals; therefore, this apocalyptic understanding deserves to be registered in the overall evangelical social discourse alongside the language of *transforming culture.* It is noteworthy that, in the same social discourse, Vietnamese evangelicals also discuss the idea of *justice,* a subject to which we now turn our attention.

CHAPTER 2

Justice

2.1 Social, Not Political, Involvement

In recent years, *justice* has emerged as an important topic for discussion among contemporary Vietnamese evangelicals. This emergence reflects the common quest for social *justice* among the Vietnamese, as their disenchantment with the failure of the socialist vision to take root in society grows, and reflects the evangelicals' struggle with their own experience of social marginalization, oppression, and inequality. The development of the Vietnamese evangelical discussion on *justice* is therefore informed mainly by the Vietnamese situation and has little interaction with the longstanding Christian philosophical-theological reflections on *justice* as a cardinal virtue that have been articulated in other parts of the world. Scanning through the Vietnamese evangelical landscape will reveal at least three trajectories of *justice* at work among contemporary Vietnamese evangelicals, namely, the understandings of *justice* as *love*, *human rights*, and *divine deliverance*.

At the onset, it is also important to note that the renewed interest in *justice* arises even though the discussion on *justice* in Vietnamese evangelicalism faces both historical and political challenges. Historically, Vietnamese evangelicals have no elaborated theory of *justice* and no well-defined policy on how to relate to the state regarding their shared commitment to social *justice*, or lack thereof, compared to, for example, Vietnamese Roman Catholics, who have rather well-documented materials on Catholic social teachings, and whose Committee on Peace and Justice, established in October 2010, provides an institutional platform to promote thinking about *justice*.[1] The century-old exhortation "do not love *the world*" has also positioned Vietnamese evangelicals mainly in the camp of maintaining minimal social involvement and seeing little use for the concept of *justice* in interacting with Vietnamese society. Furthermore, the topic of *justice* is increasingly politicized in contemporary Vietnam. Citizens who raise the issue of injustice are generally suspected of harboring a hidden agenda with the intent of challenging the State's authority

1 See, for example, Pontifical Council for Justice and Peace, *Tóm lược học thuyết xã hội của Giáo Hội Công Giáo* [*Compendium of the Social Doctrine of the Church*], trans. Caritas Vietnam (Hà Nội: Tôn Giáo, 2007).

 | DOI:10.1163/9789004383838_004

because such emphasis often gives rise to criticism of the public administration, solely determined by the CPV.

The politicization of the Vietnamese discussion on *justice*, however, is not a new development pertaining to contemporary Vietnam; it can be traced back to the late 1920s and the early 1930s, when party politics arose as an important native means of coping with colonialism. A particularly notable partnership employing party politics arose in 1930: the CPV, a merger of a few Vietnamese communist groups to build on strength. The CPV won mass conversions by offering the Vietnamese people a concrete vision of *justice* to end both colonial and class exploitation in the country and to build a new society in which people would receive equal access to goods and services according to their needs. With the rise of party politics and party discipleship, the earlier humanist aspiration for personal liberty—from the constraints of both tradition and colonialism—was elided, and the quest for *justice* was discussed along ideological lines. This particular historical configuration provided to the Vietnamese public an impression that those who talked about *justice* were in one way or another getting involved in politics, for better or for worse.

During the last century, the Vietnamese evangelical stance toward the State can be best characterized as *situational*, a description that reflects both evangelicals' lack of detailed guidelines on church-state relations and the rapid change of political power in Vietnam in the twentieth century. Since C&MA missionaries set up their first mission station in the country in 1911 and the first native evangelical church was established in 1927, Vietnamese evangelicals have engaged with several political powers. Before 1945, the main political players in Vietnam included the French colonial administration of Indochina and the Vietnamese Royalty (the Imperial Court of Vietnam), plus a legion of organized political groups whose ideas of changing Vietnam covered the entire spectrum from violent revolution to nonviolent reform. Following the Vietnamese Revolution (August 1945) and during the First Indochina War (1945–1954), a significant political power in Vietnam consisted in the League for the Independence of Vietnam (commonly known as the *Việt Minh*), a national independence coalition with a high representation of Vietnamese communists. From the end of the First Indochina War (1954) to the end of the Vietnam War (1975), Vietnam was divided into North Vietnam and South Vietnam, with the League for the Independence of Vietnam assuming political power in the North and running it as a socialist state called the Democratic Republic of Vietnam, while non-communist political leaders formed another government in the South, formally known as the Republic of Vietnam. After the Vietnam War ended, the CPV outlawed all other political parties and became the sole political power governing the current Socialist Republic of Vietnam.

The first major official document produced by the Vietnamese evangelicals consisted in the 1928 Constitution of the Evangelical Church of Indochina—predecessor of the current ECVN (South) and ECVN (North)—and was approved after the establishment of the native evangelical church in 1927. The 1928 document stated plainly that the indigenous church (as a social institution) and its members (as individual citizens) were not to get involved in any "rebellious act against the government," namely the French Administration of Indochina and the Imperial Court of Vietnam, with "rebellious act" referring to the joining of secret political parties and participating in protests. The decision showed the substantial influence of the C&MA missionaries, whose chief concern (as non-French Westerners) was to maintain good relationships with the French and to prove the missionaries were not spies trying to undermine France's interests in Indochina. Church historian Phu Le observed that the French were fairly tolerant toward the Canadian and American missionaries but were suspicious of German-born missionaries and of those of German descent due to Germany's role in the First World War.[2] At the same time, the decision showed a valid concern on the part of the early native converts and pioneer missionaries that political involvement, either by being supportive of the French colonial administration, the Imperial Court of Vietnam, or any one of the numerous opposing political groups seeking to reform or protest the French and the Imperial Court, would compromise the spiritual purity of the church and give reason for its persecution and censure for using religion to advance political agendas.

Prior to the arrival of the C&MA missionaries in 1911, Chinese versions of the four Gospels had already come to Vietnam at the same time that other revolutionist and anticolonial literature (written by the Chinese or Japanese, or translated into the Chinese languages from Western materials) began to spill over from South China to Vietnam.[3] When the French administration and the Vietnamese Imperial Court decided to ban this literature, they grouped Chinese evangelical, revolutionist, and anticolonialist materials together under the label *"yêu thư, yêu ngôn"—"heretical literature, heretical sayings."* Also unhelpful was the fact that the Gospel of Mark appeared in the form of a short booklet with a red cover. The color red and the title *Mark* caused suspicion

2 Phu Le, "A Short History of the Evangelical Church of Viet Nam (1911–1965)" (Ph.D. diss., New York University, 1972), 154.

3 For further information on the South Chinese influence of Vietnamese evangelicalism, an aspect often overlooked in the writing of Vietnamese evangelical history, see Phan Đình Liệu, "Lịch Sử Hội Thánh Tin Lành Việt Nam" [History of the Evangelical Church of Vietnam] (unpublished manuscript, 1966).

that the booklet contained Marxist communist propaganda. In response to political suspicion, the missionaries defended themselves by adopting a strict position of *non-interference-in-politics*, then instructed native believers to act likewise as they penned the first constitution for the indigenous church.

Fast forwarding to the end of the 1945 Vietnamese Revolution, the policy of *non-interference-in-politics* was invoked by pastor Lê Văn Thái, then leader of the Northern District of the ECVN, by means of his refusal to establish a patriotic organization within the church. His defiance of the recommendation to do so by communist leader Hồ Chí Minh did not go without risk to Lê Văn Thái's personal safety, for this act could have been regarded as civil disobedience.[4] The incident took place in Hà Nội immediately after the predominantly communist-led League for the Independence of Vietnam came to power, thanks to a successful uprising. Pastor Lê Văn Thái argued that all evangelicals were already patriots, in the sense that they had always loved their country, and that prior to the recommendation the church had already had the policy of *non-interference-in-politics*; therefore, evangelicals should be exempted from the recommendation to create a patriotic organization within the church. Since then, this stance has been upheld by Vietnamese evangelicals as the guiding principle for relating to the communists politically.

Following the division of Vietnam into North and South Vietnam in 1954, when most evangelicals (and Roman Catholics) moved south, the policy of *non-interference-in-politics* was altered considerably in South Vietnam. Native church leaders, less influenced by the C&MA missionaries, made a significant revision to the 1928 Constitution when they penned the 1956 Constitution of the ECVN (South): they dropped a clause that stipulated the withdrawal of membership from those getting involved in "rebellious acts against the government." In practice, while the church *as a religious organization* upheld the *non-interference-in-politics* policy, it now allowed its members *as individual citizens* to engage in politics.

Before the church revised its constitution in 1956, more importantly, the ECVN (South) had already (in early 1955) accepted the invitation of the South Vietnamese government to organize an evangelical chaplaincy in the Army of the Republic of Vietnam. Church pastor and historian Phu Le proudly reported the event by emphasizing that the ECVN (South) was second to only the Vietnamese Roman Catholic Church in receiving such an invitation from the government.[5] The existing ECVN (South) leadership justified the decision

4 See Lê Văn Thái's autobiography, *Bốn mươi sáu năm trong chức vụ* [*Forty Six Years in Ministry*] (Sài Gòn: Tin Lành, 1970), 159–61. See also Phu Le, "A Short History," 287–88.

5 Phu Le, "A Short History" 352, 409.

to accept the invitation on the ground that doing so would provide spiritual support for evangelical soldiers, care for wounded soldiers, and opportunities to share the good news with non-Christian soldiers.[6] The Vietnamese communists, after unifying Vietnam in 1975, harshly criticized Vietnamese evangelicals as ideologically aligned with the government of the former South Vietnam by operating an evangelical chaplaincy in the South Vietnamese Army. The public accusation was made directly by the communist leader Mai Chí Thọ, then chairperson of the People's Committee of HCMC, in his speech at the ECVN (South) National Assembly in June 1976.[7]

When Vietnam was unified at the end of the Vietnam War in 1975, the CPV assumed power and, in an effort to include evangelicals in the Vietnamese Fatherland Front, requested that the ECVN (South) establish a patriotic organization within the church. The ECVN (South) once again invoked pastor Lê Văn Thái's previous argument that there was no need to establish a patriotic organization within the church because all evangelicals were already patriotic.[8] The resistance was significant, given that the communist regime successfully influenced the formation of patriotic organizations within the Catholic and Buddhist churches in Vietnam—the Liaison Committee of Patriotic and Peace-Loving Vietnamese Catholics, later known as Solidarity of Vietnamese Catholics, and the Patriotic Buddhist Liaison Committee in HCMC.[9] From an insider's perspective—that of evangelical pastor Cuong Nguyen—the state-party could not do likewise in the ECVN (South) for failing to see that the national executive committee of the ECVN (South) did not have strong control over the local pastors and congregations that made up the church's national assembly, as "the local church was much on its own in almost everything."[10] It would be impossible for the state-party to propose a patriotic organization in the church when the local church network seemed to refuse to cooperate.

The *non-interference-in-politics* policy was imperfect partly due to the State's interference in church affairs. The State did so by attempting to supersede church leaders it judged as being uncooperative with those whom it viewed

6 Ibid., 353.

7 As mentioned in Cuong Nguyen, "The Growth of Certain Protestant Churches in Saigon under the Vietnamese Communist Government" (D.Min. diss., San Francisco Theological Seminary, 1995), 82–83.

8 Ibid., 78, 87.

9 On the development of the patriotic liaison in the Catholic and Buddhist churches in Vietnam in the second half of the 1970s, see Ronald Cima, "Vietnam: Historical Background," in *Vietnam: Current Issues and Historical Background*, ed. V. Largo (New York: Nova Science Publishers, 2002), 73–190, section "Religion," 164–69.

10 Cuong Nguyen, "The Growth of Certain Protestant Churches," 87.

as more tractable. In the ECVN (South)'s 1955 General Assembly, Phu Le raised the question of whether the former government of South Vietnam had tried to replace the incumbent president of the ECVN (South), pastor Lê Văn Thái, who had recently moved south from North Vietnam, with someone who would be "more amenable" to political authority.[11] In another account, Cuong Nguyen reported how the communist government explicitly wanted the church's 1976 General Assembly to replace the current president of the ECVN (South), pastor Đoàn Văn Miêng, with someone else.[12]

In retrospect, the actual political involvement of Vietnamese evangelicals is rather *situational*. Due to their preference for being left alone to focus on the task of evangelism, most Vietnamese evangelicals have strived to be good citizens and not sought to usurp the political powers that be. The degree of collaboration with the State, or the lack thereof, is determined by the attitude of the State toward the church more than by the church's own belief in the principle of *non-interference-in-politics*. Depending on which government is in power, this principle can assume different manifestations. At one end of the spectrum, a lax approach by the State toward the church may result in an evangelical chaplaincy's being held in the army and individual church members' being allowed to engage in politics according to their own personal political commitments, as in the former Republic of Vietnam (in South Vietnam from 1954 to 1975). At the other end of the spectrum, the State's insistence on a strict regulation of religious affairs may result in the church's seeing no use for church-state collaboration and prohibiting church members from engaging with the State, as shown by the attitude toward the French Administration of Indochina (before 1945) and the early-communist state of the unified Vietnam (in the late 1970s and early 1980s).

In Vietnamese evangelicalism, the thinking on *justice*, divested of its political connotation, had a clear social dimension expressed in the question of whether the church should engage in short-term social relief work in the midst of natural disasters, wars, and chronic poverty in the country.[13] Before 1955, when the United States became involved in the building of South Vietnam and the South Vietnamese Army, it can be said that Vietnamese evangelicals defined their mission mainly in terms of evangelism. This mission reflected the nature of the ECVN as originating from the missionary efforts of the C&MA, a mission organization that prioritized the work of evangelism. Unlike several mainline Protestant denominations operating in South China and South

11 Phu Le, "A Short History," 339–45.

12 Cuong Nguyen, "The Growth of Certain Protestant Churches," 81–82.

13 Ibid., 31–36.

Korea—denominations that sought, among other things, to advance their cause through long-term work in education and healthcare—the C&MA believed religious conversion was a more pressing and immediate need in Vietnam than were education and healthcare and so did not give them priority. As a result, the C&MA missionaries had to determine the right amount of effort to spend in doing social relief work, lest these activities impede the ultimate task of evangelism.

During the United States' involvement in South Vietnam during the Second Indochina War, the ECVN (South) appeared to emphasize social relief work to the detriment of the work of evangelism. The ECVN (South), rightly understood as the embodiment of Vietnamese evangelicalism at that time, began to collaborate with other non-C&MA overseas organizations (such as the Salvation Army, the Navigators, and the Eastern Mennonite Board of Missions and Charities, to name a few) to carry out relief activities in response to the hardships inflicted by the Vietnam War. With Western financial aid pouring into the church, Vietnamese evangelicals were able to organize a relief committee, an orphanage, a social service to youth, two healthcare clinics (one in Nha Trang and one in Đà Lạt), a sanatorium, a nursing school, a mobile medical team, a leprosarium in Buôn Ma Thuộc, and a hospital in Pleiku.[14] In addition, local churches were supervising a total of 75 high schools and primary schools in South Vietnam in 1970. Such development happened perhaps too quickly and exposed the inexperience of the evangelicals in the implementation of social programs:

> The US abundant economic and military aid made people pursue money and material pleasure more than spiritual need. Conversion became rare, the church could not grow through evangelism, so it turned to involvement in social relief work to soothe its conscience. Social relief work became the main concern of the church. It consumed most of the energy and time of the churches and of the pastors. The majority of the ECVN churches and pastors tended to replace evangelism by social relief work. It went from one extreme [of focusing on evangelism] to another [of focusing on social relief work].[15]

In South Vietnam, after concentrating on social relief work in the 1960s and first half of the 1970s, the ECVN (South) in early-communist Vietnam reverted

14 Information is taken from Phu Le, "A Short History," 345–60.

15 Cuong Nguyen, "The Growth of Certain Protestant Churches," 32.

to focusing on evangelism in the 1980s and 1990s, thus resulting in the "Growth of Certain Protestant Churches in Saigon under the Vietnamese Communist Government"—the title of a study of the church of that period.[16] The renewed focus on evangelism in early-communist Vietnam was due partly to the fact that Vietnamese evangelicals felt somewhat disenchanted with their experience of administering social work in previous decades. Their disenchantment sprang from seeing how monetary assistance and other aid from the United States had been managed poorly and, in some cases, had corrupted church leaders.[17] At the same time, when the strong communist party came to power, evangelical church leaders eschewed social work, in part because they no longer had material and monetary resources to do so, and also because the communist party might have interpreted the church's involvement in charity and social relief work as competing for social influence.

All told, it can be said that the Vietnamese evangelical response to the Vietnamese state and society follows a pattern of forging a situational policy toward the State based on the State's attitude toward the church, more than on the church's own understanding of the church-state relationship, and that the response oscillates between evangelism and social relief work as to what constitutes the mission of the church in Vietnam. Understandably, this pattern continues to shape the way Vietnamese evangelicals think about *justice* in today's Vietnam. But as Vietnamese evangelicalism becomes more diverse, at least three different interpretations of *justice* exist among contemporary Vietnamese evangelicals: *justice* as *love*, *justice* as the honoring of *human rights*, and *justice* as *divine deliverance*.

2.2 Love

In the light of Vietnamese evangelicals' history of conscious social but not political engagement with Vietnamese society, the discussion of *justice* among contemporary Vietnamese evangelicals is, in broad strokes, preframed by the questions of how best to engage the State and how the church should go about social relief work. In one notable development in the 2000s, the Christian virtue of *love* is proposed as the foundation of a Vietnamese evangelical understanding of *justice*: *Justice* is fulfilled when, out of *love*, Christians seeing the suffering of the Vietnamese people seek to engage with the state-party in

16 Cuong Nguyen, "The Growth of Certain Protestant Churches."

17 Ibid., 35.

collaborative efforts to provide charity and social relief to the needy.[18] With history in mind, the suggestion that the faithful should collaborate with the State in doing good work can be interpreted as following the evangelical situational approach to the State, an approach characterized by the church's willingness to cooperate when the state-party is perceived as being (relatively) less hostile to the church via a swing from evangelism (the church's focus in the 1980s to 1990s) to social relief work (the church's perceived task in the 2000s).

As the discourse goes theologically, *love* and *justice* are interrelated because, in Jesus Christ, God deals with humanity in both terms.[19] Because of the sinful condition of humanity, God's *justice* necessitates God's punishment of humankind. God's *love*, however, issues in Christ's willingness to suffer on the cross to fulfill God's requirement for *justice*; therefore, *love* is the fulfillment of *justice*. Out of *love*, cooperation with people of different faiths and ideologies for the common good constitutes *justice*.

Along similar theological lines, the idea of *harmony* is employed to characterize the divine dance of *love* and *justice*, with one particular aspect of *harmony* being achieved when evangelicals work with the state-party on cooperative terms. The concrete suggestion with respect to Vietnamese evangelicals, therefore, was that:

> While Vietnamese Protestants can show their disagreement or opposition to the Vietnam government's policies that bring injustice to religious organizations in Vietnam or to the Vietnamese people, they can still support and cooperate with the government in works that bring prosperity, harmony, and justice to the Vietnamese people.[20]

The immediate source of the Vietnamese evangelical proposal of *justice* as *love* consists in the writings of Chinese churchman K. H. Ting. The use of Ting, a Chinese author, as a representative of the Eastern (read, "non-Western") resource for Vietnamese evangelical theology is germane and justifiable, given that Ting emphasized the responsibilities of citizenship and discussed native culture in positive terms—elements that are believed to enhance the Vietnamese evangelical perspective, which is rather other-worldly and takes a negative view of culture.[21] The similarity in the political and social contexts of

18 Tu Truong, "Mệnh Trời: Toward a Vietnamese Theology of Mission" (Ph.D. diss., Graduate Theological Union, 2009).

19 Ibid., 131–40.

20 Ibid., 269.

21 Ibid., 127–28.

communist China and communist Vietnam, combined with the Vietnamese intellectual habit of consulting Chinese resources in the construction of Vietnamese thinking, also positioned Ting as an appropriate interlocutor.[22]

The suggestion to engage the Chinese communist state on collaborative terms, as in Ting's own practice, is inspired by his leadership in the establishment of the Chinese Three-Self Patriotic Movement in the early 1950s and the China Christian Council in the 1980s—the two organizations that form the only state-recognized Protestant church in mainland China. Ting also served as vice chairman of the Chinese People's Political Consultative Conference from 1989 to 2008. Although such state-sanctioned structure and political involvement were criticized by the Chinese house churches as having a political rather than a sacred nature, this state-church collaboration provided a venue for Chinese Protestants to practice their faith legally and, occasionally, offered them opportunities to work for the common good of their society. Thus the theological understanding of *justice* as *love* had its origin in the *Sitz im Leben* of Ting as a politically involved churchman who believed it was important to be cordial to the government so that Chinese Protestants would be allowed to print more Bibles, reopen more churches, publish more Christian literature, develop theological training centers, and persuade the state to allow more religious freedom.[23] As a result, the shifting away from the critical element of *justice* by emphasizing *love* should be viewed as a *diplomatic* move to advance Chinese Protestantism in communist China, rather than as a critical theological construction.[24]

The diplomatic nature of the construction of *justice* as *love* is also expressed in Ting's proposal of a *Cosmic Christology*. This proposal places emphasis on the universality of Christ by seeing Christ as caring for the whole created world and as spreading the universal love of God to all people in a non-confrontational manner. Although being a proper theological construction in

22 On K. H. Ting's theology as a proper Sinicization of Christian theology in communist China, consult the works of Philip L. Wickeri and Janice Wickeri, eds., *A Chinese Contribution to Ecumenical Theology: Selected Writings of Bishop K. H. Ting* (Geneva: WCC Publications, 2002); and Philip L. Wickeri, *Reconstructing Christianity in China: K. H. Ting and the Chinese Church* (Maryknoll, NY: Orbis, 2007). On the importance of inter-Asian referencing in doing Asian studies, see Kuan-Hsing Chen, *Asia as Method: Toward Deimperialization* (Durham, NC: Duke University Press, 2010).

23 Raymond L. Whitehead, ed., *No Longer Strangers: Selected Writings of Bishop K. H. Ting* (Maryknoll, NY: Orbis, 1989), 182.

24 On this point, see also Alexander Chow, *Theosis, Sino-Christian Theology and the Second Chinese Enlightenment: Heaven and Humanity in Unity* (New York: Palgrave Macmillan, 2013), 90.

the Christian tradition of high Christology, the image of the Cosmic Christ was used by Ting as a political means, as he insisted that the Christ from above "was not so small as to concern himself only with religious or spiritual or ecclesiastical things."[25] Here Ting's argument aimed to criticize fellow Chinese Christians who thought that church workers should simply focus on spiritual affairs and who raised concerns about the Chinese Protestant church's being (too) closely related to the State. Ting's criticism charged such Christians with being unsophisticated and lacking in knowledge as how best to engage political powers.

Ting's theology can be engaged critically from a perspective of liberation theology, which asks whether a theology starts with the experience and history of a people and whether it is being honest in its dealing with the ideological tendencies and struggles of the present day.[26] The interpretation of *justice* as *love* and the elevation of Christ to a higher place tend toward spiritualization and universalization, thus effectively avoiding contact with any concrete earthly struggle between the powerless and the powerful. As a result, the good news about "universal love and Cosmic Christ for all" is pleasant to contemplate yet illusory, for it does not deal with actual, everyday conflicts. Here advocating the idea of *justice* as *love* to Chinese Christians has an effect similar to that of presenting the gospel as "going to heaven when I die" to the African descendants who struggle with injustice on a regular basis in the United States. Black American theologian James Cone criticizes that presentation as no more than pie in the sky.[27] Here *love* becomes a harmless, non-offensive, politically correct concept that, in its practical effects according to Ting's writings, sustains rather than subverts social injustice. It results in teachings that appear to be profound, yet blur thinking about *justice*, as shown in the following argument by Ting:

> The justice of God is also God's love. If love spreads throughout humankind, it becomes justice. This is love entering into the world. Love does not come to destroy, but to sustain, heal, teach, redeem and give life.[28]

While it can be said that, for better or for worse, Ting's political theology helped free Chinese theology from the tyranny of cultural contextualization in order

25 Janice Wickeri, ed., *Love Never Ends: Papers by K. H. Ting* (Nanjing: Nanjing Amity, 2000), 411.

26 Juan Luis Segundo, *The Liberation of Theology* (Maryknoll, NY: Orbis, 1976), 7.

27 James H. Cone, *The Cross and the Lynching Tree* (Maryknoll, NY: Orbis, 2011), 155.

28 K. H. Ting, *God is Love*, New edition (Colorado Springs: David C. Cook, 2004), 317.

to address the socio-political dimension of life,[29] a ready appeal to *love* and to a Cosmic Christ as holding universal values compromises the seriousness of *justice*.

The use of *love* as a political category was also problematic from a philosophical-theological point of view, as demonstrated in Hannah Arendt's (rather unsuccessful) attempt to reconcile Christian love for God with Christian love for neighbor.[30] While Christian love for God always causes estrangement from *the world*, Christian love for neighbor usually aspires to improve *the world* by demanding the development of a genuine sense of togetherness in *the world*; this demand, however, can become a burdensome neighborly love that can distract one from loving God in solitude. In this vein, even the belief that the neighbor is created in the *Imago Dei* cannot help to reconcile Christian love for God and Christian love for neighbor. Understandably, the fundamental problem of using *love* as a political category is not adequately addressed in Ting's diplomatic use of the concept to facilitate his work in communist China. Thus, a remaining theological task after Ting in both China and Vietnam is to develop a new understanding of *justice* originating from the living conditions of grassroots Christians. Furthermore, considering this new understanding, the task must also address how *justice* and *love*, for God and for neighbor, would interpret one another and provide meaning for the marginalized in a late-communist setting.[31]

Also, a practical shortcoming of the *justice*-as-*love* proposal emerges from the concern that the theory, with its recommended practice of engaging in good deeds, can be employed to predetermine the social role of evangelicals as one of simply providing charity, as the State and society might expect from adherents to a religion of *love*. In doing so, the critical and prophetic nature of religion is marginalized. In contemporary Vietnam, the issue of the church's being co-opted into existing power structures through engaging in social relief work is a complex problem, with the State's being ambivalent about the

29 See the discussion in Chow, *Theosis, Sino-Christian Theology and the Second Chinese Enlightenment*, chapter 4.

30 The tension is revealed in Arendt's unsuccessful attempt to insert her later political activism into her former thesis arguing that love for God and love for the neighbor are fundamentally incompatible. See Hannah Arendt, *Love and Saint Augustine*, edited and with an interpretive essay by Joanna Vecchiarelli Scott and Judith Chelius Stark (Chicago: The University of Chicago Press, 1996), and George McKenna, "Review of *Love and Saint Augustine*," *First Things* 72 (April 1997): 43–47.

31 For a grassroots-sensitive exposition on *love* and *justice*, see Eldin Villafañe, *The Liberating Spirit: Toward an Hispanic American Pentecostal Social Ethic* (Grand Rapids: Eerdmans, 1993), 211–15.

church's doing good deeds. On the one hand, the State views charity as a useful vehicle for channeling the energy of religious people into activities perceived as not directly challenging the State's authority. On the other hand, organized charity work has the potential to become a platform for grooming larger social networks that may grow out from under the control of the government. The latter point is, in fact, a legitimate concern, because these platforms and the small-group settings of the evangelical networks are where ordinary people are given opportunities to acquire leadership skills, such as public speaking, committee organization, and team management.[32] Needless to say, a religious commitment to charitable work might spill over into social and political commitments, as has already happened in China.[33] As a result, the State is ambivalent toward these efforts and does not fully support religious groups in their engagement in charitable work, despite the State's wishing to use charitable work to contain and co-opt religion into the existing political power structure.

Yet it has also been noticed that co-opting runs both ways.[34] In the name of *love*, the church also co-opts the State to serving the church's own purposes. The church does so by asking the State for permission to build more churches, from which its members, as good (and loving) citizens, may exercise their harmless religious practices and gain more opportunities to provide care for fellow citizens who encounter hardship. When the State recognizes *love*, a core value of Christianity, as having the potential to contribute to society positively, pigeon-holing the faithful as being followers of a foreign religion and foreigners in their home country becomes politically incorrect. From this viewpoint, *love* is an ambiguous category—one conditioned by who uses it to advance which position in a particular context.

The use of the concept of *harmony* also invites critical engagement. Although *harmony* has long been regarded as a prominent East Asian philosophical category understood as the right way and right order of cosmic, social, and human life,[35] Ting's use of *harmony* became politicalized when the Hu Administration promoted the vision of building China as a "harmonious society" in the mid-2000s.[36] The vision of *harmony* was introduced by the Chinese government to respond to the social injustice created by unbalanced economic

32 See Harvey Cox, *Fire from Heaven: The Rise of Pentecostal Spirituality & the Reshaping of Religion in the Twenty-First Century* (Reading, MA: Addison-Wesley, 1995), 236.

33 Gerda Wielander, *Christian Values in Communist China* (New York: Routledge, 2015), 128.

34 Ibid., chapter 3.

35 For example, see Tran Van Doan, "Harmony as a Category of Asian Ethics and Theology," *Sino-Christian Studies* 7 (June 2009): 43–65.

36 For further information, see Sujian Guo and Baogang Guo, eds., *China in Search of a Harmonious Society* (Lanham, MD: Lexington Books, 2008), and Astrid Nordin, *China's*

development. This vision constituted a way for the government to present the public with evidence of a political will to focus on social well-being more than on economic growth. In reality, however, the idea of *harmony* is used to suppress dissident voices more than to promote social equality; thus there have been calls to construct a more dynamic understanding of *harmony* in order to recognize, rather than neutralize, diversity in society.[37] But the discussion's overemphasis on *harmony* betrays the likelihood that *harmony* remains wishful thinking.

In Ting's diplomatic theology, *harmony* serves the same purpose—that of neutralizing intra-church diversity. It is also used to assure the State that, in the name of *harmony*, the church does not wish to challenge the State's power or ideology. The idea of *harmony*, when it is imported from Chinese Protestantism to Vietnamese evangelicalism, is similarly vulnerable and needs to be handled with care, lest it fall prey to the political rhetoric that exploits the concepts of *love* and *harmony*—rhetoric employed by the powers that be to retain power. It has been documented that, in Vietnam, during the Vietnam War, the communists used the idea of *love* politically to advance their cause shrewdly by conflating "love of country" with "loving the communist party."[38]

One important demonstration of "the tyranny of *harmony*" was the urging by the State that Christians make their theology more compatible with the prevailing culture of the time. In communist China, for example, Protestants received pressure to construct a theology with a distinct flavor of patriotism and nationalism. Along with this development is the emergence of Sino-Christian theology, largely an academic movement begun as early as 1978—the year the Chinese Open Door policy began. Sino-Christian theology has a threefold concern: employing the Christian virtues of love and self-sacrifice in the task of nation-building, using the Christian church as an additional unifying force in society, and directing the Christian church on how to serve society better.[39] In

---

International Relations and Harmonious World: Time, Space and Multiplicity in World Politics (New York: Routledge, 2016).

37 Chan Kin-Man, "Harmonious Society," in *International Encyclopedia of Civil Society*, eds. Helmut Anheier and Stefan Toepler (New York: Springer, 2009), 821–25.

38 Tuong Vu, "'To Be Patriotic is to Build Socialism': Communist Ideology in Vietnam's Civil War," in *Dynamics of the Cold War in Asia: Ideology, Identity, and Culture*, ed. Tuong Vu and Wasana Wongsurawat (New York: Palgrave, 2009), 33–52. See also Tuong Vu, "The Party v. the People," *Journal of Vietnamese Studies* 9, no. 4 (December 1, 2014): 33–66.

39 So said Zhuo Xin Ping, director of the Institute for the Study of World Religions (Chinese Academy of Social Sciences), as quoted in Chee Pang Choong, "Studying Christianity and Doing Theology *Extra Ecclesiam* in China," in *Christian Theology in Asia*, ed. Sebastian Kim (Cambridge: Cambridge University Press, 2008), 97–98. See also Yang Huilin, "'Ethicized' Chinese-Language Christianity and the Meaning of Christianity," *Contemporary Chinese*

recent years, Sino-Christian theology has received attention as Chinese academics have considered what potential moral compasses can counterbalance the new hedonist consumerism that has resulted from China's economic development.[40]

Sino-Christian theology—a logical next step following Ting's theology—moves toward closer collaboration between church and state, with those developing this theology being members of the state-funded Chinese academy and not necessarily members of any Christian church. While some evangelicals argue that Sino-Christian theology presents opportunities to evangelize Chinese intellectuals,[41] it is important to note that Sino-Christian theology is interested only in the moral and modern character of Christianity, and not in the critical perspective of the faith. In other words, Sino-Christian theology proposes that Chinese Protestants focus on their *priestly* role (understood as serving the society under the direction of the State) and not on their *prophetic* role (that of providing criticism on social injustice), thus illustrating well one way that Ting's principle of *justice* as *love* can be further exploited.

The recent development of Sino-Christian theology, with its *justice*–as-*love* thinking, finds its Vietnamese counterpart in the elaboration of a fledgling, state-directed, *Việt-Christian theology*. An article titled "Current Issues in Vietnamese Evangelical Theology," penned by a non-Christian scholar of the Vietnamese Institute of Religious Studies, gives advice on how Vietnamese evangelicals can align their thinking and behavior with the nationalistic

Thought 35, no. 4 (2004): 68–84. Besides the already mentioned Yang Huilin's *China, Christianity, and the Question of Culture*, two other notable volumes discuss Sino-Christian theology in English: Yang Huilin and Daniel H. N. Yeung, eds., *Sino-Christian Studies in China* (Cambridge: Cambridge Scholars Publishing, 2006); and Lai Pan Chiu and Jason Lam, eds., *Sino-Christian Theology* (Frankfurt am Main: Peter Lang, 2010). For a more recent evaluation, see Wen Ge, "Engaging University Theologies with Church Theologies in China: A Postliberal Appraisal of the Emerging Sino-Christian Academic Theology," in *What Young Asian Theologians Are Thinking*, ed. Leow Theng Huat (Singapore: Trinity Theological College, 2014), 50–64.

40 On Chinese hedonism, see Jiwei Ci, *Dialectic of the Chinese Revolution: From Utopianism to Hedonism* (Stanford: Stanford University Press, 2004), and the chapter titled "Discourse of Hedonism and Extravagance: Tension Between the Agency and the Actor" in Shaoying Zhang and Derek McGhee, *China's Ethical Revolution and Regaining Legitimacy: Politics and Development of Contemporary China* (New York: Palgrave Macmillan, 2017), 135–72.

41 For example, see Richard Cook and David Pao, eds., *After Imperialism: Christian Identity in China and the Global Evangelical Movement*, Studies in Chinese Christianity 1 (Eugene, OR: Pickwick, 2011). An earlier attempt consists in Samuel Ling and Stacey Bieler, eds., *Chinese Intellectuals and the Gospel* (San Gabriel, CA: China Horizon, 1999).

culture exemplified by the state-party.[42] In an attempt to construct memories that show the evangelicals as also belonging to a united national front led by communist ideology, the same author highlighted the existence of the *Hội Tin Lành Kháng Chiến Nam Bộ* [Evangelical Association for Southern Resistance] in 1945–1946 against French, British, and Japanese troops occupying Vietnam; the author also painted evangelicals in Hà Nội as communist-friendly in the pre-1945 era.[43] As mentioned, such developments often cast the church in a supportive role—one of helping, in the name of *love*, to carry out the State's vision of society—and overlook the church's function as a social critic. As expected, some evangelicals are unsatisfied with the co-opting measures and seek other ways to define *justice* in contemporary Vietnam.

2.3 Rights

Another notable development among contemporary Vietnamese evangelicals is thinking about *justice* in terms of *human rights*, imagined mostly as legal reforms that will protect the rights of the people and bring liberty and justice for all. This rights-based *justice* is a development of legal-activist pastors who object to the state-party's harassment of religious groups. The focus on *human rights* among this group is fed by both their personal desire for social betterment and their being influenced by budding civil society in contemporary Vietnam, which also employs the concept of *human rights* in its discourse. It can also be said that the economic boom and global integration of Vietnam since the 1990s have presented urban Vietnamese evangelicals with more education and business opportunities along with a renewed awareness of their rights as citizens of a socialist republic.

42 Đỗ Quang Hưng, "Mấy vấn đề thần học Tin Lành ở Việt Nam hiện nay" [Current Issues in Vietnamese Evangelical Theology], *Tạp Chí Khoa Học Xã Hội Việt Nam* [*Vietnamese Journal of Social Sciences*] 6 (2011), accessed October 1, 2015, http://vssr.vass.gov.vn/noidung/tintuc/Lists/ngonnguvanhocvanhoa/View_Detail.aspx?ItemID=42.

43 Đỗ Quang Hưng, "Người Tin Lành ở Hà Nội" [The Evangelicals in Hà Nội], in *Đời Sống Tôn Giáo Tín Ngưỡng Thăng Long-Hà Nội* [*Religious Life of Thăng Long-Hà Nội*], ed. Đỗ Quang Hưng (Hà Nội: Hà Nội Publishers, 2010), 317–35. See also, Đỗ Quang Hưng, "Hồ Chí Minh Và Đạo Tin Lành" [Hồ Chí Minh and Evangelicalism], *Tạp Chí Khoa Học Xã Hội* [*Journal of Social Sciences*] 5 (2013), 1–12; and Nguyễn Xuân Hùng, "Relations Between Vietnamese Governments in History and the Evangelical Church," *Religious Studies Review* 1, no. 2 (May 2007): 38–50, accessed November 21, 2016, http://www.vjol.info/index.php/RSREV/article/viewFile/1324/1232.

The focus on the legal aspect of *justice* produces a particular rhetoric that often invokes the "international community" to pressure the state-party to recognize religious rights, among others, since the Vietnamese government has already signed and ratified the International Covenant on Civil and Political Rights and the International Covenant on Economic, Social and Cultural Rights—two major commitments accepting certain obligations within the International Bill of Human Rights.[44] This legal aspect of *justice* is championed by urban-intellectual house-church evangelicals, most notably the pastor-lawyers of the Mennonite Church of Vietnam Nguyễn Văn Đài and Nguyễn Hồng Quang. This position, however, gives the impression that evangelicals are appealing to a "foreign" force to deal with a domestic matter—a sensitive issue for the incumbent State.

The focus on *rights* in some urban Vietnamese evangelical circles is similar to and partly inspired by the ongoing development of Calvinist Christianity in China.[45] Since the 1980s and especially after the 1989 Tiananmen Square protest, when disenchantment with China's course of national development grew, many younger and more educated Chinese urbanites converted to Chinese Protestantism.[46] Urban Chinese house churches cater to their members

---

44 On human rights as an Asian principle, see Asian Human Rights Commission, *Asian Human Rights Charter* (Hong Kong: Asian Legal Resource Centre, 1998). For a comprehensive introduction to the field, see Philip Alston and Ryan Goodman, eds., *International Human Rights*, 2nd and rev. ed. (New York: Oxford University Press, 2012). On Vietnamese evangelicals and human rights, see James Lewis, "Christianity and Human Rights in Vietnam: The Case of the Ethnic Minorities, 1975–2007," in *Christianity and Human Rights: Christians and the Struggle for Global Justice*, ed. Frederick M. Shepherd (Lanham, MD: Lexington Books, 2009), 195–212.

45 For further information, see Alexander Chow, "Calvinist Public Theology in Urban China Today," *International Journal of Public Theology* 8, no. 2 (2014): 158–75; see also, Yang Huilin, *China, Christianity, and the Question of Culture*, trans. Zhang Jing (Waco, TX: Baylor University Press, 2014). For a discussion on the contemporary landscape of Chinese Protestantism, see Daniel H. Bays, *A New History of Christianity in China* (Malden, MA: Wiley-Blackwell, 2012), 183–208.

46 On Chinese intellectuals' role in the development of urban Chinese house churches, see Fredrik Fällman, "Calvin, Culture, and Christ? Developments of Faith among Chinese Intellectuals," in *Christianity in Contemporary China: Socio-Cultural Perspectives*, ed. Francis Khek Gee Lim, 152–68. See also, Wielander, *Christian Values in Communist China*, 108–29; Chow, "Calvinist Public Theology in Urban China Today"; and Rodney Stark and Xiuhua Wang, *A Star in the East: The Rise of Christianity in China* (West Conshohocken, PA: Templeton, 2015), 75–90. For further description of the Chinese urban house churches, see Paul Golf and Pastor Lee, *The Coming Chinese Church: How Rising Faith in China Is Spilling Over Its Boundaries* (Oxford: Monarch, 2013), 69–86. On the contemporary implication of the Tiananmen Square massacre as triggering China's embracement of a neoliberal economic agenda, resulting in an unfortunate overall global yield to Chinese political demand and a tolerance of authoritarianism in the West, see the important argument in

a more intellectual, Calvinist theology, with a few distinctive flavors. Chinese Calvinism focuses on defense of rights, including religious rights, and extends to constitutionalism from a legal perspective. In this view, *justice is understood as the protection and honoring of rights*. While the emphasis on *human rights* often put urban Chinese house-church Protestants in an alien relationship with the State, these Christians do emphasize positive dialogue with the State—a position inspired by John Calvin's own example of being both a churchman and a statesman in Geneva.

In a related development, the Chinese state also seeks to reclaim the concept of *human rights* and reasons that the Western understanding of the term is provincial. Such redefinition of concepts often happens in the context of China's criticizing the West for imposing its perspective on others. The argument goes that China, or any Oriental society for that matter, has its own way of running its society. In this particular case, the proposed Chinese concept of *human rights*, based on "Asian values," asserts that the State represents the collective will of the people and thus is entitled to its rights' being respected by its people and by other states.[47] The focus on the rights of the State effectively marginalizes, for example, John Dewey's thinking about *human rights*, which emphasizes the rule of the people. As economist and philosopher Amartya Sen pointed out, such Chinese understanding of *human rights* is both unhelpful, as it presents a salient way to justify authoritarianism, and also problematic if one accepts that the rights of the people, and not the rights of the state, are of "basic importance."[48]

In practice, the idea of *justice* as honoring *human rights* demonstrates a legal approach to *justice* in its pursuit of legal measures to bring national law into compliance with what are considered universal *human rights*, as defined in the legally binding treaties inspired by the Universal Declaration of Human Rights. At the individual level, viewing *justice* as occurring when *human rights* are honored seeks to defend individuals when injustice and oppression occur. At the institutional level, viewing *justice* as occurring when *human rights* are

Johan Lagerkvist, *Tiananmen Redux: The Hard Truth About the Expanded Neoliberal World Order* (Bern: Peter Lang, 2016).

47 Yuka Kobayashi, "*Renquan*—Chinese Human Rights: An 'Import' from the West or a Chinese 'Export'?" in *Politics of the 'Other' in India and China: Western Concepts in Non-Western Contexts*, ed. Lion Koenig and Bidisha Chaudhuri (New York: Routledge, 2016), 179–92.

48 Amartya Sen, *Human Rights and Asian Values* (New York: Carnegie Council on Ethics and International Affairs, 1997), 30. See also the chapter titled "Human Rights and Global Imperatives" in his *The Idea of Justice* (2009. Cambridge: Harvard University Press, 2011), 355–87.

honored pressures the authorities to examine legal and political systems (including constitutional order) to comply with the two previously mentioned formal statements—the International Covenant on Civil and Political Rights and the International Covenant on Economic, Social and Cultural Rights. This examination includes calls for institutional reforms and/or fostering new institutions to strengthen practices of *human rights*. In this rights-based approach, the assumption is that in every society there should be a legal structure to hold accountable those responsible for evil. Christians, as people of "righteousness," can assist the disadvantaged—Christians and non-Christians alike—through legal counsel, thereby using legal platforms to pursue social *justice*.[49] When the legal structure contains unjust laws, Christians should work to rectify them. Here the emphasis on rights and legal reforms as a Christian mission resonates with the understanding of Jesus as a lawyer who knew Levitical law well and who came to fulfill, not to destroy, the law. This emphasis further resonates with the understanding that the Calvinist accent on *covenant* provides a foundation for an adequate constitutionalism that is much needed in late-communist China (and Vietnam). Adding to this rights-based rhetoric is an emphasis on the church's being *nonviolent* when engaging the state and becoming a community that is able to develop a conscientization among the oppressed from both political ideologies and the ideologization of theology.[50] So argued Benny Tai, a law professor teaching in Hong Kong and a major figure in the Occupy Central with Love and Peace campaign there in 2013, as well as in the Umbrella Movement in 2014.[51]

In addition, Calvinist theology emphasizes the transformation of existing systems, an action judged as having relevance as a Christian mission by those who believe in the idea of *transforming the world*.[52] In a notable development,

49 Benny Tai, "Public Theology, Justice and Law: A Preliminary Note," *Chinese Graduate School of Theology Journal* 54 (January 2013): 73–96. The main source of reference for Tai is the Reformed philosophical theologian Nicholas Wolterstorff's *Justice: Rights and Wrongs* (Princeton: Princeton University Press, 2008), showing a Calvinist proclivity in Tai's proposal of *justice*. The subtitle of Tai's article, "A Preliminary Note," suggests that the discussion on justice, law, and Christian theology is still at an early stage among Chinese Protestants. The same comment holds true for Vietnamese evangelicals.

50 On Christian nonviolence, see Ronald J. Sider, *Nonviolent Action: What Christian Ethics Demands but Most Christians Have Never Really Tried* (Grand Rapids: Brazos, 2015); and Glen Stassen, *Just Peacemaking: Transforming Initiatives for Justice and Peace* (Louisville: Westminster John Knox, 1992).

51 For further information, see Justin K. H. Tse and Jonathan Y. Tan, eds., *Theological Reflections on the Hong Kong Umbrella Movement*, Asian Christianity in the Diaspora (New York: Palgrave Macmillan, 2016).

52 See, most notably, the use of Calvin in the *Christ transforming culture* proposal in H. Richard Niebuhr, *Christ and Culture* (1951. New York: Harper & Row, 2001), 217–18.

urban Chinese Calvinism carries connotations of Weberian ethics in viewing Christianity as a potential force contributing to social transformation through capitalist development and entrepreneurship based on Christian ethics and principles. Hence one sees programs such as "Chinese Entrepreneurs to Become Ethical Leaders," which organizes training tours that take Chinese Christian entrepreneurs to Europe to "learn about the roots of Christianity in Rome, and follow in the footsteps of Calvin in Geneva … to make an impact in the world through values-driven leadership and to inspire, empower and connect people worldwide to practice ethical leadership for positive impact."[53] Like the contemporary North American version of New Calvinism, which embraces the mission of redeeming (popular American) culture, the Chinese Calvinists also see Christians as having a "cultural mandate" to transform all aspects of Chinese society, with the effecting of change in the business sector being a critical component of such transformation.[54]

Similarly to the urban Christians in China, the more educated urban Vietnamese evangelicals also see affluence as attractive and the concept of *rights* convenient both to foster similarity of language with the surrounding civil society and to contribute to public pressure for legal reform. Judicially, the major limitation to the emphasis on *human rights*, as well as the related idea of legal reform, is that the concept is an imported one that is not inherent in the system of thought of grassroots evangelicals. As a result, it remains to be seen whether the concept's purchasing power will increase among rural and mountain-dwelling believers, who may have a different idea of what counts as *justice*.

---

53 *Globethics.net Newsletter*, no. 4 (2015), accessed July 20, 2015, http://www.globethics.net/-/globethics-net-newsletter-no4-2015-april-2015-. See also, Denise Austin, *"Kingdom-Minded" People: Christian Identity and the Contributions of Chinese Business Christians* (Leiden: Brill, 2011); Joy K. C. Tong, "Christian Ethics and Business Life: An Ethnographic Account of Overseas Chinese Christian Entrepreneurs in China's Economic Transition," in *Christianity in Contemporary China: Socio-Cultural Perspectives*, ed. Francis Khek Gee Lim, 169–82; Nanlai Cao, *Constructing China's Jerusalem: Christians, Power, and Place in Contemporary Wenzhou*, Contemporary Issues in Asia and the Pacific (Stanford: Stanford University Press, 2011); and the section titled "Marketplace Mission" in Golf and Lee, *The Coming Chinese Church*, 167–71.

54 For a sociological report on this phenomenon, see Brent Fulton, *China's Urban Christians: A Light That Cannot Be Hidden*, Studies in Chinese Christianity series (Eugene, OR: Pickwick, 2015), 94–108. For a theological work advancing this social approach, see Song Hong-xia, "Christ and Culture in Contemporary China: Exploring Theological Options" (Ph.D. diss., Fuller Theological Seminary, 2011).

2.4 Deliverance

Rural and mountain-dwelling Christians represent the largest evangelical demographic in Vietnam. This segment of the country's population draws attention because it comprises the subgroup that is most likely to experience marginalization and oppression today. Among these evangelicals, the most noticeable spiritual development during the last four decades, in the unified Vietnam, remains their pentecostalization, demonstrated in an increased sensitivity to *divine intervention* in daily life. Some pentecostal practices that feature more frequently in the rural areas—practices such as healing and exorcism—can be viewed by city dwellers as bordering on superstition. But for rural grassroots evangelicals, the language of *rights* that is fostered by urban lawyer-pastors is foreign to the vernacular, and the idea of pursuing legal reform lies well outside the purview of their thinking, given their limited social, political, and financial capital.

At the same time, the scholarly proposal of *justice* as *love* also faces a challenge, namely, its lack of a critical component to address the grassroots evangelicals' negative experience of marginalization and oppression. Furthermore, the *justice*-as-*love* proposal is not organic to the development of Vietnamese evangelicalism, for the proposal exemplifies a liberal theological ethos of the "modernist" side of Chinese Protestantism, while the Vietnamese evangelical tradition leans toward the "fundamentalist" pole of the spectrum.

To use the (in)famous categorization coined by Chinese Protestant leader Wang Ming-dao a few decades ago, Chinese Protestantism in the twentieth century has been sharply divided along the fundamentalist-modernist line, with Wang representing the fundamentalist trend and Ting, the modernist, liberal trend.[55] Together they embodied the conservative and liberal camps of Chinese Protestantism before the Chinese communist revolution in 1949, and the house-church movement and Three-Self Patriotic Movement of Chinese Protestantism after 1949.[56] It was Wang Ming-dao, in his doing exactly the opposite of what Ting did, who also shaped Chinese Protestantism as much as Ting.[57] While Ting advocated collaboration with the government, Wang

55 Thomas Alan Harvey, *Acquainted with Grief: Wang Mingdao's Stand for the Persecuted Church in China* (Grand Rapids: Brazos, 2002), chapter 1.

56 For a brief but informative report on Ting and Wang, see Jason Kindoff, "Protestant Resilience under Chinese Communist Party Rule," in *God and Caesar in China: Policy Implications of Church-State Tensions*, ed. Jason Kindopp and Carol Lee Hamrin (Washington, DC: The Brookings Institution, 2004), 122–45.

57 On Wang Ming-dao, besides Thomas Harvey's *Acquainted with Grief*, see also a collection of his writings in Wang Ming-dao, *A Stone Made Smooth* (Southampton, UK: OMF Books, 1982), and biographical accounts in Stephen Wang, *The Long Road to Freedom: The*

vehemently rejected doing so—a move that cost him more than twenty years in prison. Ting remained an Anglican bishop to the end of his career; he is remembered for his liberalism, rooted in the mission work of mainline Protestantism (especially the American Protestant Episcopal Mission in China), and his role in the establishment of the state-sanctioned Protestant church after the Chinese communist revolution in 1949. Wang is remembered for his rhetoric declaring mission and church institutions as not necessarily sacred, thus giving rationale for both the development of an indigenous Chinese church that broke away from Western missionary support before 1949 and the development of the Chinese house-church movement that broke away from the state-sanctioned church after 1949. As of today, rooted in Wang Ming-dao's view of the Three-Self Patriotic Movement as a politicized religious organization and not necessarily a valid Christian authority, the contemporary Chinese house-church discourse argues for the possibility of being Christian outside the state-approved church.[58] Needless to say, the fundamental and modernist labels are overly simplistic, and in recent years the lines have been blurred, with members of the Three-Self Church exploring the pentecostal beliefs and practices they see in several house churches, and the house-church Christians utilizing for their own advancement the institutional resources of the establishment.[59]

In the current discussion, however, the fundamental and modernist labels are helpful in highlighting a key difference between Chinese Protestantism and Vietnamese evangelicalism: Vietnamese evangelicalism has never in its history experienced the growth of any considerable liberal strand. Vietnamese evangelicalism is relatively homogeneous because the C&MA was virtually the only active missionary organization working in Vietnam in the first half of the twentieth century.

The above observation thus encourages a dialogue with other Chinese Protestant leaders, whose spirituality and ethos are more compatible with Vietnamese evangelicals in general than Ting's does. The names of three of these

---

Story of Wang Mingdao, trans. Ma Min (Kent, TN: Sovereign World, 2002); and Leslie Lyall, ed., *Three of China's Mighty Men: Leaders of Chinese Church under Persecution* (Scotland: Christian Focus, 2006), 101–50.

58 On Wang Ming-dao's influence on pentecostal-style Protestant groups, see Chen-yang Kao, "The House-church Identity and Preservation of Pentecostal-style Protestantism in China," in *Christianity in Contemporary China: Socio-Cultural Perspectives*, ed. Francis Khek Gee Lim (New York: Routledge, 2013): 207–19, esp. 210–13.

59 See, for example, the picture showing the house church's uses of the Three-Self Patriotic Movement's facility for Sunday school teaching in Paul Golf and Pastor Lee, *The Coming Chinese Church*, 96.

leaders quickly come to mind: Wang Ming-dao, the imprisoned conservative church leader who was also as political as Ting; Watchman Nee, whose writings provided a spiritual foundation for a sectarian response to communism among Vietnamese evangelicals in the early 1980s; and, to a lesser extent, John Sung, whose revival campaigns throughout Southeast Asia in the 1930s still live in the collective memory of Vietnamese evangelicals and whose ministry provides to their imagination a non-Western model of evangelicalism, which prompted revivalism as a Vietnamese evangelical (re)emphasis from the 1980s onward.

At the same time, it is important to note that the use of Ting and his contemporaries as interlocutors in the construction of a contemporary Vietnamese evangelical theology is primarily a reference to the Chinese Protestant responses to the State from the 1950s to the 1990s. The approach does not consider the rapid change of the Protestant landscape in China and the evangelical landscape in Vietnam over the last two decades, most notably the growth of pentecostal spirituality after the time of Ting, Wang, Nee, and Sung.[60]

Considering the above assessment, and in order to reflect the contemporary Vietnamese evangelical demographic more comprehensively, it becomes important to include contemporary grassroots evangelicals' embracing of pentecostalism in the discussion of how Vietnamese evangelicals pursue *justice*. At the present stage of the discussion, the academic discourse on Vietnamese evangelicalism considers more details on urban intellectual evangelicalism than on pentecostally oriented rural evangelicals. This situation reflecting the fact that literature on urban evangelicalism is more readily available than that on rural evangelicalism, while also revealing a perennial bias in how theology is often done, viz., by focusing on textual studies and theoretical analysis to the detriment of reflecting on beliefs and practices at the grassroots level. And the bias goes even deeper. For example, intellectuals in the church have worried that the rich language of Chinese Calvinism is difficult to explain to migrant Christians who move from the countryside to the city to find manual labor and who begin to attend urban house churches; this worry stems from the unsubstantiated assumption of limited intellectual capacity among this group of Chinese Protestants.[61]

At the same time, including the perspectives of pentecostalized evangelicals can also become a means of stabilizing their growth in Vietnam. The

60 For further information, see Edmond Tang, " 'Yellers' and Healers: Pentecostalism and the Study of Grassroots Christianity in China," in *Asian and Pentecostal: The Charismatic Face of Christianity in Asia*, 2nd ed., ed. Allan Anderson and Edmond Tang (Milton Keynes, UK: Regnum, 2011), 379–94.

61 As in Chow, "Calvinist Public Theology in Urban China Today," 174.

marginalization of pentecostals by both the State and the church's intellectuals can only produce more secretive practices among pentecostal evangelicals.[62] These congregations and home gatherings can foster paternalistic and intolerant approaches to life and faith,[63] as seen in groups such as the *Hà Mòn* and *Thìn Hùng* in the northern mountainous areas of Vietnam, or the *Việt Nam Truyền Giáo* [*Vietnam-Mission*] group in Hà Nội. Since pentecostal evangelical groups often give way to established forms of religion whenever they are given the opportunity to register with the State (as exemplified in the way that urban Vietnamese house-church groups imitate the structure of the ECVN when they become institutionalized), engagement in theological reflection benefits the pentecostal evangelicals by providing an opportunity for insiders to develop resources that may resist internal abuses of power and sectarian knowledge during the process of institutionalization.

The self-understanding that pentecostalism is a purely spiritual movement is also a major hindrance to a broader appreciation of the significance of the pentecostal way of life in social, political, and cultural terms. In other words, to describe the significance of the pentecostals in purely spiritual terms is to deny that pentecostalism has an ideological quality, that it provides a system of ideas, values, and beliefs for pentecostal evangelicals as a response to their own particular social condition. The challenges for any investigation of pentecostalism have also come from the very nature of the phenomenon: pentecostalism is an oral, spiritual, and imaginatively inhabited tradition.[64] It thus presents a kind of knowledge and way of knowing different from common academic discussion facilitated by written, intellectual sources and logical reasoning. Moreover, pentecostals emphasize miraculous *divine intervention*, a topic that causes uneasiness in some academic circles. Here the tension is twofold. On the one hand, the sociological understanding sees pentecostal practices (such as healing and exorcism) as responses to both indigenous religious expectations and the cultural-religious vacuum resulting from the eradication of organized religions as the Vietnamese (and similarly, Chinese) communists

62 This point is well made by Jason Kindoff, "Protestant Resilience under Chinese Communist Party Rule," 142.

63 At the time being, both Vietnamese state and Vietnamese Christian churches have difficulties in categorizing these groups. On a similar problem in Chinese Protestantism, see Kristen Kupfer, "Saints, Secrets, and Salvation: Emergence of Spiritual-Religious Groups in China between 1978 and 1989," in *Christianity in Contemporary China: Socio-Cultural Perspectives*, ed. Francis Khek Gee Lim, 183–203.

64 On this issue, see also Wolfgang Vondey, *Pentecostalism: A Guide for the Perplexed* (New York: T&T Clark, 2013), chapter 7, "Scholarship and Anti-Intellectualism."

came to power.[65] On the other hand, the faith-based perspective of pentecostals insists that their practices are biblical, rather than being results of indigenous or shamanist influences.[66]

Also existing in some academic circles is a popular bias that views pentecostalism more or less as an opiate of the poor and oppressed. For example, it has been argued that a large number of women in the Global South are drawn to pentecostalism because it offers them traditional values (in its fundamentalism, hierarchy, and patriarchy) in a world being challenged by modernization.[67] In order to consider a possibly pentecostal perspective on *justice*, it is thus important to give pentecostalism the benefit of the doubt by treating it first as a complex ideological space—one through which women (and other marginalized others) beget agency and become active parts of something—and second, in the process, begin to subvert some features of the dominant *status quo* in their societies for liberating purposes.

Needless to say, such agency is not always straightforward. Take the gender relations in pentecostalism as an example. Although women make up the majority of pentecostal evangelicals, to the point that pentecostalism has been portrayed as "feminized" for its reflecting, to a large extent, women's aspirations, this form of the faith appears to be a conservative throwback through which women are seldom able to exercise leadership.[68] At home, pentecostal women are often effective in using family discipline and communal church pressure to assert their will and influence in domestic affairs, even to the point of compelling husbands to put the collective needs of the household unit above the men's own freedom. But these same women seldom question the legitimacy of patriarchy as an institution.[69] It thus remains to be seen whether

65 Chen-yang Kao, "The Cultural Revolution and the Emergence of Pentecostal-style Protestantism in China," *Journal of Contemporary Religion* 24, no. 2 (2009): 171–88.

66 For an Asian defense of pentecostal practices as biblical and not shamanistic, see Lee Young-hoon, *The Holy Spirit Movement in Korea: Its Historical and Theological Development*, Regnum Studies in Mission (Milton Keynes, UK: Regnum, 2009), 13–14. See also Cox, *Fire from Heaven*, 221–28.

67 For further discussion, consult Kwok Pui-lan, *Postcolonial Imagination and Feminist Theology* (Louisville: Westminster John Knox, 2005), 208.

68 Chen-yang Kao, "Church as 'Women's Community': The Feminization of Protestantism in Contemporary China," *Journal of Archaeology and Anthropology* 78, no. 1 (2013): 107–40. See also Joy K. C. Tong and Fenggang Yang, "The Femininity of Chinese Christianity: A Study of a Chinese Charismatic Church and Its Female Leadership," in *Global Chinese Pentecostal and Charismatic Christianity*, ed. Fenggang Yang, Joy K. C. Tong, and Allan Anderson (Leiden: Brill, 2017), 329–44.

69 See Bernice Martin, "The Pentecostal Gender Paradox: A Cautionary Tale for the Sociology of Religion," in *The Blackwell Companion to Sociology of Religion*, ed. Richard K. Fenn (Malden, MA: Blackwell, 2001), 52–66; and Elizabeth Brusco, "Gender and Power," in

the gender relations manifested among pentecostal women will become active in challenging the patriarchal nature of their religious structure. The agency of pentecostal evangelicals, therefore, is ambiguous and difficult to grasp, and it may not fit well into existing theoretical frameworks.

Considering the above concerns, the proposed methodological assumption is to treat pentecostals not as passive objects but as active agents of *justice*. As the academic theological discourse has increasingly reserved more space for the poor, women, ethnic minorities, and other historically marginalized groups, as evidenced in the prolific discourses of liberation, feminist, and postcolonial theologies, it is also important to make room for religious devotees—in this particular case, the rural and mountain-dwelling pentecostalized evangelicals of Vietnam. When the problems of asymmetry of socio-political power, economic inequality, and pressure for cultural assimilation put on minority ethnic and religious others are elided (for the sake of "national harmony," as the argument goes), enacting justice for grassroots evangelicals essentially acknowledges (1) the grassroots desire for improved living conditions in the midst of oppression and (2) the grassroots aspiration for human dignity, i.e., for the affirmation of human agency within a complex social space permeated by marginalization.

From this perspective of focusing on the agency of grassroots pentecostalized evangelicals, the definition of *justice* as occurring *when the poorest, the most marginalized, or the most troubled, are cared for* carries weight.[70] On the surface, such an understanding resonates well with the self-understanding, intra-group relations, and social approach of pentecostalized evangelicals: it is an understanding of *justice* from outside social systems and structures—one that is attractive especially among the underprivileged, who otherwise have no means of help due to their limited access to structural supports. To employ

---

Studying Global Pentecostalism: Theories and Methods, ed. Allan Anderson et al. (Berkeley: University of California Press, 2010), 74–92: 85–86. On married women empowered by pentecostal spirituality, see Mark J. Cartledge, "Family Socialization, Godly Love, and Pentecostal Spirituality: A Study among the Church of God (Cleveland, TN)," in *Research in the Social Scientific Study of Religion*, vol. 23, ed. Ralph L. Piedmont and Andrew Village (Leiden: Brill, 2012), 1–27. See also, Linda Woodhead, "Feminism and the Sociology of Religion: From Gender-blindness to Gendered Difference," in *The Blackwell Companion to Sociology of Religion*, 67–84.

70 As proposed in Grace Ji-Sun Kim in *Colonialism, Han, and the Transformative Spirit* (New York: Palgrave Macmillan, 2013), 79–84. See also James C. Howell, *What Does the Lord Require?: Doing Justice, Loving Kindness, and Walking Humbly* (Louisville: Westminster John Knox, 2012), and Susan Gallagher, "Introduction: New Conversations on Postcolonial Literature," in Susan Gallagher, ed., *Postcolonial Literature and the Biblical Call for Justice* (Jackson, MS: University Press of Mississippi, 1994), 3–33.

the evangelical vernacular, it is possible to say that through the embrace of pentecostal spirituality, grassroots evangelicals believe *justice* is *divine deliverance*. This essentializing of *justice* takes its cues from the pentecostal focus on miraculous *divine intervention*, mediated through the practice of *prayer for divine deliverance*. Here *prayer for divine deliverance* is a daily religious practice that exemplifies *justice* in an important manner,[71] namely, in that *divine intervention* provides for pentecostal evangelicals in their areas of need when existing societal structures fail to provide justly and when life-threatening natural disasters decimate their livelihood through the loss of crops or livestock.

The above understanding reveals that the thinking of grassroots pentecostal evangelicals is embedded in their religious beliefs and practices.[72] From this perspective, the derivation of the meaning of *justice* from the pentecostal (1) belief in *divine deliverance* and (2) practice of prayer for miraculous *divine intervention* is essentially a construct. This construct may be described as a "thick description" of the pentecostal phenomenon, i.e., an attempt to retrieve the meaning that insiders assign to the phenomenon.[73] Without such a focus on the grassroots practice of prayer for *divine deliverance*, *justice* will appear to be only an eschatological hope rather than a social concern and mission for Vietnamese pentecostal evangelicals.[74] In the case of pentecostal evangelicals, the real-life experience of *divine deliverance* is a symbol that provides meaning to those who most need it when they encounter life's problems.

Because of the grassroots evangelical proclivity to function (relatively) outside social structures, it is conspicuous that the evangelical understanding of

71 On the everyday practices of underprivileged pentecostal Christians as having liberating effects, see Darío López Rodriguez, *The Liberating Mission of Jesus: The Message of the Gospel of Luke*, trans. Stefanie E. Israel and Richard E. Waldrop (Eugene, OR: Wipf & Stock, 2012); see also Kenneth J. Archer and Richard E. Waldrop, "Liberating Hermeneutics: Toward a Holistic Pentecostal Mission of Peace and Justice," *Journal of the European Pentecostal Theological Association* 31, no. 1 (2011): 65–80.

72 For pentecostal *practices* (and *beliefs*) as a point of reference for pentecostal studies, see James K. A. Smith, *Thinking in Tongues: Pentecostal Contributions to Christian Philosophy* (Grand Rapids: Eerdmans, 2010); Amos Yong, *In the Days of Caesar: Pentecostalism and Political Theology*, Sacra Doctrina: Christian Theology for a Postmodern Age Series (Grand Rapids: Eerdmans, 2010), chapter 3.

73 On "thick description" as an anthropological method of studies, see the seminal work of Clifford Geertz, *The Interpretation of Cultures: Selected Essays* (New York: Basic Books, 1973).

74 On this aspect of global pentecostalism, see Russell P. Spittler, "Spirituality, Pentecostal and Charismatic," in *The New International Dictionary of Pentecostal and Charismatic Movements*, revised and expanded edition, ed. Stanley M. Burgess and Eduard M. van der Maas (Grand Rapids: Zondervan, 2002), 1109–12.

justice which emerges from grassroots evangelicals' embracing of pentecostalism seems to lack a component of building structural justice. In recognizing this deficiency, the proposed grassroots pentecostal evangelical understanding of *justice* here is not meant to monopolize the discussion on *justice* among Vietnamese evangelicals. In fact, the goal of registering the possible grassroots understanding of *justice* as *divine deliverance* is, first of all, to make it available for conversing with other understandings, and second, through participating in a "polyphonic" discourse, to foster a fuller understanding of the idea of *justice* among contemporary Vietnamese evangelicals.[75]

2.5 Conclusion

A glance at the social discourse among contemporary Vietnamese evangelicals shows at least three important understandings of *justice*. The first is the scholarly understanding that *justice is fulfilled when love is made known through evangelism and social relief work*, an argument rooted in Vietnamese evangelicals' traditional approach to the State and involvement in social relief work. The idea invites further development for better addressing the problem of marginalization and oppression in late-communist Vietnam. Second, having emerged within the more educated segment of the urban house-church membership is the understanding that *justice is the honoring of human rights*. Third, the pentecostal emphasis on miraculous *divine intervention* contributes to the discussion from the perspective that *justice is divine deliverance*—a perspective popular among the underprivileged, rural evangelicals.

On reflection, the thinking about *the world* shows its imprint in these contemporary Vietnamese evangelical understandings of *justice*. For urbanites leaning more on the activist side, the condemned nature of *the world* manifests itself in the institutionalized abuse of what are perceived as the (universal) *human rights* of the common people in contemporary Vietnam. For the more scholarly inclined, the characteristic corruption of *the world* reveals itself in the widespread human suffering that only a *love* rooted in the nature of God can heal. For the ethnic-minority rural, mountain-dwelling, pentecostally oriented evangelicals, *the world* is perceived as presenting an uneasy experience of marginalization and oppression while offering very little structural support to enhance life; hence their focus on miraculous *divine deliverance* as a fulfillment of

75 On "polyphonic" discourse, see Mikhail Bakhtin, *Problems of Dostoevsky's Poetics* (Minneapolis: University of Minnesota Press, 1984), 7.

justice. In terms of theological construction, the language of *divine deliverance* has the advantage over the languages of *love* and *rights* because it can be found in the evangelical vernacular—found there because it is capable of capturing the essence of the daily experience and desire of grassroots evangelicals. The continued growth of pentecostalism among contemporary Vietnamese evangelicals can be interpreted as a phenomenon resulting from a growing number of grassroots evangelicals' finding that pentecostal spirituality provides valuable meaning as they navigate *the world*. A trialogue among the three perspectives of *justice* as *love*, *human rights*, and *divine deliverance*, therefore, is expected to enrich the understanding of *justice* in the Vietnamese evangelical tradition today. The concern for *justice* aside, the most debated topic among Vietnamese evangelical scholars remains the perennial issue of faith and culture, a subject thus deserves a careful engagement in the next chapter.

CHAPTER 3

Culture

3.1 The Vietnamization of Faith

The study of Vietnamese evangelicalism is often undertaken by two major groups in Vietnam today. The first group includes Vietnamese evangelicals (hereafter, *evangelical scholars*) who write about Vietnamese evangelicalism from a perspective of Christian historical and theological studies; many of these evangelicals doing so while studying in North American theological schools. The second group includes Vietnamese academics (hereafter, *academic* or *state scholars*), some of them members of the CPV, who are affiliated with the Institute for Religious Studies of the state-directed Vietnamese Academy of Social Sciences and the Government Committee for Religious Affairs. This group conducts research on Vietnamese evangelicalism from the perspective of the sociology of religion and, to a lesser extent, the ethnology and anthropology of religion, through a Vietnamese communist ideological lens, with particular attention given to how religion affects regime security.

The present chapter will first address the political nature of the discussion of faith and culture regarding evangelicalism in contemporary Vietnam; the chapter will go on to suggest that different ethnic groups inhabiting Vietnam, at different points in recent history, find evangelicalism attractive because its iconoclastic approach to culture resonates well with the people's desire for change, newness, and modernity. The pentecostal belief in *divine intervention* accentuates such desire for change by filling it with confidence on the part of contemporary Vietnamese evangelicals that "God is with us" in the quest for life's betterment.

Returning to the academic discussion on faith and culture, evangelical scholars, in broad strokes, entertain two ideas: first, that the gospel will need to become incarnate in culture through the use of local cultural materials to represent the gospel to the natives, and second, that once the gospel is *inculturated*, it will become a transformative agent which addresses the negative aspects of culture. In approaching the discussion on the relationship between evangelicalism and Vietnamese culture, state researchers appear to focus on the first idea; and to refer to this relationship, they use a precise term—the *Vietnamization of faith*, an undertaking they hail as a worthy endeavor for Vietnamese evangelicals.

 | DOI:10.1163/9789004383838_005

The political nature of the discussion becomes apparent when evangelicals are pressured by the State to make their beliefs and practices more aligned with Vietnamese culture, the implication being that the communist state-party serves as the ideal of culture.[1] The strong emphasis on the *Vietnamization of faith* not only pigeonholes native evangelicals into the belief that they are "not being Vietnamese enough" while pressuring them to conform to Vietnamese culture, but the emphasis also serves as a political device to build *cultural hegemony*, a process through which the CPV imposes its ideology on the beliefs and practices of other social groups to create a normative *status quo* for the purpose of protecting and expanding the CPV's privileges.

The topic deserves careful attention given that most, if not all, Vietnamese evangelical theological writings since the 1970s have been developed in the North American theological context. In that theological incubator, and based on the view that, historically, the Vietnamese evangelical tradition has inadequately engaged Vietnamese culture, Vietnamese evangelicals have been encouraged to be critical toward their missionary heritage and to begin to construct a meaningful local evangelical identity. State scholars, coming from the Vietnamese communist tradition, thus conveniently cite evangelicals' self-criticism on the matter as evidence supporting the complaint that Vietnamese evangelicals are "foreign" to their own culture. Extending this idea, state scholars suggest that evangelicals give their undivided attention to creating a cultural form for evangelicalism—a task that would effectively sidetrack evangelicals away from engaging other pressing social issues, such as the increasing inequality (at many levels) in contemporary Vietnam. Thus evangelicalism would fall into the larger *cultural hegemony* scheme of the state-party. Far from being straightforward and transparent, the political mechanism of such a request for cultural adaptation disguises the political intent behind the term *culture*, namely, the intent to use the motivation of easing cultural tension to channel evangelical energy into an activity that will not upset the *status quo* or challenge the privilege of the powerful.

In his writings on Vietnamese evangelicalism, prominent state scholar Đỗ Quang Hưng discusses the *Vietnamization of faith* in the framework of the ideas of *self-nurture* and *self-expression* advanced by evangelical pastor-scholar Phu Le in the early 1970s.[2] According to Phu Le, a mature church is not only able

1 Đỗ Quang Hưng, "Mấy vấn đề thần học Tin Lành ở Việt Nam hiện nay" [Current Issues in Vietnamese Evangelical Theology], *Tạp Chí Khoa Học Xã Hội Việt Nam* [*Vietnamese Journal of Social Sciences*] 6 (2011), accessed October 1, 2015, http://vssr.vass.gov.vn/noidung/tintuc/Lists/ngonnguvanhocvanhoa/View_Detail.aspx?ItemID=42.

2 Ibid.

to follow the "three-self" principles of self-governing, self-supporting, and self-propagating, but also to perform *self-nurture* and *self-expression*.[3] *Self-nurture* refers to the ability of the church to draw on Vietnamese cultural elements as the primary source for nurturing itself rather than relying solely on the teachings of missionaries, while *self-expression* indicates the ability of the national church to express itself through the use of local forms of worship, music, architecture, literature, and philosophy.

With this apparent understanding of culture as a "high culture" including the arts, literature, and architecture, Phu Le thus suggested that the national church should develop a form of worship which was Christian in its expression of joy and thankfulness, yet contemplative in order to accord with the nature of the traditional Vietnamese way of worship. The church was advised not only to use hymns translated from Western languages but also to pen new songs using Vietnamese musical elements. Church architecture should be redesigned to consider the tropical climate of Vietnam, instead of embracing the Western ecclesiastical architectural style. In literature, the national church should strive to construct its Christian identity in a way that is faithful to both its Christian and Vietnamese heritage.

In the last century, Vietnamese evangelicals have embarked on a few notable projects following this idea of *self-expression* as follows: narrating the Protestant Bible and evangelical catechism in the Vietnamese traditional poetic form *lục bát*;[4] writing Christian songs using either traditional Vietnamese music or contemporary Vietnamese pop music; and finding the compatible aspects, if any, between evangelicalism and Vietnamese traditional practices and values—notably, the Confucian-based filial piety and virtues of humaneness, loyalty, the proper practice of rites, knowledge, and trustworthiness.

State scholars praise the above evangelical efforts and argue that Phu Le's concept of *self-expression*, in particular, is a development in the right direction—that of showing honor and respect for Vietnamese customs and habits. They note that this attempt would eventually lessen the conflict between evangelicalism and the culture and traditional religions of the Vietnamese, most notably Buddhism, Confucianism, and the practice of ancestor worship.[5] Here the State, based on its political power and through the dissemination of doctrinal

3 Phu Le, "A Short History of the Evangelical Church of Viet Nam (1911–1965)" (Ph.D. diss., New York University, 1972), 507–509.

4 Note the efforts of evangelical pastors Phu Le and Phan Đình Liệu in providing these narrations.

5 Đỗ Quang Hưng, "Mấy vấn đề thần học Tin Lành ở Việt Nam hiện nay" [Current Issues in Vietnamese Evangelical Theology].

research, acts as a paragon of Vietnamese culture by insisting it has the right to judge the Vietnamese evangelical way of life as a derivation of that culture.

It appears that the evangelical scholars and academic authors agree on the assumption that a successful *Vietnamization of faith*, an indicator of the faith's now taking root in the heart of the people, can result in more conversions. This understanding of conversion, however, is different from the grassroots evangelical experience of conversion. In general, conversions are more likely to happen through an individual's experience of miraculous *divine deliverance* or *divine comfort* in the midst of a personal crisis or suffering than through the appreciation of an evangelical message palatable to one's native taste. On this point, the grassroots evangelical experience appears to agree with the rhetoric of Vietnamese American Catholic theologian Peter C. Phan, who frames the issue as "nobody wants to become a Christian, say, if she is happy with her Buddhist faith";[6] therefore, the assumption that the *Vietnamization of faith* might increase the evangelical population is not entirely sound.

The political nature of the discourse on the *Vietnamization of faith* shows in its recommendation that evangelicalism becomes more Vietnamese but that Vietnamese culture, especially elements constructed and expanded by the current regime, remain unchanged. For some reason, the understanding that culture is ever-changing is omitted from Vietnamese academic writings about Vietnamese evangelicalism, though Vietnamese state scholars do entertain the idea that culture is constantly receiving and revising outside elements for its own use. State scholar Đỗ Quang Hưng, for example, writes about the characteristic changing of culture when addressing his peers in the mainstream of Vietnamese cultural studies,[7] but he makes no reference to this understanding in his writings about Vietnamese evangelicalism.[8] Readers of such Vietnamese academic writings on evangelicalism, therefore, will get the impression that there is a pure, pristine, and unchanging Vietnamese culture which rightly requests a Vietnamization of evangelical faith. That unchanging core of Vietnamese culture, according to the orthodox Vietnamese communist perspective, is defined by a pure patriotism, the willingness to fight against invaders (the Chinese, Japanese, French, and Americans) to protect the freedom of the

6 Peter C. Phan, "The Socialist Republic of Vietnam," in *Christianities in Asia*, ed. Peter C. Phan (Malden, MA: Wiley-Blackwell, 2010), 140.

7 Đỗ Quang Hưng and Trần Viết Nghĩa, *Tính hiện đại và chuyển biến của văn hóa Việt Nam thời cận đại* [*Modernity and the Changing of Vietnamese Culture in Modern Time*] (Hà Nội: Chính Trị Quốc Gia, 2013), 23.

8 Đỗ Quang Hưng, "Mấy vấn đề thần học Tin Lành ở Việt Nam hiện nay" [Current Issues in Vietnamese Evangelical Theology].

Vietnamese, with the state-party serving as a contemporary exemplification of that culture.[9] Needless to say, in this case the act of narrating the past should be treated as a political construction meant to further the interests of a social group and its right to rule rather than as a piece of knowledge to advance understanding.[10]

It is notable that while several scholars working in contemporary Vietnam write as though it has an unchanging, ideal cultural core—one which is fair in all aspects and reaches its fullest form in the communist culture of the CPV—these same scholars also take pains to promote another idea, namely, that the identity of the Vietnamese people possesses perennially water-like characteristics: it is fluid, flexible, and at the same time difficult to subdue.[11] This water-like imagery—actually reminiscent of a traditional, flexible, Asian spiritual core informed by a Taoist spirituality—is employed to allude to the attitudes needed by academic scholars in order to function under ideological pressure. An example of this triad of water-like characteristics became apparent when,

---

9 Trần Văn Giàu, *Giá trị tinh thần truyền thống của dân tộc Việt Nam* [*Traditional Values of the Vietnamese People*] (Hà Nội: Khoa Học Xã Hội, 1980), 21–28, 99–145. See also Politburo of Vietnam, "Nghị quyết của Bộ Chính Trị về văn học, nghệ thuật và văn hóa" ["Resolution of the Politburo about Literature, Arts, and Culture"], December 19, 1987, accessed October 1, 2015, http://www.bvhttdl.gov.vn/vn/vb-qly-nn/4/592/index.html. On how political pressure shapes the production of prehistory in contemporary Vietnam, see Haydon Cherry, "Digging up the Past: Prehistory and the Weight of the Present in Vietnam," *Journal of Vietnamese Studies* 4, no. 1 (February 1, 2009): 84–144. On the political use of stories of history to build hegemony in contemporary Vietnam, see Wynn Wilcox, *Allegories of the Vietnamese Past: Unification and the Production of a Modern Historical Identity* (New Haven: Yale University Press, 2011). On the political construction of Vietnamese identity as primeval and powerful, consult the bibliographical essay by K. W. Taylor in his *A History of the Vietnamese* (Cambridge: Cambridge University Press, 2013), esp. 630–32; K. W. Taylor, "Nguyễn Hoàng và bước mở đầu Nam tiến của người Việt" ["Nguyễn Hoàng and the beginning of Viet Nam's southward expansion"], in *Những vấn đề lịch sử Việt Nam* [*Vietnamese Historical Problems*], by Nhiều tác giả [Many authors] (HCMC: Trẻ, 2001), 161–84; and Claudine Ang, "Regionalism in Southern Narratives of Vietnamese History: The Case of the 'Southern Advance' [*Nam Tiến*]," *Journal of Vietnamese Studies* 8, no. 3 (2013): 1–26. See also Cao Huy Thuần, *Thế giới quanh ta* [*The World around Us*] (Đà Nẵng: Đà Nẵng Publication, 2007), 317–58.

10 Argued Liam Kelly, "Bản sắc văn hóa = Ideological Position" ["Cultural Identity = Ideological Position"], July 14, 2012, accessed August 1, 2015, https://leminhkhai.wordpress.com/2012/07/14/ban-sac-van-hoa-ideological-position/. See also Stuart Hall, "Cultural Identity and Diaspora," in *The Post-Colonial Studies Reader*, ed. Bill Ashcroft, Gareth Griffiths, and Helen Tiffin, 2nd ed. (New York: Routledge, 2006), 435–38: 435.

11 Trần Quốc Vượng, *Văn hóa Việt Nam: Tìm tòi và suy gẫm* [*Vietnamese Culture: Search and Reflection*] (Hà Nội: Văn Hóa Dân Tộc, 2000), 41–49; Trần Ngọc Thêm, *Những vấn*

in the 1950s, state leaders directed North Vietnamese historians to construct a new account of Vietnamese history—an account that had to comply with the Marxist periodization of history as divided exactly into five periods. The historians had to agree to do so, but in reality they managed to delay the production of the final work for more than two decades.[12] Unfortunately, the simplistic discussion on the *Vietnamization of faith* has elided such political nuances.

To move away from the ideological hard line, Phan Ngọc, a leading Vietnamese cultural theorist, prefers to emphasize that *culture is a cultural exchange*—an emphasis based on the premise that the culture of a people group is always forged through interaction with the cultures of other people groups, near and far.[13] In the case of the Vietnamese, according to Phan Ngọc the Vietnamese culture entails at least three distinct interactions: with non-Vietnamese cultures, such as those of China, India, France, the former Soviet Union, the United States, the Western hemisphere, and Southeast Asia; with the cultures of all the ethnic groups inhabiting Vietnam; and with the modernized culture of the postindustrial age in Vietnam. To speak, therefore, of a genuine Vietnamese culture or a distinguishing characteristic of Vietnamese identity is misleading, for culture is constantly changing. If there is any distinctive feature of Vietnamese culture, it is to be found simply in the way the Vietnamese people have made decisions at crucial turning points in their history, when they have chosen to change their Southeast Asian culture by first adopting Chinese culture, then French culture, then finally socialist culture—a rather abstruse proposal by Phan Ngọc to calm critics who insist on the existence of an unchanging core of Vietnamese culture.

On reflection, the proposal of *culture is a cultural exchange* has at least two germane political implications in contemporary Vietnam. First, the idea that *culture is a cultural exchange* suggests cultural change is a gradual process, not a sudden disruption. Thus, while the CPV holds disruptive, violent revolution as a practical political approach to gain power, it is not a desirable approach to cultural development, as demonstrated well by the catastrophic effects of the communist-led Chinese Cultural Revolution (1966–1976). Second, a community

---

đề văn hóa học: Lý luận và ứng dụng [*Issues in Cultural Studies: Theory and Application*] (HCMC: Văn Hóa Văn Nghệ, 2014), 136–63.

12 On this issue, see Patricia M. Pelley, *Postcolonial Vietnam: New Histories of the National Past* (Durham, NC: Duke University Press, 2002), 17–69. On the particular stance of individual historians, see Kim Ninh, *A World Transformed: The Politics of Culture in Revolutionary Vietnam, 1945–1965* (Ann Arbor: University of Michigan Press, 2002).

13 Phan Ngọc, *Một cách tiếp cận văn hóa* [*An Approach to Culture*] (Hà Nội: Thanh Niên, 1999), 24. For similar arguments that emphasize the exchanging and interdependent nature of culture(s): in cultural studies see Edward Said, *Culture and Imperialism*

of people may need a unified political approach (a tenet of the CPV), but, as Phan Ngọc's argument goes, political unification also needs cultural pluralism in order to enrich culture and make the regime more attractive.[14]

Regarding Vietnamese evangelicalism, the understanding that *culture is a cultural exchange* encourages a reexamination of the repetitive discourse on how to make the evangelical faith compatible with the popular Vietnamese practice of ancestor worship, or how to promote the use of Vietnamese folk tunes in Christian music, to name just two readily available major examples.

From the perspective that *culture is a cultural exchange*, a discussion on the Vietnamese practice of ancestor worship does not need a romanticized approach to the practice by prematurely hailing it "the very cultural heritage of the Vietnamese."[15] A more fruitful approach is to engage with the evolution of the practice and how it changed through history, especially when it encountered different streams of Buddhism and Confucianism, and how various sectors of the Vietnamese population viewed the practice differently. In doing so, Vietnamese evangelicals can draw on a wider range of insights and construct a more reasonable approach to the practice because such practice is always changing when it encounters different cultural-religious traditions through time. A more careful investigation along this direction will discover many Vietnamese Roman Catholic materials that offer excellent historical discussions on the Vietnamese practice of ancestor worship—discussions that are helpful in developing a healthy criticism of the practice and resistance against the tendency to idealize it.[16]

On promoting the provision of Christian lyrics for Vietnamese folk tunes, or on the use of old-time folk elements to localize current Vietnamese evangelical thinking and practice, a perspective that proceeds from understanding culture as always changing may, in future evangelical thinking, call for carefully distinguishing between being "culturally traditional" and "appealing to the locals." With fast-paced changes urged by globalization and advancements in technology, traditional, "handed-down" customs are not necessarily preferred by the local people in contemporary Vietnam.[17] From the perspective

(New York: Vintage, 1994); in Christian theology see Kathryn Tanner, *Theories of Culture: A New Agenda for Theology* (Minneapolis: Fortress, 1997).

14 Phan Ngọc, *Một cách tiếp cận văn hóa* [*An Approach to Culture*], 25.

15 Quynh-Hoa Nguyen, "Tin Lành: The Bible and the Construction of an Evangelical Vietnamese Christian Identity (1975–2007)" (Ph.D. diss., Claremont Graduate University, 2013), 79.

16 See, for example, Đỗ Quang Chính, SJ, *Hòa mình vào xã hội Việt Nam* [*Blending into Vietnamese Society*] (Hà Nội: Tôn Giáo, 2008).

17 See Brian Howell, "Practical Belief and the Localization of Christianity: Pentecostal and Denominational Christianity in Global/Local Perspective," in *Religion and*

that *culture is a cultural exchange*, the cultural preference of the Vietnamese will emerge through the creative interaction of long-honored tradition(s) and new trends introduced through cultural exchanges and takes shape through a series of selection/negotiation movements within a complex set of psychological, social, political, and economic parameters. Elaboration of this understanding of local preference, with attention given to the entire living context, may provide more substance for a Vietnamese evangelical system of thought on the nature of the interaction between evangelicalism and "Vietnam"—an interaction defined in both cultural and socio-political terms. Such elaboration resists the simplistic proposal of the *Vietnamization of faith* and the state-party's agenda of *cultural hegemony*, which seeks to establish the CPV as a paragon of culture.

In brief, the state-party's concern for regime security, which calls for the construction of *cultural hegemony* based on an imagined common ancient cultural core, directs state scholars to recommend that Vietnamese evangelicals focus on the *Vietnamization of faith* as a worthy endeavor. In this debate, the issue of the *Vietnamization of faith* creates a dilemma for Vietnamese evangelicals. On the one hand, they have to be critical of their seemingly inadequate reflection on the issue of faith and culture in order to begin a meaningful construction of their local evangelical identity. On the other hand, state scholars use evangelical self-criticism as evidence that evangelicals are foreign to their own culture. The perspective that *culture is a cultural exchange* is a welcome understanding for Vietnamese evangelicals, for it reveals the political tension in the ongoing Vietnamese debate on *culture*, namely, the contesting nature of discourses that emphasize either the unchanging core of culture (an emphasis forwarded by the political powers in seeking to establish national cultural coherence) or the constructed nature of culture (an emphasis holding the potential to deconstruct hegemonic efforts).

3.2 Contextualization

Since state scholars sometimes use the terms *Vietnamization of faith* and *inculturation* (Vietnamese: *hội nhập văn hóa*) interchangeably, it is necessary to enrich the discussion with a clarification of the concept of *inculturation* and its sibling term *contextualization*. More than two decades ago, in 1994, Vietnamese evangelical pastor-scholar Dung Le wrote that evangelicalism's interaction with *culture* requires two steps: making an effort to provide cultural clothing to the evangelical faith (a *Vietnamization of faith*, so to speak), and purifying that cultural clothing once the evangelical faith is anchored in Vietnamese culture, with *inculturation* serving as the term that encapsulates both steps.[18] As mentioned in an earlier chapter, Dung Le gave the example that if evangelicals embraced the practice of ordaining women called to the ministry, the change would be looked upon as having the potential to contribute well to the purgation of patriarchal tendencies in Vietnamese culture—tendencies believed to be of Confucian influence. On the assumption that the evangelical message and way of life will remain unchanged in their interaction with the local culture, however, the proposed two-step *inculturation* remains a one-way approach.

With *inculturation's* having as a particular aspect the addressing of the cultural marginalization of women, as in the above example, the discussion can be expanded horizontally toward addressing other forms of marginalization, including political and economic forms. In fact, in the 1970s a notable development in this regard consisted in a proposal of the World Council of Churches' Theological Education Fund Ministry Program, adopted by the influential evangelical Lausanne Movement, to incorporate the concept of *inculturation* into the broader concept of *contextualization*. *Contextualization* conveys the idea that any encounter of faith and culture must employ a critical and prophetic approach not only to the cultural aspect but also to the political and economic structures of a society.[19] Thus, when the focus is on the idea of faith's engaging the whole context of life, the *contextualization* of faith includes both *inculturation* (not only to provide cultural clothing for the faith but also to deal with the areas of culture that scorn human dignity) and *liberation* (to address political and economic oppression). The term *contextualization* has thus been used to signify a way of doing theology that takes into account the dynamic interaction of the Christian faith, embodied in a particular church tradition, and local culture, including cultural changes brought by both the process of modernization and the people's struggle for justice and liberty.[20] In other

Globalization: Critical Concepts in Social Studies, ed. Véronique Altglas, vol. 2 (New York and London: Routledge, 2011), 210–29: 216.

18 Dung Le, "The Bamboo Cross: Toward a Vietnamese Theology and Christian Educational Ministry in Vietnam" (D.Min. diss., Claremont School of Theology, 1994), 134–36.

19 The Theological Education Fund, *Ministry in Context: The Third Mandate Programme of the Theological Education Fund* (London: Theological Education Fund, World Council of Churches, 1972); Lausanne Committee for World Evangelization, "The Willowbank Report: Consultation on Gospel and Culture," Lausanne Occasional Paper 2, 1978. Accessed February 1, 2016, https://www.lausanne.org/content/lop/lop-2.

20 Stephen B. Bevans, *Models of Contextual Theology* (Maryknoll, NY: Orbis, 1992), 1. See also Peter C. Phan, "Inculturation of Christianity and the Gospel," in *The Cambridge Dictionary of Christianity*, ed. Daniel Patte (Cambridge: Cambridge University Press, 2010), 593–94: 594; and Peter C. Phan, *In Our Own Tongues: Perspectives from Asia on Mission and*

words, *contextual theology* maintains that an authentic cultural manifestation of faith must go hand in hand with an attempt to uphold human dignity by addressing, for liberative purposes, the problems of human exploitation and exclusion. Hence the telling title of a recent book by a Ghanaian theologian, *African Theology: Inculturation and Liberation*.[21]

Although in contemporary Vietnam the designation *liberation* has been used in official discourse to describe the military efforts of North Vietnamese communists in unifying the country, and as a result some former citizens of South Vietnam feel an unwanted liberation has been imposed on them, *liberation* remains a helpful theological category that the Vietnamese evangelical theological enterprise may want to reclaim. The tradition of liberation theology, as seen in its development in Latin America since the 1970s, is helpful to Vietnamese evangelicals in its method of doing theology from the ground-up and in its focus on the underprivileged.[22]

Such thinking on faith as being concerned with the living conditions of the people for the purpose of their liberation also receives textual support from leading Vietnamese evangelical authors such as Phu Le and Dung Le, though these authors have not explored the idea in detail. In the 1970s, Phu Le made the mild suggestion that "potential [social] contributions can be derived from the Christian faith to help meet specific needs of a people in the here-and-now" in his support of church engagement in charity in the context of social suffering due to warfare and natural disasters.[23] In the 1990s, Dung Le wrote more explicitly that "Christian education in Vietnam must be concerned with what is happening to the people who actually live there and deal with their needs, including poverty, fear, hopelessness, loneliness, disease, and discrimination. The Gospel of salvation must prove that its power can liberate them

---

Inculturation (Maryknoll, NY: Orbis, 2003), 8. For a substantial discussion on the critical aspects of contextual theology and liberation theology, see Angie Pears, *Doing Contextual Theology* (New York: Routledge, 2009), 166–79. For a recent Vietnamese evangelical appreciation of the use of the *contextualization* category in Vietnamese Roman Catholic theology, see KimSon Nguyen, "The Catholic Church in Vietnam: An Example of Contextualization," *Asian Journal of Theology* 29, no. 1 (April 2015): 74–87.

21 Emmanuel Martey, *African Theology: Inculturation and Liberation* (Eugene, OR: Wipf & Stock, 2009).

22 In addition to Gustavo Gutierrez, *A Theology of Liberation: History, Politics, and Salvation* (Maryknoll, NY: Orbis, 1973), and Juan Luis Segundo, *The Liberation of Theology* (Maryknoll, NY: Orbis, 1976), see also the evangelical approach to liberation in C. René Padilla, *Mission Between the Times: Essays on the Kingdom*, revised and updated edition (Carlisle, UK: Langham Monographs, 2010), and Samuel Escobar, *The New Global Mission: The Gospel from Everywhere to Everyone* (Downers Grove, IL: InterVarsity, 2003).

23 Phu Le, "A Short History," 509.

from such situations."[24] The discourse on the *Vietnamization of faith*, as well as Vietnamese evangelical thinking on faith and culture, could thus adopt the category of *contextualization* as a larger frame of reference to advance the discussion.

Granted, the use of concepts such as *contextualization* and *inculturation* also has its limitations. Both terms originated in the context of a Western Christian discussion which assumed that the historical Western missionary movement was imperialistic in its dealings with indigenous cultures and that early native converts were ineffective (and slow) in creating a cultural form for and embracing the liberative aspect of the gospel. The continuous use of the terms *contextualization* and *inculturation* thus runs the risk of assuming that a non-Western evangelical identity is not organic, has limited cultural authenticity, and is alien to the life's struggle of local people, although a careful definition of terms can help resist such assumptions.

The recommendation to move toward *contextualization*, however, in evangelical thinking is germane, given the Vietnamese public's perception of evangelicalism as irrelevant to the Vietnamese people. This perception is more a result of the faith's reducing its engagement with issues of injustice arising from the actual living conditions of the people than it is a consequence of any non-*Vietnamization of faith*. Regardless of how well the evangelical message is packaged in local cultural clothing, that message will fail to be attractive if it does not address the crucial socio-political issues of people's everyday lives. This perspective is in line with the original Vietnamese evangelical use of the concept of *the world* to refer to the social context of day-to-day living and its many immediate social challenges, rather than to the beautiful cultural world of Vietnam. Revisiting the historical context through which the Vietnamese encountered evangelicalism will furnish concrete examples that illustrate this understanding more clearly.

3.3 Iconoclasm

Although to suggest so may sound elitist, revisiting the historical context through which the Vietnamese encountered evangelicalism should start at the point when the early evangelical leaders met their Vietnamese intellectual counterparts while Vietnam was turning from a relatively irenic French colony in the 1910s to a restless society in the 1920s. At that time, Vietnamese

---

24 Dung Le, "The Bamboo Cross," 157–58.

intellectuals were increasingly exposed to new (mostly Western) ideas and neologisms coming to Vietnam via China and Japan. This exposure took place as part of Vietnamese intellectuals' encounter with Chinese and Japanese writings that discussed Western political ideas. Such ideas included populist democracy, Marxism (in both the early forms of Stalinism and Trotskyism), and Social Darwinism, to name a few. In the same development, and through the tireless work of Phan Bội Châu and other like-minded Vietnamese, the idea of the *nation* became a major Vietnamese category focused on the topics of the identity and fate of the Vietnamese people in the midst of colonial exploitation.[25] In the 1920s, Vietnamese intellectuals as a whole gradually became radical in their thinking and action on how to "save the nation," so to speak.[26]

Most of the mass movements responding to colonialism—movements ranging from the political-revolutionary to the religious-millennial—were comprised of "we the people" but were led by learned individuals considered by analogy the Vietnamese *intelligentsia*.[27] The group comprised a minority within Vietnamese society, given that in the mid-1920s not more than 5 percent of the Vietnamese population could read a newspaper; but the group's intense thinking, acting, and writing about a new vision for Vietnam in terms of a completely new social and spiritual order to deal—comprehensively, simultaneously, and finally—with the exploitation perpetrated by colonialism, the bankruptcy of Vietnamese tradition, and the quest for modernity not only sustained but also greatly increased the social influence of the intellectuals.[28]

Historical evidence suggests that early evangelical leaders also belonged to the Vietnamese *intelligentsia*. The first president and vice president of the

25 Truong Buu Lam, *Colonialism Experienced: Vietnamese Writings on Colonialism, 1900–1931* (Ann Arbor: University of Michigan Press, 2000), 1; K. W. Taylor, *A History of the Vietnamese* (Cambridge: Cambridge University Press, 2013), 484. See also Haydon Cherry, "The State in Vietnam," *Journal of Vietnamese Studies* 11, no. 3–4 (Summer–Fall 2016): 1–16.

26 Tai, *Radicalism and the Origins of the Vietnamese Revolution*, 258–60.

27 The designation "Vietnamese intellectual tradition" is rather evasive. Even authoritative authors such as Trịnh Văn Thảo and Vũ Khiêu do not give a clear definition of this tradition. They instead take it for granted that the tradition is Confucian-based and includes educated members of society. See Trịnh Văn Thảo, *Ba thế hệ tri thức người Việt (1862–1954)* [*Three Generations of Vietnamese Intellectuals (1862–1954)*] (Hà Nội: Thế Giới, 2013), 17–31; and Vũ Khiêu, *Người tri thức Việt Nam qua các chặng đường lịch sử* [*The Vietnamese Intellectuals in History*] (HCMC: HCMC Publishing House, 1987), 11–31. For a discussion on the problem of using the designation "Vietnamese Confucianism," see Liam Kelley, " 'Confucianism' in Vietnam: A State of the Field Essay," *Journal of Vietnamese Studies* 1, no. 1–2 (2006): 314–70.

28 David G. Marr, *Vietnamese Tradition on Trial, 1920–1945* (Berkeley: University of California Press, 1984), 33–34.

ECVN (then the Evangelical Church of Indochina), pastors Hoàng Trọng Thừa and Trần Dĩnh, were Confucian scholars well-versed in Sinitic learning. The very first evangelical church in Central Vietnam, where pastor Hoàng Trọng Thừa was the main preacher, recorded that among its first twenty converts were four members of the Royal Family, three administrative officials from the French Administration, and three officials from the Tax Department.[29] Among the earliest converts in Hà Nội, the then capital of French Indochina, were those who held relatively high levels of education and social status: a Vietnamese professor of the *École des Beaux-Art* (School of Fine Arts), a professor of Hà Nội High School, and a high-ranking officer of *Banque de l'Indochine* (Bank of Indochina).[30] Also, the mention of "college students" as a significant bloc among early evangelical converts merits further attention, for in pre-1945, colonial Vietnam, college students were generally regarded as having relatively high social status and intellectual prowess—connotations no longer attending college students in today's Vietnam.[31]

The literacy issue was also important in recognizing the social location of early Vietnamese evangelical leaders. Prior to 1911 and the arrival of C&MA missionaries, Chinese versions of the four Gospels had already arrived in Vietnam, at the same time as revolutionist and anticolonial literature (written by the Chinese or Japanese, or translated into the Chinese languages from Western materials). This literature targeted the same audience the Gospels did, namely, the Vietnamese *intelligentsia*. When the French administration and the Vietnamese Imperial Court decided to ban this literature, they grouped Chinese evangelical, revolutionist, and anticolonialist materials together as "*yêu thư, yêu ngôn*" [heretical literature, heretical sayings]. This aspect of the *regional travel* of evangelicalism from China to Vietnam (via the interaction of the intellectuals in both countries), in contrast to the *international travel* of evangelicalism from North America to Vietnam, provides a vital link for examining early Vietnamese evangelicals in their intellectual context.

29 Lê Văn Thái, *Bốn mươi sáu năm trong chức vụ* [*Fourty Six Years in Ministry*] (Sài Gòn: Tin Lành, 1970), 90–91.

30 Ibid., 55. See also Đỗ Quang Hưng, "Người Tin Lành ở Hà Nội" ["The Evangelicals in Hà Nội"], in *Đời sống tín ngưỡng Thăng Long—Hà Nội* [*Religious Life of Thăng Long—Hà Nội*], ed. Đỗ Quang Hưng (Hà Nội: Hà Nội Publications, 2014), 317–35: 318.

31 On the Vietnamese-Franco schooling systems and the Vietnamese intellectual tradition, see Tran Thi Phuong Hoa, "Franco-Vietnamese Schools and the Transition from Confucian to a New Kind of Intellectual in the Colonial Context of Tonkin," Harvard-Yenching Institute Working Paper Series, 2009, accessed August 15, 2015, http://www.harvard-yenching.org/sites/harvard-yenching.org/files/featurefiles/TRAN%20Thi%20Phuong%20Hoa_Franco%20Vietnamese%20schools2.pdf.

Even historian Phu Le, also an evangelical pastor, who emphasized anti-intellectualism as a general trait of Vietnamese evangelicalism, noticed that most early Vietnamese evangelical pastors (between the two World Wars) had a good command of Chinese or French or both, thus allowing them to be independent researchers and, in general, showing their greater intellectual capacity than pastors of the post-World War II and post-Vietnamese Revolution eras.[32] The idea that early evangelical leaders interacted as peers with members of the upper class could also be drawn from a common practice of early native evangelical preachers: when they traveled for the purpose of establishing new preaching stations, they came directly to the most educated, wealthy people in the given area, introduced themselves (as peers), and presented to this socially influential group their plan to preach the evangelical message there.[33]

The early evangelical leaders also had some connections to Phan Bội Châu (*the* iconic anti-colonial Vietnamese of the time). Evangelical pastor Lê Văn Thái's visiting Phan Bội Châu when the latter man was detained in Huế City.[34] Phu Le even provided further evidence on Phan Bội Châu's embracing the Protestant faith while he was living in South China.[35] Also, among Phan Bội Châu's protégés was Phan Xuân Thiện, son of evangelical pastor Phan Đình Liệu. With Phan Bội Châu's help, Phan Xuân Thiện was able to travel to Japan for study, went on to become a leader and representative of the Vietnamese Nationalist Party in its Hà Nội headquarters, and was eventually appointed a member of the historic First National Assembly of the Democratic Republic of Vietnam in 1946.[36]

The existential struggle of evangelical converts also manifested itself in the sudden disappearance of some students from the evangelical Bible School to join the armed struggle against French colonizers. Such existential tension even earned the sympathy of some American missionaries. Pastor Bùi Hoành Thử was reported to have told others that William C. Cadman, a leading C&MA missionary in Hà Nội, did "give money, and hide evangelical students who

32 Phu Le, "A Short History," 499.

33 Phan Đình Liệu, "Lịch sử Hội Thánh Tin Lành Việt Nam" ["History of the Evangelical Church of Vietnam"] (unpublished manuscript, 1966).

34 Lê Văn Thái, *Bốn mươi sáu năm trong chức vụ* [*Fourty Six Years in Ministry*], 79.

35 Phu Le, "A Short History," 154.

36 Phan Xuân Thiện's political career ended in tragedy. The Vietnamese Nationalist Party believed the League for the Independence of Vietnam set him up, arrested him, and later executed him in an attempt to gain full control the First Vietnamese National Assembly in 1946. See Hoàng Văn Đào, *Việt Nam Quốc Dân Đảng* [*Vietnamese Nationalist Party*]*: A Contemporary History of a National Struggle: 1927–1954* (Pittsburgh: RoseDog Books, 2008), 307–12.

became anti-colonist revolutionists," to protect them from the persecution of the French.[37] Assuming the report about Cadman was correct, it showed a shift in Cadman's attitude toward political involvement by native evangelicals—a shift that contrasted with his official position, as revealed in his previous correspondence with the C&MA's New York headquarters in 1926. In that correspondence, Cadman advocated that a Christian should "uphold the authority of the 'powers that be,' being convinced that our Christians should be loyal to the government and obedient to its just laws, [and] therefore should take no part in the strike."[38]

Nowadays, the understanding persists among Vietnamese evangelicals that early Vietnamese evangelical leaders acted as members of the *intelligentsia* on a journey to solve existing national problems. An article written in 2013 and titled "The Pastors and the Revolutionists in Hà Nội" illustrates this collective memory.[39] Written by a Vietnamese evangelical, the article recalls the interaction and social etiquette among evangelical pastor Lê Văn Thái and communist leaders Võ Nguyên Giáp, known for his military leadership in the First Indochina War, and Hoàng Minh Giám, Minister of Foreign Affairs of the Democratic Republic of Vietnam from 1947 to 1954. The article deliberately paints early evangelical and communist leaders as equals by narrating that both groups had the same goal of addressing the problems Vietnam was facing at the beginning of the twentieth century. While the communist revolutionists focused on the political side of the problem, the evangelical pastors focused on the spiritual, moral-social side. As the article goes, after the Vietnamese Revolution, the revolutionists, who became powerful political leaders, still held evangelical pastors in high regard. General Võ Nguyên Giáp is reported to have met with pastor Lê Văn Thái, then president of the ECVN, and to have granted him special permission for free travel and visitation of churches throughout the country (during a time when restrictions on travel were being imposed for reasons of national security). Pastor Lê Văn Thái was granted this permission even though in an earlier meeting with Mr. Hồ Chí Minh, president of the new government, he had refused to organize a patriotic organization within the ECVN. In return for this privilege of free travel, Lê Văn Thái invited Mr. Tôn Đức Thắng, president of the first National Assembly, to a formal dinner

37 Đỗ Quang Hưng, "Người Tin Lành ở Hà Nội" ["The Evangelicals in Hà Nội"], 324.

38 William Cadman, "Practical Piety," *Alliance Weekly* (June 26, 1926): 418.

39 "Các mục sư tại Hà Nội và những nhà cách mạng" ["The Pastors and the Revolutionists in Hà Nội"], October 7, 2013, accessed August 1, 2015, http://www.thuvientinlanh.org/cac-muc-su-tai-ha-noi-va-nhung-nha-cach-mang/.

at the pastor's residence in Hà Nội.[40] To a large extent, the narration of these developments shows an inclination on the part of contemporary evangelicals to view early Vietnamese evangelical leaders as being on par with Vietnamese nationalist and communist leaders—all of whom were manifesting radical confidence that they knew both the problems and the solutions for their fellow Vietnamese. In the rhetoric of one Harvard historian, each group thought they had "found a map of the world, and an itinerary."[41]

Revisiting the emergence of Vietnamese evangelicals as a social group in the history of the Vietnamese intellectual response to early twentieth-century French colonization suggests something about the early evangelical leaders in Vietnam: they became radical similarly to how different segments of the Vietnamese *intelligentsia* became radical, namely, in their acting on the Western ideas they encountered in order to formulate a response to what they saw as the problems Vietnam was facing. With respect to the Vietnamese tradition of the 1920s and 1930s, it can also be said that the inability of its "old guards" to deal with colonialism left a cultural and political void in Vietnamese society—a void that the various Marxist, nationalist, and religious groups (including the evangelicals and the religious groups of *Cao Đài* and *Hòa Hảo*) emerging in this period attempted to fill. It is in this historical context that the emergence of Vietnamese evangelicals as a social group, through the establishment of the ECVN in 1927, followed a pattern similar to, for example, the emergence of Marxist and nationalist groups of the time: they were all comprised of individuals who encountered and adopted new thinking—such as revolutionist, anticolonialist, religious, or populist ideas—as the best way to bring about the total rearrangement they perceived was direly needed by their Vietnam. For the early Vietnamese evangelical converts, that new thinking was embodied by a religious idea that viewed the Vietnam of their time as *the world*, marked by moral-social problems causing chaos, tragedy, and warfare—problems which only turning to Jesus would solve. The prescription of "turning to Jesus" was radical in its offering to the Vietnamese people a unique, overarching solution, as it attempted to deal with both the personal existential quest and the demoralizing national crisis. The early evangelicals also claimed not only that the Bible was the only book that had the power to transform people, but also that every nation, every regime that followed the teachings of the Bible would be abundantly blessed.[42]

40 See Lê Văn Thái, *Bốn mươi sáu năm trong chức vụ* [*Forty Six Years in Ministry*], 160–70. Also Đỗ Quang Hưng, "Người Tin Lành ở Hà Nội" ["The Evangelicals in Hà Nội"], 325–26.

41 Tai, *Radicalism and the Origins of the Vietnamese Revolution*, 262.

42 See the front-page article "Kinh Thánh với xã hội" ["The Bible and the Society"], *Thánh Kinh Báo* [*Bible Magazine*], no. 3 (March 1931): 1–2.

In particular terms, Vietnamese evangelicalism represents a spiritualist stream emerging from the Vietnamese intellectual tradition's encounter with the North American evangelical tradition. More specifically, Vietnamese evangelicalism has the substance (spiritualism), form (radicalism in its bold and overarching claims), and contemporary aspiration (an intertwined desire for national modernization and personal freedom from the tyranny of "outdated" tradition) derived from the early twentieth-century conditions of both the Vietnamese intellectual tradition and the North American evangelical tradition.

In the context of Vietnam's being, by Western standards, a "backward" colony in the 1920s, the boldness of the evangelical message was backed up by a perception that evangelicalism represented *modernity* as much as any other Western traditions and concepts the Vietnamese encountered. Being preoccupied with the desire for *modernity*, a prominent Vietnamese scholar, who had previously helped the C&MA missionaries in their effort to translate the Bible into Vietnamese, advised the public to read the Bible as an excellent way to learn about the roots of Western civilization.[43] In being vocal about their newly founded faith, therefore, the early Vietnamese evangelical leaders resonated with other Vietnamese intellectuals' desire for the promised land of *modernity*.[44]

The radicalism of the early evangelical leaders of the 1920s and 1930s—a radicalism similar to the leaders' Vietnamese intellectual counterparts—was demonstrated most clearly in their iconoclastic, critical approach toward Vietnamese tradition, which they characterized as ineffective in dealing with the crisis created by colonialism. These leaders perceived culture as already bankrupt in the face of modernity and thus did not care about developing cultural forms of evangelicalism. After all, the Vietnamese tradition of the 1920s and 1930s was a tradition "on trial," and the evangelicals were not the only social group that would vote in favor of exchanging tradition for something new.[45] Thus the idea of Vietnamese evangelicalism as being traditionally preoccupied with the thinking about change and progress, more than with the task of easing cultural tension, invites further consideration of a few common criticisms of the faith.

---

43 Phan Khôi, "Giới thiệu và phê bình *Thánh Kinh Báo*" ["Introduction and Review of *The Bible Magazine*"], *Phụ Nữ Tân Văn* [*Women's New Literature*], no. 74 (October 16, 1930).

44 Hence the connection between evangelicalism and *modernity* will emerge as a *locus theologici* for Vietnamese evangelicals if the scholarly investigation focuses more on the relationship between the Vietnamese evangelicals and the Vietnamese intellectual tradition than on that between the Vietnamese evangelicals and the Western missionary movement.

45 Marr, *Vietnamese Tradition on Trial, 1920–1945*, 414–15. For a "genealogy" of the Vietnamese intellectual response to French colonialism, see Trịnh Văn Thảo, *Ba thế hệ tri thức người Việt* (*1862–1954*) [*Three Generations of Vietnamese Intellectuals* (*1862–1954*)], 79ff.

Taking the early Vietnamese evangelicals' rejection of ancestor worship as an example, to say that the evangelicals did so only because they were blind followers of the culturally ignorant Western missionaries does not do justice to the complex social, political, and cultural webs of meaning that the native evangelicals were navigating and within which they were asserting their choices. The discussion should register the view that the early Vietnamese evangelicals had sought a radical, iconoclastic interpretation and revision of ancestor worship—a practice they perceived as having become exceedingly ritualized and less meaningful in the 1920s, when the entire Vietnamese tradition was in crisis. In this context, the early native adopters of evangelicalism argued that ancestor worship should not be limited to the ancestors one knows; rather, it should be expanded to include all ancestors, thus pointing to the worship of God as the Creator of the first ancestor. Of course, such an argument is always open for debate; the agency of early native evangelicals in asserting their adoption of evangelical elements and developing their own interpretation of those elements—their cultural right to do—is, nonetheless, what needs to be acknowledged.

In another example, as early as December 1931, one Vietnamese evangelical had the courage to ask whether Vietnamese evangelicals should continue to observe the Vietnamese traditional new-year's celebration on the grounds that the celebration, in its current configuration, was fraught with drinking, gambling, and superstitious practices. Thus the celebration caused the wasting of money, competition among the participants to present themselves as wealthy (when they were not!), and opportunity for indulging in sinful behaviors—all outcomes that failed to uphold the original meaning of the celebration as an occasion for resting after a year of hard work.[46] The article, which hailed the evangelical church as "widely known [within Vietnamese society] for rejecting old things and embracing new things," urged the faithful to drop the new-year's celebration once and for all since the practice had lost its meaning.[47] Interestingly, while the C&MA missionaries, who produced *Thánh Kinh Báo* [*Bible Magazine*], agreed to print the opinion, they inserted a disclaimer informing readers that the magazine provided only the opinion of an author, not an endorsement of it—the author was fully responsible for the content of the comments. This disclaimer thus showed there was a considerable difference of views on the matter of "embracing newness" and also reflected the independence of thought prevalent among the early native evangelicals of the period.

46 This observed was made by Gabrielle M. Vassal in *Ba năm ở An Nam* [*Three Years in Annam*], trans. Nguyễn Nam Huân (1910. HCMC: Hội Nhà Văn, 2015), 113–15.

47 Kính Thiên, "Tín đồ có nên giữ Tết Nguyên Đán?" ["Should Believers Observe the Traditional New Year?"], *Thánh Kinh Báo* [*Bible Magazine*], no. 10 (December 1931): 11–12.

The understanding that the evangelical church stood in the vanguard of embracing new ideas to achieve social progress also ran parallel to the call of social humanists to "embrace newness," understood as following "European-American culture."[48] This call for progress was also seen as a means of enabling Vietnamese young people's ability to pursue noble aspirations for Vietnam through their commitment to social engagement, as promoted, for example, by *Tự Lực Văn Đoàn* [*Self-Strengthening Literary Group*], an influential literary movement then aspiring for social progress in Vietnam.

The situation of early Vietnamese evangelical leaders within the radical faction of the Vietnamese intellectual tradition in the 1920s to 1930s can also add insights into contemporary concern that evangelicalism appears to attract only the less educated Vietnamese. Such concern can be traced back to the anti-intellectualism of the Western missionary movement and the failure of the national church leadership to emphasize theological and ministerial education, thus creating a clergy that had less formal education and that, therefore, attracted only less educated people. From an alternative perspective, it can be argued otherwise, namely, that the evangelical faith, especially its contemporary pentecostal segment, offers a message which prioritizes care for the socially disadvantaged. As a result, in most cases the body of believers had less intellectual power. The continuing devotion to the more socially disadvantaged shows yet another radical aspect of evangelicalism, as the wealthy and educated must acknowledge they are at least (in principle) "poor in spirit" in order for the evangelical message to have meaning in their lives. This Vietnamese evangelical radicalism, a kind of preferential option for the poor and vulnerable, shows continuity with the radical and liberative spirit of the early Vietnamese intellectuals who sought to dismantle colonial exploitation. In today's Vietnam, this radicalism positions the evangelical faith as a social critic of, say, the Vietnamese communist tradition, which abandons its radicalism in opting to entertain the rent-seekers instead of speaking for the socially disadvantaged.[49] At the same time, the discussion can also register an alternative socio-political argument: it is the marginalization of religious people

48 Hoàng Đạo, "Mười điều tâm niệm của bạn trẻ: Điều thứ nhất—Theo mới" ["Ten Things for the Youth to Live By: The First Tenet—Embrace Newness"], *Ngày Nay* [*Modern Times*], no. 25 (September 13, 1936), accessed October 1, 2016, http://baochi.nlv.gov.vn/baochi/cgi-bin/baochi?a=d&d=Hxsu19360913.2.2&e=-------vi-20--1--img-txIN------#.

49 On rent-seeking behavior in contemporary Vietnam, see Alexander L. Vuving, "Vietnam in 2012: A Rent-Seeking State on the Verge of a Crisis," in *Southeast Asian Affairs 2013*, ed., Daljit Singh (Singapore: Institute of Southeast Asian Studies, 2013), 325–47; Adam Forde, "Rethinking the Political Economy of Conservative Transition: The Case of Vietnam," *Journal of Communist Studies & Transition Politics* 26, no. 1 (March 2010): 126–46.

in early-communist Vietnam that limited Vietnamese evangelicals' access to opportunities for higher education, and this limitation has resulted in the so-called problem of evangelicals' now being less educated.

In the wake of the 1945 Vietnamese Revolution, prominent Vietnamese scholar and linguist Phan Khôi began to view Vietnam as having not merely a political problem that a regime change would solve (a naïve approach prevalent in the Vietnamese anti-colonial movement) but actually a deeper cultural problem that prevented progress (a problem that needed much self-criticism, humility, and multigenerational efforts to address).[50] The evangelical insistence on taking little interest in party politics and functioning in a critical capacity toward culture may have connections to Phan Khôi's argument of Vietnam's having an unsolved cultural rather than political crisis, created in or before colonial times—a crisis that yet today remains unsolved. Such an observation provides an intellectual space to engage critically with the communist argument that there has been no problem with the communist cultural and socio-political arrangement in contemporary Vietnam, because in 1943 the CPV had already dealt thoroughly with the effects of colonialism, including culturally embedded challenges, in its *Đề cương văn hóa Việt Nam* [*Outline of Vietnamese Culture*].[51] Granted, the cultural-political framework as discussed above is simplistic, but it is helpful to call attention to the State's adoption of a "quick-fix" solution when dealing with the problem of culture, and also to the troublesome idea of regarding the communist culture as fair in all ways. The Vietnamese evangelical tradition has the potential to contribute to this discussion based on its long-standing function in a critical capacity within the Vietnamese intellectual tradition. Vietnamese evangelicalism can do so by calling attention to the state-party's project of *cultural hegemony* as glossing over cultural problems—a *cultural hegemony* that would not benefit Vietnamese society in the long run.

---

50 Đỗ Lai Thúy, "Phan Khôi và bước chuyển từ chính trị sang văn hóa" ["Phan Khôi and the Transition from Politics to Culture"], *Văn Hóa Nghệ An* [*Culture of Nghệ An*], November 5, 2014, accessed August 1, 2015, http://www.vanhoanghean.com.vn/chuyen-muc-goc-nhin-van-hoa/nhung-goc-nhin-van-hoa/phan-khoi-va-buoc-chuyen-tu-chinh-tri-sang-van-hoa.

51 Nguyễn Hòa, "Nghiên cứu hậu thực dân ở Việt Nam: một nhu cầu thực tế hay một giả vấn đề?" ["Postcolonial Research in Vietnam: An Actual Need or a False Perception?"], *Nhân Dân*, November 17–26, 2014, accessed March 20, 2015, http://www.nhandan.com.vn/mobile/_mobile_vanhoa/_mobile_diendan/item/24937602.html. Cf. Đỗ Thị Thoan, "Vị trí của kẻ bên lề: Thực hành thơ của nhóm *Mở Miệng* từ góc nhìn văn hóa" ["The Role of the Marginalized: Engaging the Group *Mở Miệng*'s Practices of Poetry from a Cultural Perspective"] (M.A. thesis, Vietnam National University, Hanoi, 2010), 103.

With the benefit of hindsight, it can be said that the cultural agency of the early Vietnamese evangelicals manifested more strongly in the intention to employ faith for the purposes of improving culture and promoting change toward modernity, rather than in efforts to ease cultural tension. The understanding of early Vietnamese evangelicals as a radical stream of Vietnamese intellectuals calling, in an iconoclastic manner, for the discontinuing rather than the continuing of traditional cultural and social practices thus rejects the simplistic political assessment that Vietnamese evangelicalism is foreign to Vietnam because its origin, content, and form are unfamiliar to the country's native people. This understanding also warrants a review of the relationship of Vietnamese evangelicalism and Vietnamese culture in both the contemporary, communist-led Vietnamese academy and the Vietnamese evangelical theological academy.

Revisiting early Vietnamese evangelicalism in context also reveals an important aspect of the Vietnam of the 1920s to 1930s: the country was, in many respects, a plurivocal society. These characteristics have implications for contesting the state-party's efforts of *cultural hegemony* to establish contemporary Vietnam as a univocal society that uncritically attaches to a single ideology.[52] Here contemporary Vietnam may find inspiration in reviewing the intellectual integrity of the Vietnamese intellectuals of the 1920s and 1930s, for they possessed a healthy, non-ideological attachment that has long been admired:

> Vietnamese intellectuals of half a century ago ... possessed both boundless curiosity and firm moral commitments. Neither their knowledge nor their principles were subject to strict external control. No tradition was so sacred as to be above debate. No intellectual felt fulfilled by simple contemplation or idle discussion; the purpose of thinking was to learn how, when, and where to act. There was no single court before which every action could be judged, but rather a variety of courts, to include History, Fate, Science, the People, the State, the Party, and one's family, friends, and peers.[53]

52 On the contemporary Vietnamese intellectual trend of revisiting the 1920s–1930s, see Nguyên Ngọc, "Chương trình vĩ đại bị dở dang của Phan Châu Trinh" ["The Great Unfinished Project of Phan Châu Trinh"] (university lecture, Hoa Sen University, HCMC, March 23, 2011), and Bùi Trân Phượng, "Diễn từ nhận giải thưởng 'Vì sự nghiệp văn hoá giáo dục' của Quỹ Văn Hoá Phan Châu Trinh" ["Speech on Accepting the Honorary Award for Lifetime Achievement on Cultural and Educational Development by Phan Châu Trinh Cultural Fund"], HCMC, March 29, 2013.

53 Marr, *Vietnamese Tradition on Trial, 1920–1945*, 420.

3.4 Multi-Ethnicity

In today's Vietnam, it is noteworthy that Vietnamese culture, as described in the preceding discussion of its interaction with evangelicalism, is primarily the culture of the majority *Việt* people, with little being said about the culture(s) of the country's non-*Việt* minority ethnic groups. When Phu Le completed his writings on Vietnamese evangelicalism in 1972, he noted that the ECVN was perhaps the only evangelical church in Southeast Asia in which the majority ethnic people of the nation also comprised the majority within the church demographic (as compared, for example, to the mostly ethnic minority evangelicals of Myanmar).[54] This statistic does not hold true in contemporary Vietnam, where ethnic minority groups now represent the majority of Vietnamese evangelicals.

While the state-party's measurement of *cultural hegemony* is manifested in a rather cordial manner toward the *Việt* evangelicals—via the state-party's suggestion of their *Vietnamization of [the] faith*—the State instructs, sometimes through coercive means, that people belonging to ethnic minority groups must not convert to Christianity—that it is important for these people to keep their traditional beliefs and practices, even though the same state sometimes judges those indigenous beliefs and practices to be "unrefined."[55] Here the State is acting in a paternalistic manner by instructing people of ethnic minority groups not to trust "bad people," where the term "bad people" points ambiguously to both the religious others (who are mostly evangelicals or Roman Catholics) and political others (who pretend to be itinerant Christian evangelists in order to travel and spread propaganda against the regime). The coercive manner in which this ambiguity translates into reality is recorded by a Western evangelical sociologist as follows:

> Hamlet by hamlet, officials gathered H'Mong Christians [the H'Mong is a non-Việt minority people] and forced them to sit through educational sessions to study the correct meaning of religious liberty and learn to recognize 'bad people' who promote evangelical religion. The statement of promise reads: "I promise to implement the following: 1) Neither my family nor I will take part in any *Tin Lành* [evangelical] practices or study of the *Tin Lành* religion, and we will return to the traditional practices of our H'Mong people … 4) If I should in any way not abide by these

54 Phu Le, "A Short History," 485.

55 As well documented by former C&MA missionary Reg Reimer in his *Vietnam's Christians: A Century of Growth in Adversity* (Pasadena: William Carey Library, 2011).

> promises, I please request that I be held accountable to the laws and legal authorities."[56]

Since contemporary Vietnam can be rightly considered a postcolonial society, the above method used by the state-party can be interpreted as a postcolonial practice rooted in the colonial experience. Here *Việt* ethnicity in contemporary Vietnam fosters a rhetoric that portrays them as the "eldest brother" to non-*Việt* ethnic minority groups and as bearing the "burden" of looking after all the "younger brothers" to prevent the influence of "bad people." The mentality mimics the old Chinese and French presumption of responsibility for civilizing the inhabitants of Vietnam—thinking that resulted in the paternalistic attitude of the incumbent state toward the ethnic Other.[57]

The instruction that people of ethnic minority groups should not adopt the evangelical faith also reveals the State's direct concern over the evangelical pulpit's potential to serve as a political platform giving rise to secessionism based on the ethnic difference—a potential that, if realized, may threaten the security of the regime. Evangelicalism grows mostly among the ethnic minorities residing in the Central Highlands and Northwest Highlands, two geographically strategic regions of the country. While the Central Highlands allow control over the whole of Indochina, the Northwest Highlands function as a buffer between Vietnam and China; thus, the Vietnamese state views this latter region as critical for asserting sovereignty over the nation's borders. In terms of the modern history of these regions, in 2001 and 2004 the Montagnards mounted mass demonstrations in the Central Highlands due to land disputes; statistics showed that fully half of the Montagnard population was evangelical. Similarly, by the time of a similar rally of the H'Mong people in the Northern Highlands in 2009, statistics showed a 750 percent growth rate for evangelicalism among the H'Mong from 1999 to 2009.[58] Here the mass of ethnic-minority

56 James Lewis, "The Evangelical Religious Movement among the H'Mong of Northern Vietnam and the Government Response to It: 1989–2000," *Crossroad: An Interdisciplinary Journal of Southeast Asian Studies* 16, no. 2 (2002): 79–112: 97. See also Tam T. T. Ngo, "Protestant Conversion and Social Conflict: The Case of the Hmong in Contemporary Vietnam," *Journal of Southeast Asian Studies* 46 (2015): 274–92.

57 As a rhetoric used by Vietnamese communists in North Vietnam (1954–1975), see Patricia M. Pelley, " 'Barbarians' and 'Younger Brothers': The Remaking of Race in Postcolonial Vietnam," *Journal of Southeast Asian Studies* 29, no. 2 (September 1998): 374–91. See also Pelley, *Postcolonial Vietnam*, 62. On the challenge of using the category "colonialism" to prioritize the history of Western interpretation over other histories, see Aijaz Ahmad, "The Politics of Literary Postcoloniality," *Race and Class* 36, no. 3 (1995): 1–20: 6–7.

58 On the conversion of the H'Mong people as a result of their listening to Christian radio or their interaction with evangelical Christians along the borders, see Tam T. T. Ngo,

evangelicals is viewed by the State as a potential mobilizing force that could challenge both state sovereignty and border integrity. In the Central Highlands, for example, the United Front for the Liberation of Oppressed Races, which was involved in armed conflict with both the former South Vietnam and the current communist regime, and whose members were identified as adherents of evangelicalism, only ceased to function in 1992. The State has also directed criticism at C&MA missionaries for following French colonialists in considering the ethnic peoples inhabiting the highlands and mountainous areas to be separate people groups that do not necessarily belong to the modern nation of Vietnam, thus creating a precedent for contemporary evangelicals to disturb the nation's territorial integrity.[59] Hence the regime's concern that there was a troubling mixture of evangelicalism and ethnic politics in Vietnam.[60]

Further, state scholars viewed ethnic evangelicals as law-breakers when they mass migrated from North Vietnam to the Central Highlands and eventually to Cambodia, where they sought refugee status by appealing to the United Nations' High Commissioner for Refugees. In doing so, they accused the Vietnamese government of violating their religious freedom and grabbing their land, thus jeopardizing Vietnam's international relations and standing.[61] Also viewed critically by the State as creators of separate socio-political structures that compete with established local political structures are the organized women's groups, youth groups, and elder committees within evangelical bodies.[62]

"'The Short-waved Faith': Christian Broadcastings and the Transformation of the Spiritual Landscape of the Hmong in Northern Vietnam," in *Mediated Piety: Technology and Religion in Contemporary Asia*, ed. Francis Khek Gee Lim (Leiden: Brill, 2009), 139–59.

59 Lê Thị Giang, "Hệ phái Tin Lành Việt Nam (Miền Nam) ở Lâm Đồng" ["The Evangelical Church of Vietnam (South) in Lâm Đồng Province"], (M.A. thesis, Đà Lạt University, 2006), 51.

60 For an elaboration of this concern from the perspective of the state-party, see section "Thủ đoạn phá hoại khối đại đoàn kết toàn dân tộc Việt Nam của các thế lực thù địch" ["Malicious Move of Hatred to Undermine the Solidarity of People Groups in Vietnam"], in Nguyễn Đình Minh, ed., *Đoàn kết dân tộc ở Việt Nam* [*Solidarity among People Groups in Vietnam*] (Hà Nội: Chính Trị Quốc Gia—Sự Thật, 2016), 172–204. See also the discussion on evangelicalism and secessionism among ethnic people groups in the Central Highlands in Lương Thị Thoa, ed., *Nhân tố tôn giáo trong chủ nghĩa ly khai ở một số nước Đông Nam Á* [*The Religious Factor in Secessionism in Some Southeast Asian Countries*] (Hà Nội: Chính Trị Quốc Gia, 2013), 111–22.

61 Nguyễn Văn Minh, "Một số vấn đề về đạo Tin Lành trong cộng đồng người Hmông di cư tự do vào Tây Nguyên hiện nay" ["Some Issues Related to Evangelicalism in the H'Mong Community Migrating to the Central Highland at the Present"], *Tạp Chí Dân Tộc Học* [*Journal of Ethnology*], no. 5 (2010): 38–47.

62 Vương Thị Kim Oanh, "Các yếu tố tâm lý—xã hội ảnh hưởng tới sự phục hồi và phát triển đạo Tin Lành tại tỉnh Kon Tum trong giai đoạn hiện nay" ["Social-Psychological Factors

The *Việt* evangelicals are also criticized by the state-party as being "colonialists" in their promoting among ethnic peoples evangelical materials written in the *Việt* language, thus weakening the use of tribal languages and causing cultural assimilation; it has, however, been noted that Vietnamese evangelicals of former generations maintained a rather consistent approach of striving to communicate with the ethnic groups in their own languages.[63] But the criticism is fairly accurate, given the low level of promoting indigenous languages among contemporary Vietnamese evangelicals, who in church communication use mainly the *Việt* language for the sake of convenience, without thinking much of the practice's cultural impact. At the same time, the incumbent State is subject to an equal share of criticism on the basis of its slow development of elementary schooling programs in the languages of the ethnic minority groups, thus forcing their children to study mainly in *Việt*.

Because of the above understandings, to date state scholars still hold a rather negative view of Vietnamese evangelicalism. While Vietnamese evangelicals insist they have no intent to challenge any powers that be by citing their long-standing *non-interference-in-politics* policy to substantiate this claim,[64] state authors, possibly having utmost concern for regime security, often voice suspicion that evangelicals' overt insistence on the *non-interference-in-politics* policy is meant to hide a political agenda. Here the evangelical rejection of political involvement is interpreted as a tacit posture showing their unwillingness to cooperate with the state-party, thus implying their opposition rather than real intention to stay out of politics.[65]

Based on the above concerns, a state scholar consulted the State to foster a "double" approach to evangelicalism: on the one hand, the State should exercise

---

that Influence the Resurgence and Development of Evangelicalism in Kon Tum Province in the Present Time"], *Tạp Chí Tâm Lý Học* [*Journal of Psychology*], no. 3 (2001): 60–62.

63 Hồ Tấn Sáng, "Đạo Tin Lành và ảnh hưởng của nó đối với một số lĩnh vực xã hội ở Tây Nguyên" ["Evangelicalism and Its Influence on Certain Aspects of Society in the Central Highlands"], *Tạp Chí Nghiên Cứu Tôn Giáo* [*Journal of Religious Studies*], no. 4 (2008): 30–35; Nguyễn Văn Năm, "Ảnh hưởng của Đạo Tin Lành với thiết chế xã hội truyền thống của đồng bào các dân tộc thiểu số ở Tây Nguyên" ["The Influence of Evangelicalism on Traditional Social Institutions of Ethnic Peoples in the Central Highlands"], *Tạp Chí Nghiên Cứu Tôn Giáo* [*Journal of Religious Studies*], no. 4 (2008): 36–42.

64 See, for example, the writing of Thái Phước Trường in his *Hội Thánh Tin Lành Việt Nam: 100 năm hình thành và phát triển* [*The Evangelical Church of Vietnam: 100 Years of Forming and Development*] (HCMC: Hội Thánh Tin Lành Việt Nam Miền Nam, 2011), 164–65.

65 Lê Thị Giang, "Hệ phái Tin Lành Việt Nam (Miền Nam) ở Lâm Đồng" ["The Evangelical Church of Vietnam (South) in Lâm Đồng Province"], 51.

tight control on religious and ethnic affairs to contain the risk of people's using religious and ethnic differences to challenge the sovereignty of the State; on the other hand, the State should continue to uphold the socialist vision of "protecting national independence and unification for prosperity, strength, justice, and democracy" in order to persuade and co-opt evangelicals into the Vietnamese Fatherland Front to ensure one nation under the leadership of one political party.[66] This "double" approach reveals the state-party's willingness to balance both force and consent in order to achieve *cultural hegemony* and maintain sovereign power.[67]

The phenomenal growth of evangelicalism among minority ethnic groups in contemporary Vietnam, however, has resulted in evangelical institutions' becoming, among many of these people groups, the largest social organizations outside the state-controlled institutions. This development has placed evangelicalism in a strategic position in the ongoing public debate on the multi-ethnic nature of contemporary Vietnam, especially whenever the state-party fails to include the perspective of minority ethnic people groups in its attempts to build political and cultural consensus. This case also applies whenever the political powers resort to condescending colonial rhetoric that suggests they have a moral responsibility to bring civilization and modernity to the "backward" ethnic others. Finally, any attempt to define and elaborate the "Vietnamese-ness" of Vietnamese evangelicalism that gives preference to evangelicalism's interaction with the *Việt* intellectual tradition and its Sinitic foundation (though acknowledged in this study as an important research direction for improving the overall historical understanding of Vietnamese evangelicalism) will need to be held in creative tension with the contemporary Vietnamese evangelical demographic, which includes members of several minority ethnic groups that may, historically, have lower levels of engagement with Sinitic learning.

3.5 Conclusion

On reflection, the chief concern of the Vietnamese evangelical tradition appears to be how to posit the faith as a liberating force that is able to free people

66 Hồ Tấn Sáng, "Đạo Tin Lành và ảnh hưởng của nó đối với một số lĩnh vực xã hội ở Tây Nguyên" ["Evangelicalism and Its Influence on Certain Aspects of Society in the Central Highlands"], 34.

67 For a theoretical discussion, see Antonio Gramsci, *Selections from the Prison Notebooks* (New York: International Publishers, 1971), 215.

from cultural elements that impede their human flourishing. In doing so, evangelicalism may take an iconoclastic approach to the cultural *status quo* that it judges to have negative effects on the people. It can be argued that, for both the *Việt* evangelical converts in the 1920s and 1930s and for several underprivileged ethnic minority populations in today's Vietnam, evangelicalism is attractive because the faith has presented itself as a positive force which can help people achieve newness, progress, and modernity while countering dehumanizing aspects of culture. In the entire development of Vietnamese evangelicalism, little evidence shows that people inhabiting Vietnam are drawn to this form of the faith because it has adequately created a cultural cloth that makes it more local.[68] In today's Vietnam, the pentecostal emphasis on *divine intervention* accentuates the desire for change in its providing believers with positive faith that God is on their side as they seek the alterations necessary to improve their lot in life.

It is also important to note that the idea of a *Vietnamization of faith* has been used politically to marginalize Vietnamese evangelicals and pressure them to conform to the state-controlled culture of contemporary Vietnam. Within the ongoing discussion concerning the relationship between evangelicalism and Vietnamese culture, therefore, it is germane to promote the concept of *contextualization* as including at least the two tasks of *inculturation* and *liberation*. In other words, the scholarly discussion should register an additional perspective that no attractive *Vietnamization of faith* would exist in the midst of social injustice. Further, "writing" early Vietnamese evangelical leaders "back into history" has the capacity to promote the understanding that, in the 1920s and 1930s, Vietnam was a plurivocal society. This understanding, in turn, calls into question the need for enforcing univocality and *cultural hegemony* in contemporary Vietnam.

In this discussion of faith and culture, the importance of the typical Vietnamese person's aspiration for *modernity*—an aspiration found among both the majority and minority ethnic groups—cannot be overemphasized. It was within the overall Vietnamese quest for *modernity* in the 1920s and 1930s that the concern for "change" became a fixture in the writings of the *Việt* intellectuals, the early evangelical leaders included; and that same

68 For further discussion, see Tam T. T. Ngo, *The New Way: Protestantism and the Hmong in Vietnam* (Seattle: University of Washington Press, 2016), and Nguyễn Văn Thắng, ed., *Giữ 'lý cũ' hay theo 'lý mới'? Bản chất của những cách phản ứng khác nhau của người H'Mong tại Việt Nam với ảnh hưởng của đạo Tin Lành* [*Keep 'Old Reason' or Follow 'New Reason'? Natures of the Responses of H'Mong people to Evangelicalism*] (Hà Nội: Khoa Học Xã Hội, 2009).

aspiration for newness and progress is important for the ethnic minority people groups in contemporary Vietnam. As of today, the quest for *modernity* remains vigorous, as currently expressed through aspirations such as *development* and *prosperity*; therefore, this quest requires further investigation.

CHAPTER 4

Development

4.1 National Development

Modernization, understood as the acquisition and application of Western technology and scientific methodology for the betterment of society, has been a long-desired outcome for the Vietnamese intellectual tradition since its first encounter with Westerners. The most significant encounter with the West—arguably, via the roughly century-long experience of being a French colony from the mid-nineteenth to the mid-twentieth century—has left the people groups inhabiting contemporary Vietnam ambivalent: on the one hand, they struggle against Western influence in their attempts to define and assert a native culture; on the other hand, they desire indigenous society to become Western-like through modernization.

In contemporary Vietnam, the longtime desire for modernization is manifested in an intense thinking about *development*, the overarching framework for thought and action aiming at materializing the collective Vietnamese desire for modernity. In a larger sense, the concept of *development* creates the distinct subcategories of *developed* and *developing* countries, a division that has been criticized as a continuation of the colonial division along the line of civilized colonizing powers and uncivilized colonized territories.[1] *Development*, however, still functions as a foundational concept that guides many political and economic behavioral patterns in postcolonial international relations, thus rendering it a prominent concept that requires careful engagement. The present chapter will discuss three perspectives on *development*: *national development, transformational development*, and *prosperity teaching*. These different perspectives will serve as a frame of reference for discussing the issue of *development* among contemporary Vietnamese evangelicals—a frame of reference in which *prosperity teaching*, rightly situated within the pentecostal emphasis on *divine intervention*, represents a helpful grassroots perspective that can improve the overall social discourse of Vietnamese evangelicals.

For a quick historical overview, as early as 1858, Vietnamese official Nguyễn Trường Tộ, after a diplomatic mission to France, submitted "A Plan

1 For example, see Gustavo Esteva, "Development," in *The Development Dictionary*, ed. Wolfgang Sachs, 2nd ed. (London and New York: Zed Books, 2010), 1–23, especially pages 1–3.

 | DOI:10.1163/9789004383838_006

for Making the People Wealthy and the Country Strong" to the Imperial Court based on what he saw about the wealth, scientific advancement, and military strength of France. His concerns were then echoed in 1904 in the textbooks of the Tonkin Free School (a school, yes, but also an embodiment of a cultural and political movement) through their emphasis on the idea of "civilizing" Vietnam.[2] This emphasis on civilizing then became a concern of many native Vietnamese for modernization, or *development*, a term perhaps first used and discussed as the modernization proponents' ultimate goal for Vietnam (or any colonized country for that matter) in a famous political treatise believed to be put forth by a Tùng Phong—a pen name allegedly used in 1964 by Ngô Đình Nhu, the younger brother and chief political advisor of South Vietnam's first president, Ngô Đình Diệm.[3] Last but not least, the Constitution of the Socialist Republic of Vietnam, which went through five revisions from 1946 to 2013, also insisted that the state-party has as its primary goals the "striving to build a wealthy and strong country in which social justice prevails, all men have enough to eat and to wear, [and] enjoy freedom, happiness, and all necessary conditions for complete development."[4]

Concerning *national development*, the prominence of the issue of *development* in contemporary Vietnam is demonstrated in the fact that the CPV builds its legitimacy to rule on the claim that the party is the most capable social group to lead Vietnam toward modernity through the course of *development*—a major claim put forth in the party's doctrine of *socialist-oriented development*.[5] Coincidentally, the first-ever independent think-tank of Vietnam, organized by intellectuals discontent with the country's leadership, was named the *Institute for Development Studies* (2007–2009), thus exampling again the importance of the concept of *development* in contemporary Vietnam.

2 For excerpts from the writings of Nguyễn Trường Tộ and the Tonkin Free School, see George E. Dutton, Jayne S. Werner, and John K. Whitmore, eds., *Sources of Vietnamese Tradition*, Introduction to Asian Civilizations Series (New York: Columbia University Press, 2012), 284–89, 369–75.

3 Tùng Phong, *Chính đề Việt Nam* [*Main Issues of Vietnam*] (Sài Gòn: Đồng Nai, 1965).

4 Textual excerpts from the online English translation of "Constitution of the Socialist Republic of Vietnam," available at the official website of the National Assembly of Vietnam, accessed March 20, 2015, http://www.na.gov.vn/htx/English/C1479/default.asp?Newid=24766#gQNqmQstOBFE.

5 Nguyễn Văn Thạo and Nguyễn Viết Thông, eds., *Tìm hiểu một số thuật ngữ trong văn kiện Đại Hội XI của Đảng* [*Studying the Terminologies of the Documents of the Eleventh Congress of the Communist Party of Vietnam*] (Hà Nội: Chính Trị Quốc Gia, 2011), 226–28.

According to the Socio-Economic Development Strategy of the 11th Congress of the CPV (2011), *national development* is *fast and sustainable development*.[6] The concept of *fast development* aims at a high and increasing annual economic growth rate, expressed in concrete terms asserting that Vietnam will be "by and large an industrialized country on the way to modernity by 2020"—an ambitious goal that in 2011 academic critics judged as "impatient."[7]

Sustainable development, referring to a political will to mitigate the adverse effects of rapid economic development in society and the environment, is also a prominent conceptual byproduct of the *development* discourse in Vietnam.[8] Following the common usage of *sustainable development* as "development that meets the needs of the present without compromising the ability of future generations to meet their own needs,"[9] the concept of *sustainable development* in Vietnam does include environmental care and responsible use of resources as one important aspect. But in local usage *sustainable development* is also used to convey two other ideas. First, *sustainable development* as it is employed in Vietnam implies concern for equality, since the State acknowledges that increased income *inequality* is an impediment to the sustainability of *national development*. Second, the state-party emphasizes that sustainability can only be achieved in a politically stable context, thus calling social consensus and support of the CPV's leadership a virtue in contemporary Vietnam.[10] Dissident voices are therefore marginalized in the name of *sustainable development*.

In a related development, the CPV, for the purpose of protecting political hegemony, borrows and promotes the Chinese communist concept of *harmonious development*, which views critical arguments as upsetting "harmony" and impeding *development*.[11] Needless to say, critics seek to reclaim the concepts of

6 The Communist Party of Vietnam, *Văn kiện Đại hội Đại biểu toàn quốc lần thứ XI* [*Documents of the 11th Congress of the Party*] (Hà Nội: Chính Trị Quốc Gia, 2011).

7 Hồ Sĩ Quý, *Tiến bộ xã hội: Một số vấn đề về mô hình phát triển ở Đông Á và Đông Nam Á* [*Social Progress: Some Issues in East Asian's and Southeast Asian's Development Models*] (Hà Nội: Tri Thức, 2011), 227–31.

8 For a historical overview of the use of the concept of *sustainable development* in Vietnam, see Nguyễn Văn Dân, *Văn hóa và phát triển trong bối cảnh toàn cầu hóa* [*Culture and Development in the Context of Globalization*] (Hà Nội: Khoa Học Xã Hội, 2006), 221–29.

9 United Nations World Commission on Environment and Development, *Our Common Future* (*Brundtland Report*) (Oxford: Oxford University Press, 1987), 43.

10 For example, Vũ Hữu Ngoạn, "Giải quyết tốt mối quan hệ giữa đổi mới, ổn định và phát triển" ["Solving Well the Relationship of Reform, Sustainability, and Development"], *Tạp Chí Cộng Sản* [*Journal of Communism*] 826 (August 2011): 47–50. The term "relationship" actually means "tension" in this context.

11 For example, Phạm Văn Đức et al., eds., *Vấn đề dân sinh và xã hội hài hòa* [*The Issue of Livelihood and Social Harmony*] (Hà Nội: Khoa Học Xã Hội, 2010); Vũ Văn Hà, "Kết hợp hài hòa

sustainability and *harmony* by arguing that it is the CPV's monopoly on leadership that hinders *development* and causes unsustainability.[12]

In addition to *sustainable development*, both the state-party and academic scholars on *development* also entertain the concept of *human development*, advocated by the United Nations Development Programme (UNDP) since 1990. In the UNDP proposal, *human development* is defined by non-economic indicators based on the assumption that the well-being of the people results from focusing on improving their lives, not from focusing on economic growth.[13] The concept of *human development* proposed by the UNDP includes both directly enhancing human abilities (manifested through good health, good education, and a decent standard of living) and creating healthy conditions for human development (including participation in political and community life, environmental sustainability, human security and human rights, and gender equality).

Moving beyond *human development*, Hồ Sĩ Quý, a leading scholar in development studies in Vietnam and director of the Institute of Social Sciences Information of the Vietnam Academy of Social Sciences, calls attention to the idea of *free development*, meaning that human development is ultimately "the free development of each person within the free development of all." This idea carries weight in communist Vietnam because Hồ Sĩ Quý is able to quote "canonical" communist writers such as Marx, Engels, and Hồ Chí Minh to support his thesis.[14] At the same time, the concept of *free development* also shows the influence of development thinker Amartya Sen, 1998 Nobel Prize winner in economic sciences.[15] In *free development*, *democracy*, understood

chính sách kinh tế với chính sách xã hội" ["Harmonious Integration of Economic Policy with Social Policy"], *Tạp chí Cộng Sản* [*Journal of Communism*] 861 (July 2014): 70–75.

12 This argument is evident in various calls to reconsider Article 4 of the Constitution of Vietnam, which posits the CPV is the only institution assuming leadership of the Vietnamese state and society. On this issue, see Bùi Hải Thiêm, "Pluralism Unleashed: The Politics of Reforming the Vietnamese Constitution," *Journal of Vietnamese Studies* 9, no. 4 (December 1, 2014): 1–32.

13 For further information on *human development*, see UNDP, with an introduction by Amartya Sen, "Human Development Report 2010," November 2010, accessed October 25, 2015, http://hdr.undp.org/en/content/human-development-report-2010. For a review of literature critical of the Human Development Index, see the UNDP publication of Milorad Kovacevic, "Review of HDI Critiques and Potential Improvements," February 2011, accessed October 25, 2015, http://hdr.undp.org/en/content/review-hdi-critiques-and-potential-improvements. On the revised HDI as still inviting further refinement, see Stephen Morse, *Indices and Indicators in Development: An Unhealthy Obsession with Numbers* (New York: Routledge, 2013): chapter 4, "Integrating Development Indicators," 83–117.

14 Hồ Sĩ Quý, *Tiến bộ xã hội* [*Social Progress*], 93–94.

15 Amartya Sen, *Development as Freedom* (New York: Oxford University Press, 1999).

conservatively as the freedom to express political opinions, is defended as an important contributing factor in the process of *development* and a key indicator of social progress.[16]

The proliferation of definitions gathered under the *development* umbrella, including *fast [economic] development, sustainable development, harmonious development, human development*, and *free development*, demonstrates both the national contestation of what counts as *development* and the implicit national struggle in the search for a configuration of power to facilitate *development*.

With the benefit of hindsight, the increased preoccupation with *development* among Vietnamese policymakers and intellectual critics in the past two decades can be situated within the global context of the end of the Cold War. Within this global context, the dissolution of the Soviet Union in 1991 caused Vietnam to become more proactive in rethinking *development* in two directions: first *globally*, by showing a willingness to work with Western powers, by accepting the Western premise of *development*, and by seeking international integration via cooperation with various agencies of the United Nations (UN) and with International Financial Institutions (IFIS) such as the World Bank (WB);[17] and second *regionally*, by situating Vietnam in the context of East Asian development.

One of the most significant global influences on the Vietnamese *development* discourse remains the reception by the state-party of the neoliberalism manifested in the Washington Consensus—a reception evidenced in the state-party's reliance upon Western donors for financial support to carry out development projects.[18] In the 1970s, *development* was thought of mainly in terms of providing an impoverished population with *basic needs* (such as food, water, shelter, healthcare, education, and the promotion of human dignity and integrity) through state intervention in the market and society. In this line of thinking, *development* focused on the reduction of poverty. Since the 1990s, however, neoliberalism, embodied in the economic-policy prescriptions promoted by the Washington Consensus, abandoned thinking about *basic needs* in favor of focusing on *structural adjustment*, the belief that economic growth

---

16 Hồ Sĩ Quý, *Tiến bộ xã hội* [*Social Progress*], 241–61.

17 For detailed documentation of the influence of international policy on Vietnam's post-Cold War development, see David W. P. Elliott, *Changing Worlds: Vietnam's Transition from Cold War to Globalization* (New York: Oxford University Press, 2012).

18 On the CPV's presiding over a neoliberal economy, read through the prism of property rights, see Hue-Tam Ho Tai and Mark Sidel, eds., *State, Society and the Market in Contemporary Vietnam: Property, Power and Values* (New York: Routledge, 2013).

(or development) could be achieved through the promotion of fiscal transparency, institutional accountability, and a credible legal framework.[19] Neoliberalism did so on the assumption that *structural adjustment* was an indirect yet more efficient way of reducing poverty than working to address *basic needs*.

The Socio-Economic Development Strategy of the 11th Congress (2011) of the CPV shows the Vietnamese state's receptiveness to neoliberalism by embracing *structural adjustment* as the strategic direction to achieve development. This strategic direction is in line with what the IFIs suggested as good practices for developing countries, thus showing the influence of Western donors and experts on the Vietnamese state as the recipient of *structural adjustment* loans.[20] In practice, however, that the Vietnamese state has managed to delay the implementation of several *structural adjustment* standards invites different interpretations: the delay evidences either the State's incompetence to carry out an agreed upon plan, or the subtle resistance of those who feel they carry the short end of the stick in an asymmetric relationship, thus illustrating James C. Scott's theory of everyday resistance by the less powerful party in a power-governed relationship.[21] Moreover, in the context of an expanding open economic market in Vietnam, the delay of the Vietnamese state in implementing *structural adjustment* standards can be interpreted as a means to open windows of opportunity for creating *crony capitalism*, a collaboration between state officials and business people in exploiting loopholes for gains in material and power.[22] From an academic perspective, Vietnamese critics' main objections to the adoption of the *structural adjustment* approach to

19 For a historical account of the shift from *basic needs* to *structural adjustment* in development practice, see Gilbert Rist, *The History of Development: From Western Origins to Global Faith*, 4th ed. (London and New York: Zed Books, 2014), chapter 9, "The Triumph of Third-Worldism," 140–70. See also Richard Peet and Elaine Hartwick, *Theories of Development: Contentions, Arguments, Alternatives*, 3rd ed. (New York and London: The Guilford Press, 2015), chapter 3, "From Keynesian Economics to Neoliberalism," 63–118.

20 In the case of Vietnam, see Pietro Masina, *Vietnam's Development Strategies* (New York: Routledge, 2006), 3. As a global phenomenon, see Dani Rodrik, *One Economics, Many Recipes: Globalization, Institutions, and Economic Growth* (Princeton: Princeton University Press, 2009), chapter 1; Ha-Joon Chang, *Bad Samaritans: The Myth of Free Trade and the Secret History of Capitalism* (New York: Bloomsbury Press, 2008), chapter 2.

21 James C. Scott, *Domination and the Arts of Resistance: Hidden Transcripts* (New Haven: Yale University Press, 1990).

22 On crony capitalism and rent-seekers in Vietnam, see Alexander L. Vuving, "Vietnam in 2012: A Rent-Seeking State on the Verge of a Crisis," in *Southeast Asian Affairs 2013*, ed., Daljit Singh (Singapore: Institute of Southeast Asian Studies, 2013), 325–47; Adam Forde, "Rethinking the Political Economy of Conservative Transition: The Case of Vietnam," *Journal of Communist Studies & Transition Politics* 26, no. 1 (March 2010): 126–46.

development include the argument that using expert advice from IFIs and UN agencies is problematic because these inputs simply reflect the ideology of the given international institution—an ideology that often arises from the study of a particular historical context (such as the East Asian countries in the 1960s) then inadequately proposed to other countries in the 2000s.[23]

Of equal import as the state-party's reception of neoliberalism is the problem that the Vietnamese discussion on the concept of *development* appears to lack engagement with the critical perspective of *postdevelopment*. This perspective maintains that the imposition of neoliberalism on postcolonial societies is a practice of ongoing colonialism—one through which Western institutions continue to act according to the assumption that they possess superior knowledge and ethics. The existing discourse on *development* is criticized as prefiguring the people of former colonies as *underdeveloped* and treating them as such. The *postdevelopment* proposal, therefore, is to jettison *development*, in both thinking and action, in order to provide social space for alternative social movements.[24] In many cases, the solutions proposed by *postdevelopment theory* involve the indigenization of *development* and a preference for social and spiritual well-being over material growth. These solutions are reflected in the suggestions of thinking locally (at the expense of acknowledging the global links of the community), and living a simple life (at the expense of acknowledging the potential benefits of modern science and technology for the community).[25] But their shortcoming raises ethical concerns about the denial of rights to "modernity for all," a theoretical tension that has not yet been adequately resolved.[26] Although the creative solutions offered by *postdevelopment* criticism continue to invite refinement, the critical analysis of the *postdevelopment*

23 Hồ Sĩ Quý, *Tiến bộ xã hội* [*Social Progress*], 210. A similar criticism is raised by Joseph Stiglitz, winner of the 2001 Nobel Prize in economic sciences, in his *Globalization and Its Discontents* (New York: Penguin Books, 2002). For detailed case studies to illustrate this issue, see William Easterly, *The Tyranny of Experts: Economists, Dictators, and the Forgotten Rights of the Poor* (New York: Basic Books, 2013).

24 Arturo Escobar, "'Post-Development' as Concept and Social Practice," in *Exploring Post-Development: Theory and Practice, Problems and Perspectives*, ed. Aram Ziai (New York: Routledge, 2007), 18–32: 20–21. See also Escobar's influential work *Encountering Development: The Making and Unmaking of the Third World* (Princeton: Princeton University Press, 1995). For a helpful review of post-development literature, see James D. Sidaway, "Spaces of Postdevelopment," *Progress in Human Geography* 31, no. 3 (June 2007): 345–61.

25 For brief but helpful summaries of this literature, see Peet and Hartwick, *Theories of Development*, 228–30, and Nalani Hennayake, *Culture, Politics, and Development in Postcolonial Sri Lanka* (Lanham, MD: Lexington Books, 2006), 34–35.

26 Peet and Hartwick, *Theories of Development*, 285–86.

perspective is helpful in calling attention to colonial-like thinking and practice in the contemporary discourse on *development*.

The situation of Vietnam as an Asian country also generates debate over whether Vietnam should embrace the *East Asian model of development* (thus trying to imitate the success stories of Taiwan, South Korea, and China, and to a lesser extent the stories of Japan, Hong Kong, and Singapore) or indulge itself in the *Southeast Asian model of development* (thus attempting to avoid the not-so-successful stories of other neighboring Southeast Asian countries, such as Thailand and the Philippines). The discussion is valid if one accepts the premise of the Vietnamese tradition's belonging to the East Asian cultural sphere (the so-called Sinosphere), though Vietnam is geographically situated in Southeast Asia.[27]

Such a framework for analysis received even further attention after it was used in a consulting report by the Asia Programs of the John F. Kennedy School of Government at Harvard University. The report advised Vietnam to follow the *East Asian model of development*, i.e., to foster *development* by creating a national political will to push society toward modernity through the practices of strong government over an extended period of time.[28] Such a proposal is attractive because it provides both an image of modernity (making Vietnam appear more like Taiwan or South Korea) that the people might easily accept, and leeway for justifying why the CPV's monopoly of power is a prerequisite for *development*. Vietnamese scholars criticize the proposal as insensitive to the political context of Vietnam.[29]

Preoccupation with the East Asian model of *development* also prompts questions about the role of *culture* in *development*. Since the Vietnamese intellectual tradition often views itself as part of the East Asian cultural-intellectual sphere, *development* becomes a pressing issue for Vietnam because it seems to be the only Confucian-based country that has not yet achieved modernity; in

27 On comparative studies of Vietnam in its East Asian and Southeast Asian contexts, for example, see James C. Scott, *The Art of Not Being Governed: An Anarchist History of Upland Southeast Asia* (New Haven: Yale University Press, 2010), and Tuong Vu, *Paths to Development in Asia: South Korea, Vietnam, China, and Indonesia* (Cambridge: Cambridge University Press, 2010).

28 David Papice, "Choosing Success: The Lessons of East and Southeast Asia and Vietnam's Future—A Policy Framework for Vietnam's Socioeconomic Development 2011–2020," accessed October 25, 2015, http://ash.harvard.edu/files/choosing_success.pdf.

29 Hồ Sĩ Quý, *Tiến bộ xã hội* [*Social Progress*], 215–20. See also Trần Hữu Dũng, "Dân chủ và phát triển: Lý thuyết và chứng cớ" ["Democracy and Development: Theory and Evidence"], *Thời Đại Mới* [*Vietnamese Review of Studies and Discussions*] 10, March 2007, accessed October 25, 2015, http://www.tapchithoidai.org/ThoiDai10/200710_THDung.htm.

this regard, Vietnam trails not only Taiwan and South Korea but also mainland China.[30] Here the focus is not on culture *per se*, but on how the *Confucian-based cultural values*, specified as high regard for education, discipline, diligence, hard work, and respect for community and family, can support *development*.[31] A significant additional value consists in high esteem for social consensus and homogeneity to create a strong will for *development*, a value that gets a mixed reception among intellectuals because it can be used to promote the authoritarian practices of the state-party.

This line of inquiry regarding the relationship between *culture* and *development* shows a change in the cultural concerns of the Vietnamese intellectual tradition. During the pre-1945 colonial period, the concern was more about how modernization, mediated through colonialism, might cause the loss of national cultural characteristics. In post-1975 postcolonial times the concern is more about how traditional culture can be an effective force in modernization. Yet the contemporary promotion of Confucian-based values raises challenges for modernization because, since Vietnam's encountering of French colonialism, Confucianism has been viewed as a hindrance to scientific advancement, trade, personal freedom, and social progress.[32]

As the discussion unfolds, it is important to note that the heavily Confucian-influenced culture, which is evident in the ethnic majority *Việt* people, is not necessarily as apparent among the ethnic minority groups inhabiting the mountainous areas of Vietnam. Keith Taylor, a prominent historian of Vietnam, therefore titles his recent work *A History of the Vietnamese* (i.e., a history of the *Việt* people), not *A History of Vietnam*, to highlight the fact that the ethnic majority *Việt* people, though representing about 86 percent of the population, cannot represent "Vietnam" as a whole.[33] The importance of the ethnic issue is also demonstrated in the government's approval of a Strategy on Ethnic Minorities. Approved in 2013 toward achieving socio-economic development in areas with a high percentage of ethnic minorities, this strategy aims at building a more coherent approach to the goal than do other national

30 Hồ Sĩ Quý, *Tiến bộ xã hội* [*Social Progress*], 208.

31 Ibid., 201.

32 This criticism of Confucianism was put forth most famously by the anti-colonialist Nguyễn An Ninh in his speech "The Ideal of Annamite Youth," October 15, 1923, reprinted in Mai Quốc Liên and Nguyễn Sơn, eds., *Nguyễn An Ninh—tác phẩm* [*Nguyễn An Ninh—Collected Works*] (HCMC: Văn Học, 2009), 57–78.

33 K. W. Taylor, *A History of the Vietnamese* (Cambridge: Cambridge University Press, 2013). See also Christopher Goscha, *Vietnam: A New History* (New York: Basic Books, 2016), xi–xiii.

strategies, which discuss minority ethnic peoples in a rather *ad hoc* manner.[34] Thus the question of *culture* that Vietnamese intellectual critics pose on how the Confucian-based cultural values of the *Việt* people can contribute to *national development* must be broadened to ask how the multicultural nature and interculturation of the people groups currently occupying Vietnam can contribute to their common *development*.[35]

In summary, the Vietnamese discussion on *national development* has local, regional, and global dimensions that are deeply rooted in the historical colonial encounter between "the West and the rest," with attendant tensions pertaining to the politics of: (1) defining and measuring *development*, (2) the *basic needs–structural adjustment* framework of *development*, and (3) articulating the contribution of cultural values to *development*. Emerging from a different framework of thought, Vietnamese evangelicals use the term *development* differently by focusing mainly on the transformational aspect of *development*.

4.2 Transformational Development

Among Vietnamese evangelicals, *development* is not a strange word, but they do not think of *development* in terms of national modernization. With a religious commitment to charity, Vietnamese evangelicals are more interested in direct engagement with the poor to alleviate suffering. As the theory goes, engagement with the poor includes *relief* and *development*, in addition to evangelism. *Relief* is conceived as a short-term engagement to support the poor in crises such as famine, war, and natural disasters. *Development* is defined as a long-term commitment to bring transformation to a targeted poorer community, hence the term *transformational development* in evangelicals' theoretical studies of *development*.[36] Vietnamese evangelicals' understanding of *relief*

---

34 Office of the Prime Minister, The Socialist Republic of Vietnam, "Approval of Strategy on Ethnic Minorities to the Year 2020," March 20, 2013, accessed October 30, 2015, http://www.chinhphu.vn/portal/page/portal/chinhphu/noidungchienluocphattrienkinhtexahoi?_piref135_16002_135_15999_15999.strutsAction=ViewDetailAction.do&_piref135_16002_135_15999_15999.docid=1777&_piref135_16002_135_15999_15999.substract=.

35 Hence the call for development initiatives to be built on strong knowledge of local cultures in order to be effective. See Jean Michaud and Tim Forsyth, eds., *Moving Mountains: Ethnicity and Livelihoods in Highland China, Vietnam, and Laos* (Seattle: University of Washington Press, 2011).

36 See, most notably, Bryant Myers, *Walking with the Poor: Principles and Practices of Transformational Development*, revised and expanded edition (Maryknoll, NY: Orbis, 2011). For a more recent theological reflection, see Ruth Padilla DeBorst, "An Integral Transformation

and *development* as worthy social engagements results from their interaction with foreign international evangelical relief and development agencies, such as World Vision International, with very limited concern for progress toward modernity.[37] It is therefore appropriate to employ the term *transformational development* to refer to Vietnamese evangelicals' commitment to work with the poor, and to use *national development* to refer to the common Vietnamese intellectual desire for modernity—two somewhat overlapping concepts with different nuances.

The intersection of national developmental studies and religious studies of evangelicalism in Vietnam begs an inquiry into the past contribution (if any) of evangelicalism to national modernization, with the hope of gaining insights for the present *development* of Vietnam and identifying the potential role of evangelicalism in that effort. Such an inquiry becomes of particular interest when scholars begin to investigate Vietnamese evangelicalism from a regional perspective, namely, by comparing the historical impact of evangelicalism on Vietnam, South China, and South Korea, with special attention given to the role evangelicalism played in the modernization of South China and South Korea as Confucian-based societies with considerable resemblances.[38]

Approach," in *The Mission of the Church: Five Views in Conversation*, ed. Craig Ott (Grand Rapids: Baker Academic, 2016), 41–68.

37 For a recent assessment of the global influence of World Vision International, see David King, "The New Internationalists: World Vision and the Revival of American Evangelical Humanitarianism, 1950–2010," *Religions* 3, no. 4 (October 2012): 922–49.

38 For further information on comparative-historical studies of evangelicalism in Vietnam and China, consult Vũ Thị Thu Hà, "Những đóng góp của đạo Tin Lành trong qua trình truyền giáo vào Trung quốc cuối thế kỉ XIX đầu thế kỉ XX" ["The (Social) Contribution of Protestantism During Its Coming to China in the Late Nineteenth Century and the Early Twentieth Century"], *Tạp Chí Nghiên Cứu Tôn Giáo* [*Journal of Religious Studies*], no. 6 (2009): 47–55; no. 7–8 (2009): 95–102; Vũ Thị Thu Hà, "Lực lượng truyền giáo của đạo Tin Lành ở Trung Quốc trước Cách Mạng Văn Hóa" ["Evangelist Manpower of Evangelicalism in China before the Chinese Cultural Revolution"], *Tạp Chí Nghiên Cứu Tôn Giáo* [*Journal of Religious Studies*], no. 5 (2012): 55–62; no. 6 (2012): 58–71; Nhiều tác giả [Many authors], *Tôn giáo và đời sống hiện đại ở Trung Quốc* [*Religion and Modern Life in China*] (Hà Nội: Khoa Học Xã Hội, 2014).

On comparative historical studies of evangelicalism in Vietnam and South Korea, consult Lý Xuân Chung, "Vai trò của đạo Tin Lành ở Hàn Quốc và nguyên nhân suy giảm tốc độ phát triển những năm gần đây" ["The Role of Evangelicalism in South Korea and Reasons of its Decreasing Growth Rate in Recent Years"], *Tạp Chí Nghiên Cứu Đông Bắc Á* [*Journal of East Asian Studies*] no. 9 (2009), accessed August 1, 2015, http://www.inas.gov.vn/590-vai-tro-cua-dao-tin-lanh-o-han-quoc-va-nguyen-nhan-suy-giam-toc-do-phat-trien-nhung-nam-gan-day.html; Nguyễn Quang Hưng, "Chính sách tôn giáo so sánh với Hàn Quốc" ["Vietnam's Religious Policy in the Regional Context (In Comparison with the Republic of Korea)"], *Tạp Chí Nghiên Cứu Tôn Giáo* [*Journal of Religious Studies*], no. 7

In a nutshell, the Vietnamese evangelical understanding of *transformational development* is drawn from two evangelical commitments—those to charity and to spiritual change. Here a social commitment to charity causes evangelicals to understand development in terms of working with the poor, as can be seen, for example, in the working principle of the Socio-Medical Committee of the ECVN (South), the most notable arm of the church that works with the poor through *relief* and *development*. Stated succinctly, the Committee's working principle is "to show love in concrete actions" toward all Vietnamese, Christian and non-Christian alike, and, in doing so, to demonstrate the responsibility assumed by evangelicals as Vietnamese citizens.[39] Major Vietnamese evangelical efforts to benefit the poor in contemporary Vietnam include, but are not limited to, the provision of medical care, educational scholarships, emergency aid in response to wars and natural disasters, construction assistance for rebuilding houses after natural disasters, and seed funds and microloans for small family businesses and women—an initiative influenced by the Grameen Bank of Mohammad Yunus.[40] One of the major principles of the Socio-Medical Committee of the ECVN (South), as well as of other Vietnamese evangelical groups committed to charity, stems from belief in the maxim, "Providing fishing poles is better than providing fish," thus suggesting a preference for acts of charity that have long-term benefits for the people.[41] Vietnamese evangelicals also operate from the perspective that *development* work should be a conduit of the divine influence that brings about *transformation*; in turn, they understand *transformation* as an all-encompassing positive change not only in people's physical well-being and living conditions but also in their spiritual condition, as well as the overall improvement of the social and natural environment of the community.[42]

(2014): 21–35; and Đỗ Quang Hưng, "Đạo Tin Lành ở Việt Nam và Hàn Quốc: Hai số phận văn hóa" ["Evangelicalism in Vietnam and South Korea: Two Cultural Destinations"], *Tạp Chí Khoa Học Xã Hội Việt Nam* [*Journal of Vietnamese Social Sciences*], no. 9 (2013): 49–64. See also Alexander Woodside, *Lost Modernities: China, Vietnam, Korea, and the Hazards of World History* (Cambridge: Harvard University Press, 2006).

39 Socio-Medical Committee, ECVN (South), "Những quan điểm về công tác xã hội" ["Perspective on Social Work"], accessed October 25, 2015, http://somedco.blogspot.com.

40 On the Grameen Bank and Yunus, see his *Banker to the Poor: Micro-Lending and the Battle against World Poverty* (New York: PublicAffairs, 2007). For an evangelical appropriation of the Grameen Bank approach, see Brian Fikkert and Russell Mask, *From Dependence to Dignity: How to Alleviate Poverty through Church-Centered Microfinance* (Grand Rapids: Zondervan, 2015).

41 Socio-Medical Committee, ECVN (South), "Giới thiệu" ["About Us"], accessed October 25, 2015, http://httlvn.org/ubytxh/index.php?do=page&id=146.

42 Socio-Medical Committee, ECVN (South), "Những quan điểm về công tác xã hội" ["Perspective on Social Work"], accessed October 25, 2015, http://somedco.blogspot.com.

The Vietnamese evangelical understanding of *development* shows it has been influenced by the understanding of *poverty* and *development* held by Western evangelical relief and development agencies, such as World Vision International. This agency's former Vice President for International Program Strategy offers a spiritual understanding of *poverty* and *development*: *poverty* is fundamentally relational—the poor suffer from broken relationships with others and with God;[43] *development* is, therefore, activity that aims first at changing people, both the poor and those who work with the poor, so they can discover their true identity as children of God. The changed people then begin to establish right relationships with God and with their neighbors in a chain of effects resulting in overall peace, justice, and righteousness. The inclusion of the spiritual aspect of the discussion is thought of as presenting the idea of *transformational development* in a holistic manner that addresses the physical, mental, social, spiritual, and even environmental, challenges of the poor.[44]

Not surprisingly, this understanding of development work as dealing with spiritual poverty—as *transformational*—is novel with respect to the typical Vietnamese understanding of *development* as aiming at modernity. As an initial interaction between the two ideas of *national development* and *transformational development*, the latter can offer a critical perspective on the former by calling for special attention to the economically disadvantaged religious groups as the nation embarks on the course of modernization. It is not uncommon to find that many of the areas in which developmental programs are implemented represent deeply religious communities, so the invitation to consider the spiritual dimension of development work has generated research initiatives at the intersection of development studies and religious studies.[45] At the same time, the demographic of Vietnamese evangelicalism (which includes more people of ethnic minorities than people of the ethnic majority, more women

43 Myers, *Walking with the Poor*, 14–18. See also Jayakumar Christian, *God of the Empty-Handed: Poverty, Power, and the Kingdom of God*, 2nd ed. (Victoria, Australia: Acorn Press, 2011), 146–47.

44 For a comprehensive proposal of *transformational development*, consult Melba Padilla Maggay, *Transforming Society* (Manila, Philippines: Institute for Studies in Asian Church and Culture, 1996).

45 In the context of Asia, see Philip Fountain et al., eds., *Religion and the Politics of Development: Critical Perspectives on Asia* (New York: Palgrave Macmillan, 2015). For an interdisciplinary study of religion and development in religious studies, see Barbara Bompani, "Beyond Disciplinarity: Reflections on the Study of Religion in International Development," *Religion and Theology* 21, no. 3–4 (2014): 309–33. For a similar argument in theological studies, see Anthony Balcomb, "What Theology? Whose Development?: Interrogating Theology and Development in the Secular Academy," *Journal of Theology for Southern Africa* 142 (March 2012): 6–20.

than men, and more people with little economic power than people with notable economic power) calls attention to the combined issue encompassing *ethnic minority*, *women*, and *development*—an issue that has not been adequately addressed by Vietnamese scholars and policymakers, whose status mostly as financially secure men belonging to the majority *Việt* ethnic group means that, in general, their perspectives may not necessarily represent the best interests of the women, ethnic minorities, and economically poor.

The evangelical perspective on *development* also calls attention to the issue of *dependency*. Evangelicals engaging in research on the practice of charity have argued that charity may create *dependency* and weaken the people on the receiving end.[46] In evangelicalism, *dependency* is part of a broader phenomenon experienced by churches on the mission field who end up relying on their counterparts in more affluent countries for theological resources, structures, and material support—hence the promotion of the missional evangelical principles of self-governance, self-support, self-propagation, and self-theologizing to counter *dependency*.[47] In some extreme cases, it has even been argued that international aid is doing harm to the people receiving the aid.[48]

Evangelicalism's experience with the inadvertent creation of *dependency* also reveals an important aspect of the phenomenon, namely, that most foreign donors not only provide financial support but, more importantly, also provide theories on how the native church should deal with poverty. They do the latter mostly through reference to practices developed by international Christian non-governmental organizations (NGOs) or denominational relief

46 On almsgivings as problematic from the perspectives of Christian practitioners, see Brian Fikkert and Steve Corbett, *When Helping Hurts: Alleviating Poverty Without Hurting the Poor … and Yourself* (Chicago: Moody, 2009); Robert D. Lupton, *Toxic Charity: How the Church Hurts Those They Help and How to Reverse It* (New York: HarperOne, 2011). On short-term mission trips as not producing changes, see the sociological-empirical study of Kurt Alan Ver Beek, "The Impact of Short-Term Missions: A Case Study of House Construction in Honduras after Hurricane Mitch," *Missiology* 34, no. 4 (October 2006): 477–95; and Kurt Alan Ver Beek, "Lessons from the Sapling: Review of Quantitative Research on Short-Term Missions," in *Effective Engagement in Short-Term Missions: Doing It Right!*, ed. Robert J. Priest (Pasadena: William Carey Library, 2008), 474–502.

47 For a Vietnamese evangelical use of these principles, see Phu Le, "A Short History of the Evangelical Church of Viet Nam (1911–1965)" (Ph.D. diss., New York University, 1972), 213–20, 503–509.

48 Angus Deaton, winner of the 2015 Nobel Prize in economic sciences, argues so in his *The Great Escape: Health, Wealth, and the Origins of Inequality* (Princeton: Princeton University Press, 2013), 294–307. See also the case study on Cambodia by the Cambodian-born Sophal Ear, *Aid Dependence in Cambodia: How Foreign Assistance Undermines Democracy* (New York: Columbia University Press, 2012).

and aid agencies.[49] Similarly, the phenomenon of *dependency* can also arise between developmental programs and governmental agencies when such programs rely on governmental structures to implement activities (and are thus able to increase grant expenditure rates, thereby boosting their perception as efficient and, in turn, their ability to attract continuing donations). The phenomenon arises in the other direction as well when governmental officials rely on the human and financial resources provided by international NGOs to address pressing local issues that the officials themselves are supposed to address (thus decreasing the capacity of local governmental officials to provide public services). As a result, the evangelical practice of providing *basic needs* to the poor is a two-edged sword: it is a helpful moral act that can contribute to the noble fight against poverty, and it is a harmful act in its creation of *dependency*. As the evangelical theory of *transformational development* goes through the process of revision, theorists such as Myers propose a solution to doing good without harming people: by doing additional work in policy advocacy.[50] The assumption is that policy advocacy contributes to the creation of a living environment in which the poor gain autonomy to fight poverty, and local agencies gain increased awareness of the need to build up their own capacities; as a result, *dependency* will not occur.

In addition to the problem of *dependency* are the challenges posed by the professionalization of charity, demonstrated in the trend of church denominations' setting up their relief and development arms as international NGOs holding consultative status with the UN. The professionalization of religious charity results in a mutual co-opting between church development agencies and mainstream development organizations such as the IFIs, UN agencies, and Western government-funding relief agencies. While mainstream development organizations become increasingly aware of the religious dimension of *development*, evangelical development agencies are influenced by the ideologies and practices of secular development institutions, as demonstrated in the evangelical agencies' promotion of policy advocacy activity when mainstream development institutions shift their focus from *basic needs* to *structural adjustment*. For the Vietnamese state, this collaboration also raises a particular concern over large international NGOs' having ties to and receiving funding from Western governments—a relationship seen by the Vietnamese state as

49 On the problem of dependency from an evangelical perspective, see Bryant Myers, "Relief and Development," in *Global Dictionary of Theology: A Resource for the Worldwide Church*, ed. William A. Dyrness and Veli-Matti Kärkkäinen (Downers Grove, IL: IVP Academic, 2008), 739–45.

50 Ibid., 742–43.

providing opportunities for input from and the promotion of the foreign policy of global powers such as the United States while the given NGO is working in Vietnam.[51] The work of international NGOs is also perceived as supporting the growth of a "civil society," a network of voluntary organizations outside the State's control, and is thus viewed within conservative circles of Vietnamese communists as a way to groom alternative political powers to challenge the CPV's right to rule; civil society networks in Vietnam, however, remain on a small scale and are unlikely to coalesce to mount a challenge for regime change in the near future.[52]

The evangelicals' *transformational development* proposal is also subject to a few internal problems, most notably its failure in acknowledging the agency of the poor. *Transformational development* tends to see the poor as passive people who have little agency and are thus in need of "empowerment" through the initiative of the non-poor in order to "participate" and assert their "rights" in the public square. The approach assumes that "people change by becoming less passive and more the primary actors in their own development."[53] The conclusion that "participation has become empowerment" also suggests an overall evangelical struggle to understand the agency of the poor, who are also often the powerless.[54]

This inability to appreciate the agency of the poor is caused, in part, by the challenge of listening to the powerless. A call for the poor, the ethnic minorities, and women to exercise agency by speaking up on issues that matter to them is crucial; but, as the postcolonial theorist Gayatri Chakravorty Spivak reminds us, both their speaking up and the listening to them by others is challenging because the combination of class, gender, and racial issues deepens the asymmetry of power between the speakers and listeners and effectively silences the powerless speakers.[55] The frustrations of not being able to access the perspectives of the poor are reflected in a willful insistence that "the subaltern must speak" (reflected in the field of development studies),[56] and that the poor should "become less passive" (reflected in the field of evangelical development

51 For further information, see Rachel M. McCleary, *Global Compassion: Private Voluntary Organizations and U.S. Foreign Policy since 1939* (New York: Oxford University Press, 2009).

52 So argues Andrew Wells-Dang in *Civil Society Networks in China and Vietnam: Informal Pathbreakers in Health and the Environment* (New York: Palgrave Macmillan, 2012).

53 Myers, *Walking with the Poor*, 18.

54 Ibid.

55 Gayatri Chakravorty Spivak, "Can the Subaltern Speak?" in *The Post-Colonial Studies Reader*, ed. Bill Ashcroft, Gareth Griffiths, and Helen Tiffin, 2nd ed. (New York: Routledge, 2006), 28–38.

56 Ilan Kapoor, *The Postcolonial Politics of Development* (New York: Routledge, 2008), 149.

studies).[57] The idea of *transformational development* is problematic because it asks the powerless to make efforts to associate with the structure that renders them powerless in the first place, and it depends on the goodwill of the powerful to engender such speaking up. Furthermore, the concepts used to encourage women and minority persons to speak up—concepts such as *participation, empowerment, rights,* and *capacity building*—belong to an institutional language that is foreign to grassroots language. A more proper vehicle for encouraging such engagement by the powerless is probably their association with an alternative structure so as to counter the dominating structure that is causing their oppression and marginalization. This observation prompts the intriguing question as to whether *religion*, and *evangelicalism* in particular, might provide one such alternative structure for the grassroots poor in contemporary Vietnam, since the poor often speak in religious language.[58]

To sum up, Vietnamese evangelicals, in their understanding of *transformational development,* have potentially added two points of discussion to the public debate on *development.* The first point consists in their call to consider new methods and efforts to bring the voices of religious and underprivileged people to the discussion on *development.* The second consists in their call to attentiveness to the issue of generating *dependency* in the areas of both fundings and thought—a dependency that can weaken the people on the receiving end and thus fail to bring about long-term change in their quality of life. These two points of discussion render the evangelical perspective critical to the Vietnamese debate on *national development.* Nevertheless, this crucial evangelical perspective has its own challenges: the problem of imagining the agency of the poor in pursuing *development,* and the professionalization of charity, which results in the mutual co-opting of secular development institutions and church development agencies and in the codependency of governments receiving foreign (mostly Western) aid and professional development organizations.

4.3 Prosperity Teaching

Among pentecostally informed Vietnamese evangelicals, *prosperity teaching* emerges as a positive belief that God wants to bless the faithful with physical

57 Myers, *Walking with the Poor,* 18. On the thinking of the poor, consult Abhijit Banerjee and Esther Duflo, *Poor Economics: A Radical Rethinking of the Way to Fight Global Poverty,* (New York: PublicAffairs, 2011).

58 On the religiousness of the poor, see Aloysius Pieris, *An Asian Theology of Liberation,* Faith Meets Faith Series (Maryknoll, NY: Orbis, 1988), 20–23.

and material well-being. This belief exemplifies the pentecostal belief in *divine intervention* in a very this-worldly manner. In other words, in addition to the salvation of their souls, Christians should expect to receive health and wealth from God, hence the other name of *prosperity teaching*: "the health-and-wealth gospel."[59] The teaching of *prosperity*, which came to Vietnam via the spread of the contemporary global pentecostal movement, is adopted by several Vietnamese evangelical groups but thrives among the more pentecostally oriented ones.

The teaching of *health*, including God's miraculous healing of diseases and benevolence in granting good health to believers, enjoys a long history in Vietnamese evangelicalism—one that dates back to the C&MA missionaries' teaching of the Fourfold Gospel, with *Jesus is Healer* as the third tenet. Vietnamese evangelicalism finds the scriptural foundation for this belief in Mathew 8:16–17, referring back to Isaiah 53:4–5:

> When evening came, many who were demon-possessed were brought to him, and he drove out the spirits with a word and healed all the sick. This was to fulfill what was spoken through the prophet Isaiah: he took up our infirmities and bore our diseases. (Matthew 8:16–17, NRSV)
>
> Surely he has borne our infirmities and carried our diseases; yet we accounted him stricken, struck down by God, and afflicted. But he was wounded for our transgressions, crushed for our iniquities; upon him was the punishment that made us whole, and by his bruises we are healed. (Isaiah 53:4–5, NRSV)

As the argument goes, because "Jesus Christ is the same yesterday and today and forever" (Hebrews 13:8, NRSV), he continues to be the Healer of the faithful. Biographies of early missionaries and native evangelical leaders recounted several experiences of divine healing.[60] Today, testimonies of thanksgiving for

59 On *prosperity teaching* in global pentecostalism, see Katherine Attanasi and Amos Yong, eds., *Pentecostalism and Prosperity: The Socioeconomics of the Global Charismatic Movement* (New York: Palgrave Macmillan, 2012). For statistical data on the popularity of *prosperity teaching* on the global scene, see The Pew Forum on Religion & Public Life, "Spirit and Power: A 10-Country Survey of Pentecostals" (Washington, DC: Pew Research Center, 2006).

60 For example, E. F. Irwin, *With Christ in Indo-China* (Harrisburg, PA: Christian Publications, 1937); I. R. Stebbins, *41 năm hầu việc Chúa với Hội Thánh Tin Lành Việt Nam (1920–1961)* [*41 Years Serving God with the Evangelical Church of Vietnam (1920–1961)*] (Akron, OH: Spiritual Light Magazine, 2004).

divine healing are still common within several evangelical circles regardless of their denominational affiliations.

The teaching of God's granting *wealth* to believers is a more recent development. In contrast to the teaching on *health*, which dates to the early twentieth century, the teaching on *wealth* did not become a frequent part of Vietnamese evangelicalism till contemporary times. *Wealth* teaching receives scriptural support from 3 John 1:2: "Beloved, I wish above all things that thou mayest prosper and be in health, even as thy soul prospereth" (KJV). Here *prosperity* includes the prosperity of the soul (referring to salvation and spiritual well-being), good health (indicating physical, bodily well-being), and material prosperity (showing outward evidence of prosperity through material possessions). The names of the famed South Korean Assemblies of God minister Cho Yong-gi and the prominent preacher in the North American Word of Faith movement Kenneth E. Hagin are often associated with the teaching of *prosperity* in Vietnam.[61]

In contemporary Vietnam, the teaching of God's granting *wealth* to the faithful receives resistance from the traditional evangelical belief that *holiness* is best demonstrated in a simple, sufficient material life. Philippians 4:9 is cited in support of this belief: "God shall supply all your need according to his riches in glory by Christ Jesus" (KJV), but with the added caution, "God has never promised us an extravagant lifestyle according to our limitless avarice."[62] This belief in material simplicity is shaped by both a missionary emphasis on the virtue of sacrifice (i.e., denying the material comforts of one's home country to travel to a place of less material comfort for the sake of the gospel) and an older Vietnamese Confucian tradition of promoting modesty as the best path for intellectuals and others aspiring to a more spiritually enriching way of life. From

61 See, for example, Cho Yong-gi, *Salvation, Health & Prosperity: Our Threefold Blessings in Christ* (Altamonte Springs, FL: Creation House, 1987); Kenneth E. Hagin, *How God Taught Me About Prosperity* (Oklahoma City: Kenneth Hagin Ministries, 1985). The most comprehensive evaluation of Cho Yong-gi's theology and ministry to date is perhaps Young San Theological Institute, ed., *Dr. Yonggi Cho's Ministry & Theology: A Commemorative Collection for the 50th Anniversary of Dr. Yonggi Cho's Ministry*, 2 vols. (Seoul: Hansei University Logos, 2008). A more accessible and shorter collection is Wonsuk Ma, William W. Menzies, and Hyeon-Sung Bae, eds., *David Yonggi Cho: A Close Look at His Theology and Ministry* (Baguio City, Philippines: APTS Press, 2004). For a biography of Cho, see Nell L. Kennedy, *Dream Your Way to Success: The Story of Dr. Yonggi Cho and Korea* (Plainfield, NJ: Logos International, 1980). For a socio-historical background of Cho's ministry, see Young-hoon Lee, *The Holy Spirit Movement in Korea: Its Historical and Theological Development* (Oxford: Regnum, 2009).

62 "Đầy đủ mọi nhu cầu" ["Fulfill All Your Needs"], *Thánh Kinh Báo* [*Bible Magazine*] no. 412 (1974): 3–4.

the 1990s onward, however, economic growth has generated increasing social admiration for material surplus, and this admiration, in turn, has contributed to a change in evangelicals' thinking about wealth, namely, that wealth, rather than poverty, is a virtue. This observation points to a possible and intriguing link that may connect the reception of *prosperity teaching* and the way *development* is configured in Vietnam.

In late-communist Vietnam, *development* that emphasizes *rapid economic growth* has brought *health* and *wealth* to the fore as major concerns. For the most part, economic growth has relied on the provision of cheap manual labor in industrial zones and the exporting of natural resources.[63] The working and living conditions of laborers in industrial zones and the process of extracting non-renewable natural resources have been criticized as "non-sustainable" due to their causing environmental pollution and degrading the health of the masses.[64] In this context, surveys continue to show *health* as the leading concern of the Vietnamese people.[65] At the same time, the emphasis on *rapid economic growth* also produces income inequality, deepened by ineffectual measures of the State to address the issue. *Crony capitalists*—state officials who exploit legal loopholes for material gains, their allies in the market, and other rent-seekers—have effectively converted the Vietnamese Marxist utopianism to hedonism; hence the observation of Peter C. Phan, a Vietnamese-born American theologian, that people only pay lip service to Marxist ideology in Vietnam these days.[66] It is crony capitalism that rules in contemporary Vietnam, with a state-controlled media that has no choice but to promote *wealth* and even opportunism as virtuous and desirable while playing down the problem of distributive injustice. The end result is a desire of the masses quickly to become better off financially. Thus, even a state-sponsored academic research

63 For further information see Eren Zink, *Hot Science, High Water: Assembling Nature, Society and Environmental Policy in Contemporary Vietnam* (Copenhagen: Nordic Institute of Asian Studies Press, 2013).

64 On the living conditions and protests of workers in contemporary Vietnam, see Benedict J. Kerkvliet, "Workers' Protests in Contemporary Vietnam (with Some Comparisons to Those in the Pre-1975 South)," *Journal of Vietnamese Studies* 5, no. 1 (February 1, 2010): 162–204.

65 Reported in Nguyễn Ngọc Hà, "Đặc điểm tư duy và lối sống của con người Việt Nam hiện nay và những vấn đề đặt ra trước yêu cầu đổi mới và hội nhập quốc tế" ["Contemporary Thinking and Living Characteristics of the Vietnamese and Emerging Issues Due to Social Change and International Integration"] (Working paper of Viện Triết Học [Institute of Philosophy], 2010), 10–11.

66 Peter C. Phan, "Christianity in Vietnam Today (1975–2013): Contemporary Challenges and Opportunities," *International Journal of the Study of the Christian Church* 14, no. 1 (2014): 3–21.

project on the values of contemporary Vietnamese people has to agree with the Vietnamese Catholic Bishop Nguyễn Thái Hợp that a major problem in contemporary Vietnam is the phenomenon of the people's "going after money restlessly, seeking pleasure mercilessly" [Vietnamese: *nóng ruột kiếm tiền, cắm đầu hưởng thụ*].[67]

It is in this context of *development* through *rapid economic growth*, resulting in the people's decreased *health* and increased desire to become wealthy, that *prosperity teaching* can be situated socially. The teaching of *health* is attractive because it provides an alternative approach to attaining physical well-being for a mass of people who have limited purchasing power to obtain decent health care and make decisions on how their living, working, and environmental conditions can help them maintain good health. At the same time, the teaching of *wealth* is attractive because it meets the grassroots desire for material well-being in a world becoming increasingly unfriendly and offering less security to the *have-nots*. Thus *prosperity teaching* provides a glimpse into what grassroots people really want in the context of what has, instead, been a "top-down" approach to *development* that has not always represented the interests of the masses. The teaching of *health and wealth* deserves attention, therefore, not only because of its contribution to the growth of evangelicalism in contemporary Vietnam, but also, and more importantly, because of its being congruent with the common Vietnamese desire for *health, wealth*, and *upward social mobility* in market-oriented, late-communist Vietnam. Understandably, *prosperity teaching* can be rejected on the grounds of being unorthodox, as it is in Vietnamese evangelical circles skeptical of claims of miraculous *divine intervention* in modern-day contexts, or of being unscientific, as it is in Vietnamese intellectual circles that subscribe to empirical scientism. (The former objection arose via Vietnamese evangelicals' exposure to fundamentalist teaching through the connection between Vietnamese evangelicalism and North American evangelicalism, especially during the United States' involvement in the Vietnam War.) The social situating

67 Nguyễn Ngọc Hà et al., "Đặc điểm tư duy và lối sống của con người Việt Nam hiện nay và những vấn đề đặt ra trước yêu cầu đổi mới và hội nhập quốc tế" ["Contemporary Thinking and Living Characteristics of the Vietnamese and Emerging Issues Due to Social Change and International Integration"], 174. See also Allison Truitt, *Dreaming of Money in Ho Chi Minh City*, Critical Dialogues in Southeast Asian Studies (Seattle: University of Washington Press, 2013), and Catherine Earl, *Vietnam's New Middle Classes: Gender, Career, City* (Copenhagen: Nordic Institute of Asian Studies Press, 2014). On the problem of Vietnam's middle class as growing rapidly in size but not yet becoming a contributing factor to economic and social stability, see Le Thu Huong, "Vietnam's Urban Middle Class: Rapidly Growing, Slowly Awakening," in *The Blooming Years: Kyoto Review of Southeast Asia*, ed. Pavin Chachavalpongpun (Kyoto: Center for Southeast Asian Studies, 2017), 528–31.

of *prosperity teaching* in the context of *development* as it is done in Vietnam, however, can yield a different result—one that presents *prosperity teaching* as an embodiment of the desire of ordinary people in late-communist Vietnam.

4.4 The Value of Prosperity Teaching

Prosperity teaching can contribute to the Vietnamese public discussion on *development* in at least three aspects: *concept, value,* and *practice*. These aspects are elaborated below.

In terms of *concept,* the register of *prosperity teaching* as a particular perspective on *development* creates an enhanced conceptual framework for rethinking *development* in contemporary Vietnam. In the wider context of *national development,* and in the immediate context set up by evangelicalism's institutional adoption of *transformational development, prosperity teaching* becomes both a grassroots, this-worldly evangelical response to the other-worldly institutional use of *transformational development,* and, at the same time, part of a grassroots Vietnamese response to the top-down design of *national development*. While the macro vision of *national development* emphasizes the growth in size of the economy and how such growth results in a stronger, more prosperous Vietnam, with the effect of allowing the Vietnamese state to enjoy increasing influence in international relations, the *prosperity* approach, through its focus on individual health, wealth, and upward social mobility, reminds systemic thinkers and visionaries as clearly as possible what the grassroots wants. As such, *modernity for the nation* and *prosperity for all* occupy the two polar opposite positions; that they do so expresses the intellectual-versus-grassroots tension which speaks well to the contemporary Vietnamese experience.

Prosperity teaching, understood as an improvement in the quality of life (as a religious economy), also stands both for and against the intellectual, critical theory of *postdevelopment* (as a political economy). On the one hand, both *prosperity teaching* and *postdevelopment theory* are skeptical of the current neoliberal configuration of *development,* especially its belief in the free market and that the market is able to protect itself against manipulation. On the other hand, while *postdevelopment theory,* and many other critical theories for that matter, seeks the deconstruction of *development* in favor of preserving spaces for new social movements to construct alternatives,[68] grassroots

68 On this issue, see a summary of the criticism of Marxist and neo-Marxist theories, poststructural theory, and feminist theories in Peet and Hartwick, *Theories of Development*, 310–12.

evangelicalism, in its emphasis on *prosperity*, is rather inert about the concept of *development* and its measurement and focuses instead on *basic needs*, i.e., the health and wealth of the people and the potential for their upward mobility.

Regarding language, *prosperity teaching's* vocabulary of *health*, *wealth*, and *blessings* is easily understood by the Vietnamese because these words belong to the Vietnamese vernacular and in general do not require explanation. Keywords in the *national development* discourse—words such as *development*, *growth*, *modernization*, and *industrialization*—have been used very frequently in Vietnamese media and secondary education. In contrast, evangelical terms such as *relational poverty* and *transformation* present a linguistic and conceptual problem, because these words do not belong to the vocabulary and thinking patterns of the Vietnamese; thus such words require additional clarification when used in engaging the public. The evangelical proposal for *transformational development* is also represented by a plethora of concepts such as *empowerment*, *participation*, and *human rights*—common language among the IFIs, UN agencies, and development organizations of the church, but foreign to the Vietnamese; thus the usefulness and effectiveness of these words are often questioned.[69]

For another example, note that the concept of *community* as used by foreign (including evangelical) development agencies still carries the vague connotation of a targeted rural area for a development project, thus revealing the struggle to make sense of local territories. Traditionally, the Vietnamese community is primarily the village, functioning as a self-contained unit. For centuries, central governments worked with villages and not with individual citizens. In contemporary Vietnam, the state-party's aspiration for strong government has resulted in the abandonment of the village as the mediator between the State and individual citizens. The village, however, still functions as a prominent social structure outside the country's chart of administrative units. Thus the efforts to create a *community*, and the promotion of community property and grassroots democracy, entail the enormous task of dealing with the already-existing village structure and its unofficial status—a task that neither foreign

69 This issue is also mentioned in recent discussions on pentecostals and development in Ben Jones's "Pentecostalism, Development NGOs and Meaning in Eastern Uganda," in *Pentecostalism and Development: Churches, NGOs and Social Change in Africa*, ed. Dena Freeman (New York: Palgrave Macmillan, 2012), 181–202: 200; and Christine Schliesser, "On a Long Neglected Player: The Religious Factor in Poverty Alleviation," *Exchange (Online)* 43, no. 4 (2014): 339–59: 353.

practitioners of developmental strategies nor Vietnamese evangelical scholars have adequately addressed.[70]

If Vietnamese evangelicals would consult the terminology of the Vietnamese Catholic tradition, they would see that, due to the translation of the documents of the Vatican II Council into Vietnamese, concepts such as the *common good* and *human flourishing* are proposed in the construction of the Catholic vision of a better Vietnam.[71] Outside Vietnamese Catholic theological writings and preaching, however, these terms have not become part of the Vietnamese vernacular. Similarly, all the other concepts being entertained by the evangelicals—concepts such as *shalom* and *peace*—will face the same linguistic problem.[72] Amid this cacophony, it is noteworthy that the vocabularies of *prosperity*, *health*, and *wealth* receive as much scriptural support as other concepts proposed by evangelical scholars (such as *transformation* and *shalom*) or employed by Roman Catholics (such as *common good* and *human flourishing*). While *prosperity teaching* has a foreign origin and shows signs of relying on thinking supplied by the West, its relative ignorance of the evangelical, national, and global discourses on *development* and its emphasis on health, wealth, and upward social mobility at the grassroots level at least accidentally gives birth to an autonomy that appears to help reveal actual grassroots concerns.

Prosperity teaching also has implications for the ongoing discussion on how cultural (and religious) *values* can contribute to the *development* of Vietnam. This study is related to the Vietnamese academic inquiry into whether

70 On the Vietnamese village, consult Nguyễn Văn Huyên, *Văn minh Việt Nam* [*The Civilization of Vietnam*] (Hà Nội: Thế Giới, 1995); see also the initiation of an interdisciplinary study of the Vietnamese village in Đỗ Danh Huấn, "Làng Việt—đối tượng nghiên cứu của khu vực học" ["*Việt* Village—A Case Study in Area Studies"], *Tạp Chí Khoa Học Xã Hội và Nhân Văn* [*Journal of Social Sciences and Humanities*] 26 (2010): 15–23. For an early Vietnamese evangelical discussion on the village structure, see Phu Le, "A Short History of the Evangelical Church of Viet Nam (1911–1965)" (Ph.D. diss., New York University, 1972): 29–30, 242–43.

71 For the Vietnamese translation of the official documents of Second Vatican Council, see especially "Pastoral Constitution on the Church in the Modern World—*Gaudium et spes*," December 7, 1965, available online, accessed October 25, 2015, https://www.catholic.org.tw/vntaiwan/vatican2/vatican2.htm and http://www.simonhoadalat.com/HOCHOI/NamThanh/DucTin/47TongHopGiaoHuanVat2.htm.

72 For an attempt to reorient Christian mission and development practices using the category of *shalom*, within a discussion of healthcare mission, see Bryant Myers et al., eds., *Health, Healing, and Shalom: Frontiers and Challenges for Christian Health Missions* (Pasadena: William Carey Library, 2015), especially the two theoretical chapters written by Myers: "Health, Healing, and Wholeness: Theological Reflections on Shalom and Salvation" (pp. 15–39) and "Announcing the Whole Gospel: Health, Healing, and Christian Witness" (pp. 41–55).

Protestant ethics can assist the Vietnamese in their quest for modernity.[73] The Vietnamese study of evangelicalism has given attention to Weber's thesis of Protestant ethics, which argues that growth in wealth and capital is a result of a disciplined attitude toward work and life and a deferral of instant gratification (thus increasing saving and building up capital). Vietnamese scholars thus ask not only about the contribution of Confucian-based values (retrievable from within Vietnamese tradition) but also about the contribution of Protestant values (adoptable from outside Vietnamese tradition) to the national project of *development*.

Attention to *prosperity teaching* can expand the Vietnamese consideration of Weberian Protestant ethics. At the grassroots level, the groups that are attracted to *prosperity teaching* often assist in the creation of local volunteer organizations, which provide a forum for evangelical commoners, especially the women, to socialize. Through their volunteering in this social space, their habits, skills, and knowledge are mutually reinforced, and information on upcoming opportunities is exchanged, thus leading to greater chances for experiencing upward social mobility.[74] Further, the grassroots nature of having a loose structure of leadership among groups enacting *prosperity teaching* offers more opportunities for the groups' members to acquire the skills necessary to succeed in modern-day society—skills such as time management, planning, coordination, and leadership, which are conducive to upward social mobility.[75] From this perspective, *prosperity teaching* helps believers become active and make progress in life, even under unfavorable social conditions.[76]

---

73 This issue is discussed most explicitly in the final section of Đỗ Quang Hưng, "Mấy vấn đề thần học Tin Lành ở Việt Nam hiện nay" ["Current Issues in Vietnamese Evangelical Theology"], *Tạp Chí Khoa Học Xã Hội Việt Nam* [*Vietnamese Journal of Social Sciences*] 6 (2011), accessed October 1, 2015, http://vssr.vass.gov.vn/noidung/tintuc/Lists/ngonnguvanhocvanhoa/View_Detail.aspx?ItemID=42.

74 Peter Berger, "Max Weber is Alive and Well, and Living in Guatemala: The Protestant Ethic Today," *The Review of Faith and International Affairs* 8, no. 4 (2010): 3–9; Tomas Sundnes Drønen, "Weber, Prosperity and the Protestant Ethic: Some Reflections on Pentecostalism and Economic Development," *Svensk Missionstidskrift* 100, no. 3 (2012): 321–35. For an empirical study on the reliability of the belief on hard work as a means to honor God and the belief on prosperity as God's promise, see Mitchell J. Neubert et al., "Beliefs about Faith and Work: Development and Validation of Honoring God and Prosperity Gospel Scales," *Review of Religious Research* 56, no. 1 (March 2014): 129–46.

75 Harvey Cox, *Fire from Heaven: The Rise of Pentecostal Spirituality & the Reshaping of Religion in the Twenty-First Century* (Reading, MA: Addison-Wesley, 1995), 234–38.

76 See the excellent anthropological account by Naomi Haynes, *Moving by the Spirit: Pentecostal Social Life on the Zambian Copperbelt* (Berkeley: University of California Press, 2017).

Prosperity teaching, as a "re-enchanting" phenomenon, also takes on a magical worldview that health, wealth, and upward social mobility are due to the faith and generous giving of believers to the church.[77] This approach creates a potential counter-thesis to Weber's proposal, which emphasizes the role of discipline, entrepreneurship, and hard work in achieving upward social mobility. The belief in getting rich "magically" is evident among urban Vietnamese pentecostals through their attraction to what is judged as acquiring material gain with minimal efforts, such as property flipping and multi-level marketing. For rural and mountain-dwelling evangelicals, however, *prosperity teaching* is more of a survival strategy rather than a means to get rich, for the procurement of *basic needs* is more pressing in remote areas. In either case, however, it has been argued that Christians who believe in healing and prosperity are "often duly rewarded" by the nature of their penchant for miraculous divine intervention, while disbelieving liberals obtain no such experience and, as a result, remain doubting outsiders.[78]

By comparison, the *prosperity-teaching* model shows how pentecostal values support upward social mobility through such means as people's acquisition of critical working skills for the modern world, the strengthening of the household unit, and positive results emanating from belief in generous divine assistance, to name a few. The Vietnamese intellectual model of *national development* shows evidence of developing thinking on how Confucian values can direct actions toward achieving modernity. By contrast, the *transformational development* model offers the values of "recovering true identity and vocation" and "just and peaceful relationships," but it has not explained how these values create a culture that can alleviate material poverty or create material security.[79]

In terms of *practice*, a significant contribution of *prosperity teaching* to the discussion on *development* in Vietnam is its practical, "can-do" spirit on the small-scale level. Poorer pentecostals have already initiated their own pursuit of *development*. More precisely, poorer people are often involved in an *informal economy*, understood as activities and income that exist outside government

77 Paul Gifford and Trad Nogueira-Godsey, "The Protestant Ethic and African Pentecostalism: A Case Study," *Journal for the Study of Religion* 24, no. 1 (2011): 5–22.

78 David Martin, *Pentecostalism: The World Their Parish*, Religion & Modernity Series (Malden, MA: Blackwell, 2002), 172.

79 Myers, *Walking with the Poor*, 177–82. Myers' book *Walking with the Poor* has only a two-page section (pages 203–204) providing a handful of links to helpful resources on what have been considered best practices for livelihood security, sustainable agriculture, microenterprise development, and community-based healthcare. This theoretical work fails to discuss how economic activities would fit under the overarching evangelical category of *transformational development*.

regulations and official economic statistics. As the theory goes, an informal economy includes both a *productive economy*, which makes profits through services and production, and a *reproductive economy*, which meets the *basic needs* of local people.[80] Both aspects are necessary to the success of an informal economy, as it is one driven by both the needs of local populations and their own capacity to address those needs outside the purview of the formal economic structure of the State. Importantly, *informal economies* include many groups traditionally marginalized in formal economies, namely, women, ethnic minorities, and the poor.[81] It is in an *informal economy* that the underprivileged have at their disposal the flexibility to initiate projects neglected by the State yet proposed by intellectual critics—projects that focus, for example, on agricultural production and local trades through small-scale businesses.[82] Considering the long term, global evangelical and pentecostal networks also show the potential to facilitate people's acquisition of skills and technologies for improving their economies if health, wealth, and upward social mobility continue among pentecostal evangelicals in the Global South.

Although it is too early to reach a definite conclusion regarding the best way to fight poverty in Vietnam, it has been argued that the small-scale economic practices and "can-do" spirit of the adherents of *prosperity teaching* are more effective than the interventions designed by international faith-based NGOs.[83] Best practices often point to mutual cooperation between the groups

---

80 On the concept of and information about the estimated size of informal economies, see Philip McMichael, *Development and Social Change: A Global Perspective*, 5th ed. (Thousand Oaks, CA: SAGE Publications, 2011), 166–74. For a pentecostal discussion on informal economy, see Amos Yong, *In the Days of Caesar: Pentecostalism and Political Theology*, Sacra Doctrina: Christian Theology for a Postmodern Age Series (Grand Rapids: Eerdmans, 2010), 304–11. For an example of a sociological discussion on pentecostalism and informal economies, see Kate Meagher, "Trading on Faith: Religious Movements and Informal Economic Governance in Nigeria," *Journal of Modern African Studies* 47, no. 3 (2009): 397–423.

81 On poor women and informal economies, see Martha Alter Chen, "The Informal Economy: Definitions, Theories, and Policies," Women in Informal Employment Globalizing and Organizing Working Paper No. 1, August 2012, accessed November 1, 2015, http://wiego.org/sites/wiego.org/files/publications/files/Chen_WIEGO_WP1.pdf.

82 On agricultural production as a strategic direction for *development*, see Đặng Kim Sơn, *Công nghiệp hóa từ nông nghiệp* [*Industrialization through* (*the Industrialization of*) *Agriculture*] (Hà Nội: Nông Nghiệp, 2001), chapter 6. On the importance of local micro trades and small-scale businesses, see Shozo Sakata, "Rural Industries in Northern Vietnam: Strategies of Small-Scale Business Establishments in the Formation of Craft Villages," in *Vietnam's Economic Entities in Transition*, ed. Shozo Sakata (New York: Palgrave Macmillan, 2013), 204–26.

83 So goes the overall assessment of Dena Freeman, ed., *Pentecostalism and Development: Churches, NGOs and Social Change in Africa*. In global evangelical studies of

preaching *prosperity* and the faith-based NGOs as a sure way to effect positive change.[84] Such mutual cooperation (a sort of "middle way" approach), however, needs to be handled with care, because, as in the case with Vietnam, it has been argued that many rural development policies implemented by the State and NGOs have adopted criteria that are inappropriate to the situation and needs of rural people, and that most success stories belong to those who have done creative small-scale work outside the structures set up by the State and NGOs.[85] At the same time, the effectiveness of helping the poor has become a politicized issue in which evidence is used to advance political agendas and institutional ideologies.[86] In this respect, people who believe they experience upward social mobility through *prosperity teaching* actually join a political debate in which case studies are used to illuminate different sets of social, economic, and even religious relationships that affect the process of upward social mobility. Such people cannot simply invite development practitioners to assess the impacts of *prosperity teaching* and assign correct meanings to the phenomenon of their upward social mobility.

4.5 Conclusion

To sum up, contemporary Vietnamese evangelicals are encouraged to engage with at least three major *development* perspectives, namely, *national*

---

international development, see also a recent appreciation of the role of pentecostalism in bringing about *development* in Bryant Myers, "Progressive Pentecostalism, Development, and Christian Development NGOs: A Challenge and an Opportunity," *International Bulletin of Missionary Research* 39, no. 3 (2015): 115–20. On the social engagement of pentecostalism, see Donald E. Miller and Tetsunao Yamamori, *Global Pentecostalism: The New Face of Christian Social Engagement* (Berkeley: University of California Press, 2007), and more recently Ivan Satyavrata, *Pentecostals and the Poor: Reflections from the Indian Context* (Baguio City, Philippines: Asia Pacific Theological Seminary Press, 2017), 1–18.

84 Schliesser, "On a Long Neglected Player," 355.

85 Philip Taylor, "Poor Policies, Wealthy Peasants: Alternative Trajectories of Rural Development in Vietnam," *Journal of Vietnamese Studies* 2, no. 2 (August 1, 2007): 3–56. For a promotion of the agency of ethnic minority groups in transforming their worlds, see Philip Taylor, "Minorities at Large: New Approaches to Minority Ethnicity in Vietnam," *Journal of Vietnamese Studies* 3, no. 3 (October 1, 2008): 3–43. On governments as having little knowledge of the livelihoods of ethnic minorities, see Sarah Turner, Christine Bonnin, and Jean Michaud, *Frontier Livelihoods: Hmong in the Sino-Vietnamese Borderlands* (Seattle: University of Washington Press, 2015).

86 Rosalind Eyben et al., *The Politics of Evidence and Results in International Development: Playing the Game to Change the Rules?* (Warwickshire, UK: Practical Action Publishing, 2015).

development, *transformational development*, and *prosperity teaching*. Situated as a critical perspective on *development*, the two evangelical approaches to *development*—*transformational development* and *prosperity teaching*—call attention to the religious dimension of *development* and the need to continue finding ways to retrieve grassroots perspectives, especially from women and ethnic minority groups, for input into *development* planning. In the intellectual quest to determine the relationship between *culture* and *development*, a critical evangelical perspective can help by refocusing the question on how the interculturation of Vietnamese culture, based on the multi-ethnicity of the people currently inhabiting Vietnam rather than the mono-ethnic Confucian-based culture of the ethnically *Việt* people, can contribute to the *development* of the nation.

On a different note, both the *national development* and *transformational development* perspectives show dependency of thought and finance on Western ideologies and donations. *Prosperity teaching* also has a foreign origin, but its relative ignorance of the wider discussion on *development* at least accidentally give birth to an autonomy that appears to help resist dependency and enhance the ability to engage with actual grassroots concerns.

In the configuration of *development*, *prosperity teaching* can be interpreted as a criticism of national developmental policy that fails to respond to the *basic needs* of the masses by focusing on *structural adjustment* and dealing ineffectively with crony capitalism. In this regard, the grassroots argument of *prosperity for all* is a fitting counterbalance to the top-down design of *modernity for the nation*. Equally importantly, the ongoing discussion on the issue of cultural values, upward social mobility, and modernity is furthered by suggestions on how socially disadvantaged people can acquire skills, knowledge, and opportunities by virtue of socialization within the evangelical groups that offer *prosperity teaching*. This chapter also calls for further studies on the activity of women, ethnic minorities, and economically poor people in *informal economies* that focus on creating income and meeting local *basic needs* through the industrialization of agriculture, the operation of small businesses, and the building of capacity for the future acquisition of technologies, to name a few examples.

Prosperity teaching exemplifies an important aspect of the pentecostal belief in *divine intervention*, that it is God's will to intervene and bless the underprivileged faithful with health, wealth, and upward social mobility in their context of economic inequality. It can also be said that the addition of *prosperity teaching* to the overall set of evangelical teachings in Vietnam from the 1990s onward represents both the materialization and "re-enchanting" of a society that is growing in material wealth but creates more inequality. Marginalized evangelicals, perceived as left behind in the course of *national development*, embrace *prosperity teaching* as their own path to *development* in an alienating world.[87] Here, the emphasis falls on the positive aspect of the apocalypse of *the world*, namely, that a new, improved condition of life will emerge as the old one passes away. Being otherworldly and this-worldly at the same time, *the world* thinking provides an internal logic for the growth of *prosperity teaching* among evangelicals in today's Vietnam.

With the benefit of hindsight, while the approach of *transformational development* is geared toward spiritualization, as evidenced in the definition of poverty in relational terms (i.e., broken relationships with God and others), the use of *prosperity teaching* is faced with a challenge in the opposite direction—that of being caught up in materialism. Divinely granted health and wealth may only prepare those who experience upward social mobility fully to function as newly minted capitalists ready to be integrated into the capitalist system.[88] Further, *prosperity teaching* runs the social risk of endorsing hedonism. Missing from *prosperity teaching* are resources to address socio-structural problems and the ability to motivate solidarity with the poor who have not yet experienced upward mobility. Bearing in mind these shortcomings, the successful practice of *prosperity teaching* needs at least two elements: a "can-do" attitude toward enhancing life, and a critical outlook for resistance to being co-opted into a problematic economy and forgetting those who are left behind. As a result, the use of *prosperity teaching* needs to be evaluated as part of a larger set of pentecostal beliefs and practices adopted and utilized by underprivileged contemporary Vietnamese evangelicals as they face *the world* in its multifaceted expression—it is this particular set of beliefs and practices that the next chapter will discuss.

87 Seb Rumsby argues similarly in "Vietnam Wrestles with Christianity: Why Hundreds of Thousands of Ethnic Hmong Have Converted to Christianity in Vietnam over the Past 30 Years," *The Diplomat*, November 13, 2017, accessed November 22, 2017, https://thediplomat.com/2017/11/vietnam-wrestles-with-christianity/.

88 Argued Daniel M. Bell, *The Economy of Desire: Christianity and Capitalism in a Postmodern World* (Grand Rapids: Eerdmans, 2012), 23–24.

CHAPTER 5

The Underprivileged

5.1 Becoming Pentecostal

The growth of pentecostalism is the most important spiritual development among contemporary Vietnamese grassroots evangelicals. Within this movement, the emphasis on *divine intervention* represents a grassroots perspective on some important social, political, cultural, and economic issues that evangelicals are facing in today's Vietnam. Concisely stated, the faithful believe the conditions of their life and the *status quo* of their society can be disrupted, so that as they embrace pentecostalism their life can improve through their experience of *divine deliverance* and *divine blessings*. This grassroots perspective can be ascertained by looking at the different pentecostal beliefs and practices that have emerged through the course of pentecostalism's development in contemporary Vietnam. They include the beliefs that Jesus is Lord, as well as Spirit Baptizer, Healer, and Coming King—a particular version of the so-called Full Gospel pattern—and practices such as *tongues-speaking*, *worship*, *prayer*, and to a lesser extent *fasting*. These beliefs and practices, common among contemporary Vietnamese pentecostal evangelicals, are also popular among pentecostal Christians elsewhere around the globe and manifest the pentecostal movement's natural predisposition toward *divine intervention*.

Chronologically, the development of pentecostalism among contemporary Vietnamese evangelicals began in the 1980s, with *tongues-speaking* considered the signature practice of the movement. In the context of early-communist Vietnam, the State, informed by communist ideology, did not encourage religious practices. Throughout the country, local evangelical churches could open only two hours per week on Sunday for a worship service. Several pastors were put in re-education camps, or worse, in jail, while others fled the country. The two national church bodies, the ECVN (North) and the ECVN (South), kept their operations and evangelistic activities at a minimal level to avoid drawing unnecessary attention from the government.

Amid this difficulty, several urban lay evangelicals in HCMC, formerly known as Sài Gòn, began to gather quietly in small groups in private houses to pray for revival, that God would intervene and help the faithful in their time of difficulty.[1]

1 Pastor Đinh Thiên Tứ of the local evangelical church of Tuy Lý Vương (HCMC) was credited with developing this cell-group system. Tongues-speaking evangelical pastors who led the

 | DOI:10.1163/9789004383838_007

While they prayed, a strange thing happened: some people began to voice utterances that do not belong to the Vietnamese language—in fact, that may not represent any human language. The utterers contended that they had experienced *tongues-speaking*, a sign that the Spirit of God had visited them and baptized them with fire. The newly flamed fire then resulted in the people's sharing with fellow believers the necessity of seeking the Holy Spirit and undertaking evangelism in novel ways, among which was the taking of long and risky journeys from South to North Vietnam to share the gospel. Some even quipped that the communists had done an excellent service to the church by unifying the country so that the evangelicals could travel to the North. While it is not accurate to equate the pentecostal movement with the practice of *tongues-speaking*, it is important to note that the prominent practice of *tongues-speaking* was often used to define the pentecostal movement in its early days in Vietnam.

As with several historical occurrences, it is difficult to pinpoint when, and to whom, the first *tongues-speaking* experience happened in postwar Vietnam, for different pentecostal leaders and groups remember this event differently. Most accounts, however, would narrate that the inception of *tongues-speaking* occurred in the 1980s, first among the Southern *Việt* evangelicals in HCMC, who in turn missionized the *Việt* people, living in the North, and the ethnic minorities, living in the highlands and mountainous areas. As of today, little has been written about the early pentecostal experience and agency of the ethnic minority groups, who make up three quarters of the evangelical population of the country.

While *tongues-speaking* appeared to emerge out of nowhere, two converging historical streams fed the development of pentecostalism among Vietnamese evangelicals in the 1980s. The first stream pairs the revival among the students of the ECVN's Bible Institute in Nha Trang in 1971 and the preaching tour of the Chinese revivalist/evangelist John Sung in 1938, which continue to shape the Vietnamese evangelical and pentecostal understanding of revival.[2] The second

early pentecostal movement picked up the understanding of the cell-group system as one among several valid church models during their pre-1975 seminary training at the ECVN's Nha Trang Bible Institute, where faculty members Reg Reimer and Trương Văn Tốt, who had previously studied church growth under Donald McGavran at Fuller Theological Seminary in 1970–71, served as key teaching resources.

2 On the 1971 revival, see Orrel Steinkamp, *The Holy Spirit in Vietnam* (Carol Stream, IL: Creation House, 1973). On the 1938 revival, see Phan Đình Liệu, "Lịch sử Hội Thánh Tin Lành Việt Nam" ["History of the Evangelical Church of Vietnam"] (unpublished manuscript, 1966); also Ruth Goforth Jeffrey, *Amazing Grace: A Brief Account of My Life in China and Vietnam* (Stouffville, ON: D. I. Jeffrey, 1975), 27–28.

stream consists in Vietnamese evangelicalism's awareness of *tongues-speaking* as a spiritual practice since the early days of the tradition. R. A. Jaffray, the field secretary of the South China Alliance Mission and chief architect of the C&MA's work in Vietnam in the 1910s and 1920s, was himself a tongues-speaker,[3] and most if not all the earliest C&MA missionaries had worked in South China (where the manifestation of tongues among C&MA missionaries and native believers was evident) before coming to Vietnam.[4] The pentecostal Assemblies of God denomination had also done considerable work in South Vietnam from 1972 to 1975; its Vietnamese members, who joined the ECVN (South) in and after 1975, brought to the denomination renewed attention to the practice of *tongues-speaking*.[5] Knowledge of the practice thus survived among Vietnamese evangelicals and contributed to the proliferation of pentecostalism in Vietnam in the 1980s. It has also been noted that the earliest incidents of *tongues-speaking* occurred without the intervention of foreign missionaries.[6]

3 R. A. Jaffray, "'Speaking in Tongues'—Some Words of Kindly Counsel," *Alliance Weekly*, March 13, 1909, 395–96, 406. On the C&MA and pentecostalism, see Charles Nienkirchen, *A. B. Simpson and the Pentecostal Movement* (Peabody, MA: Hendrickson, 1992); and Paul King, *Genuine Gold: The Cautiously Charismatic Story of the Early Christian and Missionary Alliance* (Tulsa: Word & Spirit, 2006).

4 R. A. Jaffray, "South China: Selections from the Annual Reports from the Southern Provinces of China," *Alliance Weekly*, August 1, 1908, 287–90. See also Nienkirchen, *A. B. Simpson and the Pentecostal Movement*, 88, 125–28, and King, *Genuine Gold*, 102–104.

5 A generous estimate of postwar Assemblies of God leader Trần Đình Ái contended that "there were 10,000 to 15,000 adherents in the Assemblies of God [in Vietnam] in 1975"; see Trần Đình Ái, "The History of Pentecostalism in Vietnam," paper presented at the 10th Anniversary of the Pentecostal Movement, Vũng Tàu, August 1998, quoted in Joshua (pseudonym), "Pentecostalism in Vietnam: A History of the Assemblies of God," *Asian Journal of Pentecostal Studies* 4, no. 2 (2001): 307–26. Note that the Vietnamese Assemblies of God dated the beginning of the pentecostal movement as late as 1988, thus bringing it closer to the time its leaders were excommunicated from the ECVN (South) in 1989.

6 Lê Thị Hồng Ân, email message to author, November 24, 2014. This observation may be accurate, for Vietnamese evangelicals had limited overseas contacts in the early 1980s. Also, a group of Vietnamese evangelicals who experienced tongues-speaking did visit a charismatic Catholic priest, father Đinh Khắc Tiệu (in HCMC), to learn more about the nature of the experience of tongues-speaking. Given the limited contact between Vietnamese evangelicals and Catholics in the past, this group of evangelicals must have exhausted their own sources before they decided to consult a Catholic priest.

Additionally, the French Assemblies of God missionary Roland Cosnard, who worked in South Vietnam before 1975, did not revisit Vietnam until 1986 (or 1988—sources conflict). Although Cosnard, in his collaboration with a Mrs. Hồng Phước, had a significant influence on postwar Vietnamese pentecostal leaders during his time in Vietnam, his first post-1975 visit appears to have come later than the earliest surge of tongues-speaking.

Given the context of early-communist Vietnam, in which expressions of difference and deviation from the established course of the state-party would meet severe intolerance, the political implication of speaking in different, unknown tongues is straightforward: *while the state-party enforced univocality and threatened the exhibition of difference, there existed, nevertheless, a minority religious group whose insistence on speaking plurivocally constituted a political act against hegemonic measurements of the current political powers. Tongues-speaking* represented the promotion of *plurivocality* as a subversive act against the State's effort to enforce univocality.

At the same time, while the established church decided to lie low by curbing public engagement in order to not attract attention from the government (a move judged by fervent evangelicals as limiting the church's missional identity), the making of strange noises through *tongues-speaking* by evangelicals-turned-pentecostals was also an act of ecclesial subversion; it argued for the renewal of a religious commitment to God requiring expression through outward evangelism. As it actually went, the strange noise was loud enough to deliver the message of political and ecclesial subversion, thus resulting in the imprisonment of a number of the main leaders of the movement and the excommunication of all tongues-speakers from the ECVN (South) in the late 1980s and early 1990s.[7]

The employment of *tongues-speaking* as an act of subversion has a long history in Christianity. The most famous story of *tongues-speaking* is obviously the story of the Holy Spirit's visiting the early believers in Jesus on the Day of Pentecost in Jerusalem (recorded in Acts 2), through which event the "pentecostal" movement gets its name. A study of the use of this story in medieval and early-modern European Christianity leads church historian Albert Hernández to identify a pattern of revisiting the story of the Day of Pentecost by Christian thinkers and visionaries and to argue that they did so because this story "inspired and empowered them to subvert dominant ecclesiastical and political paradigms for the betterment of society and for the emancipation of God's children," just as the speaking of tongues in Acts 2 represents an act of subversion to both the Jewish religious and the Roman political paradigms.[8]

7 The ECVN (South), Church Memo 21/TLH/VP, dated June 24, 1989, quoted in Trần Thái Sơn, "Sau hai mươi năm" ["After Twenty Years"] (unpublished manuscript, 1995). See also Võ Hữu Đức, "Lược sử Hội Thánh Tin Lành Việt Nam (1975–1991)" ["A Brief History of the Evangelical Church of Vietnam (1975–1991)"] (unpublished manuscript, 1991).

8 Albert Hernández, *Subversive Fire: The Untold Story of Pentecost* (Lexington, KY: Emeth Press, 2010), xii. See also similar observations in James K. A. Smith, "Tongues as 'Resistance Discourse'—A Philosophical Perspective," in *Speaking in Tongues*, ed. Mark J. Cartledge (Milton Keynes, UK: Paternoster, 2006), 81–110; and Robert G. Reid, "Spirit Empowerment as Resistance Discourse: An Imperial-Critical Reading of Acts 2," in *Trajectories in*

As such, *tongues-speaking* represents an irruptive response in a crisis-inducing event that includes both religious and political constituents.[9] It is noteworthy that, in Acts 2, the disciples "were filled with the Holy Spirit and began to speak in other languages, as the Spirit gave them the ability," and people heard of "God's deeds of power" through the tongues being spoken. In contemporary Vietnam, speaking in tongues rarely has that or a similar effect, but it does not stop believers from associating their experience with the event recorded in Acts 2.

The *tongues-speaking* that emerged among evangelicals in early-communist Vietnam can also be further explored as a multifaceted phenomenon. *Politically* and *religiously*, it is an act of subversion of the dominant ecclesiastical and political paradigms, as mentioned above. Here, utterances that may or may not have meaning to lay evangelicals constitutes a grassroots resistance to the rhetorical devices employed by the State and by church leadership to establish dominance. *Culturally*, *tongues-speaking* represents a break from the evangelical tradition, judged as being bankrupt in the face of political change.[10] *Socially*, *tongues-speaking* fosters a particular identity through similar commitments (to the affective love of God, the revival of faith, and evangelism) and experience (that of *tongues-speaking*). Socialization with tongues-speakers also allowed many people to learn about the practice and gave rise to the use of *tongues-speaking* as a defining practice that set a group boundary.[11] *Psychologically*, *tongues-speaking* provides a therapeutic moment of relieving stressors and has the cathartic quality of releasing the anger of, and providing opportunities to grieve about, the injustice caused by ethnic, religious, and class discrimination experienced by the underprivileged such as migrant manual workers and several ethnic minority groups in contemporary Vietnam.[12]

---

the Book of Acts: Essays in Honor of John Wesley Wyckoff, ed. Paul Alexander, Jordan Daniel May, and Robert G. Reid (Eugene, OR: Wipf & Stock, 2015), 21–45.

9 Peter Hocken, *You He Made Alive: A Total Christian View of Prayer, Communal, Individual and with Special Reference to the Work of the Spirit in Prayer Groups* (London: Darton, Longman and Todd, 1974), 69.

10 On this position, see also Henry I. Lederle, who argues, "the keynote of their experience was that of jubilant freedom—the break with the confinements of previous traditional styles of Christianity and a refusal to be limited again in any way in their faith experience," in his *Treasures Old and New: Interpretations of "Spirit-Baptism" in the Charismatic Renewal Movement* (Peabody, MA: Hendrickson, 1988), 222.

11 On socialization and tongues, see Mark J. Cartledge, "The Socialization of *Glossolalia*," in *Sociology, Theology and the Curriculum*, ed. Leslie J. Francis (London: Cassell, 1999): 125–34.

12 For tongues as having therapeutic benefits, see Amos Yong, *The Spirit of Creation: Modern Science and Divine Action in the Pentecostal-Charismatic Imagination* (Grand Rapids: Eerdmans?, 2011), 67n110. For a similar observation from the field of psychological studies, see

Among Vietnamese pentecostal evangelicals, the practice of *tongues-speaking* is closely associated with the belief that *Jesus is Spirit Baptizer*, an important doctrinal tenet confirming continuity in the ministry of Jesus: after Jesus' ascension, the Holy Spirit continues Jesus' work in the three realms of the church, individual believers, and the world.[13] Differing views suggest that a person may receive the Spirit, or Spirit Baptism, at different times: the moment of conversion, the moment of receiving water baptism, or the moment of speaking in tongues. In the early years of the Vietnamese pentecostal movement in the 1980s, *tongues-speaking* was thought of as the sole indicator of Spirit Baptism—a historical-theological point that remains open for theological reflection and debate.[14]

With regard to belief, the confession of *Jesus is Spirit Baptizer* is one component of the pentecostal fourfold Full Gospel pattern, which narrates Jesus as Savior, Spirit Baptizer, Healer, and Coming King. Two of the larger Vietnamese pentecostal evangelical groups, currently affiliated with the International Church of the Foursquare Gospel and the World Assemblies of God Fellowship, have familiarized Vietnamese pentecostal evangelicals with this pattern for belief.

Another popular version of the Full Gospel pattern among Vietnamese evangelicals is the C&MA's fourfold pattern, which portrays Jesus as Savior, Sanctifier, Healer, and Coming King.[15] The difference between the pentecostal and C&MA fourfold patterns is evident: the former depicts Jesus as *Spirit Baptizer*, while the latter depicts him as *Sanctifier*. The tenet *Jesus is Sanctifier*,

---

Fraser Watts's discussion of tongues in "Psychology and Theology," in *The Cambridge Companion to Science and Religion*, ed. Peter Harrison (New York: Cambridge University Press, 2010), 190–206. For an empirical study that suggests tongues leads to "experiences of love, power, liberty, joy, and transformation" among practitioners, see Cartledge, *Testimony in the Spirit*, 104. For a review of the psychological research on *tongues-speaking* (up to the 1990s), see William Kay, "The Mind, Behaviour and Glossolalia—A Psychological Perspective," in *Speaking in Tongues*, ed. Mark J. Cartledge (Milton Keynes, UK: Paternoster, 2006), 174–205.

13 The belief, in fact, has a long history in Vietnamese evangelicalism. See John D. Olsen, *Thần đạo học* [*Theology*] (Sài Gòn: Tin Lành, 1958): 570–79.

14 On the identification of *tongues-speaking* with Spirit Baptism as not necessarily a helpful theological decision, see Lederle, *Treasures Old and New*, 221–22.

15 A. B. Simpson, *The Fourfold Gospel* (1890. Reprint, Harrisburg, PA: Christian Publications, 1984). See also Bernie Van De Walle, *The Heart of the Gospel: A. B. Simpson, the Fourfold Gospel, and Late Nineteenth-Century Evangelical Theology* (Eugene, OR: Pickwick, 2009). For a historical discussion of the genealogy of the Full Gospel pattern in North America, in its connection to the development of pentecostalism, see Vinson Synan, *The Holiness-Pentecostal Tradition: Charismatic Movements in the Twentieth Century*, 2nd ed. (Grand Rapids: Eerdmans, 1997).

which originated in the Holiness circles of North American evangelicals to refer to a distinct crisis-moment of total sanctification in the Christian life that happens after initial conversion, is not a prominent belief among Vietnamese evangelicals; they emphasize, instead, sanctification as a lifelong process of increasing holiness by upholding the principles of moral living. For Vietnamese evangelicals who have experienced *tongues-speaking*, the *ordo salutis* thus includes only two precise moments: the moment of water baptism as an outward manifestation of regeneration and a public acknowledgment of conversion, and the moment of Spirit Baptism as an evidence of being filled with the Spirit, expressed outwardly in the act of *tongues-speaking*. From this perspective, the pentecostal fourfold pattern, which attests Jesus as Savior, Spirit Baptizer, Healer, and Coming King expresses more unambiguously the internal logic of the soteriological thinking of Vietnamese pentecostal evangelicals.[16]

In retrospect, the practice of *tongues-speaking* and the related belief in *Jesus is Spirit Baptizer* are germane to the overall development of Vietnamese evangelical theology in several respects: they both promote social *inclusivity* and *hybridity*, and they both represent acts of subversion of cultural hegemony. Furthermore, they both provide social and psychological support to believers in times of need.

The idea that Spirit Baptism and *tongues-speaking* encourage social inclusivity is supported by Acts 2:17 (NRSV), which reads: "In the last days it will be, God declares, that I will pour out my Spirit upon all flesh, and your sons and your daughters shall prophesy, and your young men shall see visions, and your old men shall dream dreams." In its emphasis on *all* flesh, sons and daughters, and young men and old men, Acts 2:17 offers a theology of *inclusivity* in the outpouring of the Holy Spirit.[17]

The practices of early pentecostals in the contemporary pentecostal movement in the United States further illustrate this point: During America's Jim Crow era in 1906, many Holiness and pentecostal Christians claimed that it was possible for blacks, whites, and people of other races to attend the same worship service together in Los Angeles because the Spirit had been poured out on *all* of them. "The 'color line' was washed away in the blood [of Jesus]," declared reporter Frank Bartleman, an insider of the movement.[18] For those

16 See also a similar discussion on North American pentecostalism in Donald W. Dayton, *Theological Roots of Pentecostalism* (Peabody, MA: Hendrickson, 1987), 17–23.

17 For further information, see Amos Yong, *The Spirit Poured Out on All Flesh: Pentecostalism and the Possibility of Global Theology* (Grand Rapids: Baker Academic, 2005).

18 Frank Bartleman, *Azusa Street*, centennial edition (1906. Gainesville, FL: Bridge-Logos, 2006), 61.

who believe, the comprehensive scope of the pouring out of the Spirit has potential to redraw racial, gender, and social boundaries. This understanding of the *inclusivity* of Acts 2:17 is critical for the development of a Vietnamese evangelical theology that needs to be sensitive to the ethnic dynamics within the Vietnamese evangelical demographic.

A carefully edited editorial report on the front page of the very first issue of *The Apostolic Faith* newspaper, published more than a century ago in North America, also illustrated pentecostal spirituality's tendency toward social inclusivity and egalitarianism. This tendency may provide inspiration for contemporary Vietnamese evangelical thinking about the work of the Spirit in the life of believers, given the ethnic diversity within Vietnamese evangelicalism:

> Bro. Campbell, a Nazarene brother, 83 years of age, who has been for 53 years serving the Lord, was receiving the baptism with the Holy Ghost and gift of tongues in his own home. His son, who was a physician, was called and came to see if he was sick, but found him only happy in the Lord. Not only old men and old women, but boys and girls, are receiving their Pentecost. Viola Price, a little orphan colored girl eight years of age, has received the gift of tongues.[19]

In the above report, the image of an elderly minister, who had a son holding a highly regarded profession, was put in sharp contrast with a little colored girl, who was parentless. Spirit Baptism, as shown in this carefully crafted piece, was a Christian experience that could widely embrace people of different age, gender, race, social status, and family situation. This editorial report was both a theological and a social statement about the inclusive characteristic of the pentecostal movement in its early development in North America—a characteristic the contemporary pentecostal movement in Vietnam would do well to adopt.

The pentecostal evangelical thinking about *tongues-speaking* also intersects with the notion of *hybridity*, referring to a mixture or an intersection of two races, two cultures, or two phenomena.[20] As the theory goes, the stage of *hybridity* is a significant third space that allows much creativity and valid criticism to emerge as one interacts with the two original spaces that give rise to *hybridity*. The phenomenon of *tongues-speaking* signifies *hybridity* since, in the practice, one person (located in a particular culture) is speaking another

19 *The Apostolic Faith* vol. 1, no. 1 (September 1906), p. 1.

20 On *hybridity*, see Homi K. Bhabha, *The Location of Culture* (New York: Routledge, 1994).

language (representing another culture—perhaps even a heavenly one). The advantage of thinking about *tongues-speaking* as a sign of *hybridity* is that it invites Vietnamese pentecostal evangelicals to rethink their identity as a mixture drawing from several traditions. *Hybridity* thus rejects the belief in a pure and pristine Vietnamese identity as disseminated in the dominant political discourse for the purpose of building cultural hegemony. When engaging with Vietnamese intellectuals and evangelicals who belong to the majority *Việt* people, therefore, the idea of *hybridity* is relevant due to these groups' privileged ethnic status in contemporary Vietnam. There is, however, a disadvantage of inviting thinking about *hybridity* to Vietnamese evangelical theology, namely, its creation of a problem from the perspective of evangelicals belonging to minority ethnic groups. Their concern is for cultural locatedness, preservation, and specificity. So in reference to them, one must guard against the misuse of *hybridity* to justify cultural assimilation and at the expense of their own agency. As a result, the idea of *hybridity* shows the potential to contribute to a more inclusive, interrelated, and interdependent Vietnamese evangelical theology but requires careful administration, given the ethnic dynamics within both Vietnamese evangelicals as a group and the wider Vietnamese society.[21]

Looking back, the major historico-political significance of the pentecostal belief in Jesus as *Spirit Baptizer* and the practice of *tongues-speaking* in contemporary Vietnam remains their promotion of *plurivocality*, an act to subvert the ecclesial and/or political enforcement of univocality and obedience. As the Vietnamese state has pursued an open door economic policy and sought "international integration" since the 1990s, the social space for pentecostal evangelicals to practice their faith has been significantly enhanced. As a result, there has been an attendant decline in focus on the teaching of *Spirit Baptism* and the practice of *tongues-speaking*, for there is (relatively) less opposition against which to show resistance. In today's Vietnam, the practice of *tongues-speaking* is thought of as one among many gifts of the Spirit, with each of these gifts demonstrating the fact that the Spirit abides within a believer. The Spirit's gifts cover a wide range, from spiritual gifts such as prophecy, exorcism, and the performance of physical healings, to very this-worldly gifts such as church administration, almsgiving, and hospitality, to name a few. But an argument arises for reclaiming the significance of *tongues-speaking* on the basis of the

21 For further exploration of the theological use of the concept of *hybridity*, see Néstor Medina, *Mestizaje: (Re)mapping Race, Culture, and Faith in Latina/o Catholicism* (Maryknoll, NY: Orbis, 2009); and Néstor Medina, "Discerning the Spirit in Culture: Toward Pentecostal Interculturality," *Canadian Journal of Pentecostal-Charismatic Christianity*, no. 2 (2011): 131–65.

suggestion that *tongues-speaking* is the practice which shows a believer's willingness to work with the Spirit, thus unlocking other gifts of Spirit in the life of that believer.[22] Although *tongues-speaking* is losing its prominent status as the "signature" practice among Vietnamese pentecostal evangelicals, it is expected that if determined hegemonic efforts are carried out by any political or ecclesial authority in the future, *tongues-speaking* will once again be invoked for the purpose of subverting the dominant paradigms.

5.2 Aspiring Newness

In addition to the emergence of *tongues-speaking*, the most noticeable change among "pentecostalized" evangelicals in early-communist Vietnam was the change in their style of worship. Their worship became more expressive, with more bodily movement and the expression of a wide range of emotions, from crying out of grief and repentance to laughing out of exuberant joy in divine love. *Worship* was important, for it was thought of as a way to experience "the presence of the Lord" or "the touch of the Spirit." Since the late 1990s, the music of well-known pentecostal musicians such as Don Moen and Darlene Zschech has set a standard for the development of expressive worship in Vietnamese evangelicalism. More recently, the internet has informed Vietnamese pentecostal evangelicals of new, global trends in pentecostal worship. In its current configuration, the musical style of Vietnamese pentecostal evangelicalism mixes the influences of the older evangelical tradition (coming from the early C&MA missionaries and other South China evangelical sources), the contemporary (mostly North American) pentecostal way of worship, and Vietnamese pop music. This area is one in which Vietnamese pentecostal evangelicals influence other evangelical and charismatic Catholic groups, both of whose worship services incorporate pentecostal songs, sometimes with accompanying bodily expressions.

As similarly with regard to the practice of *tongues-speaking*, *worship* is conducive to the subversion of the *status quo*. Through *worship*, Vietnamese pentecostal evangelicals confess that *Jesus is Savior* or, alternatively, *Jesus is Lord*. In early Christianity, the proclamation that *Jesus is Lord* had political implications, for the designation *Lord* had been used to refer to the Emperor, who was widely thought of as a deity acting in a salvific capacity and thus demanding

22 On tongues as "the crown jewel of pentecostal distinctives," see Frank D. Macchia, *Baptized in the Spirit: A Global Pentecostal Theology* (Grand Rapids: Zondervan, 2006), 20.

worship and loyalty.[23] Thus the enduring political significance of the Christian confession that *Jesus is Lord* lies in its function of publicly rejecting the state's (*any* state's) illusory rhetoric of omnipotence, omniscience, and omnibenevolence to substantiate its claim to deserve the submission of the people.

In contemporary Vietnam, the state-party relies for the most part on the argument that it, as an institution, is the most knowledgeable, capable, and philanthropic entity for leading the country in a salvific manner; thus the state-party buttresses its claim to retain power. The commemorations and construction of museum-shrines for past communist leaders have already raised questions about whether this practice is cult-like in nature.[24] Marxist thinking, once serving in an iconoclastic capacity in colonial Vietnam, has been used in contemporary times as an ideology to build a belief system to protect the State's right to rule. Religion, once criticized as the "opium of the poor" in Marxist argumentation, has ironically seen increasing potential to become iconoclastic in communist Vietnam—a society being categorized as re-enchanted.[25]

Standing within this trend of religious re-enchantment in contemporary Vietnam, the pentecostal evangelical confession *Jesus is Lord*, manifested in expressive worship, is a public statement that sovereignty, salvation, and history do not belong to the State. Accordingly, the mass conversion to evangelicalism by the ethnic minorities in the mountainous areas of the North and Central Highlands of Vietnam can be viewed as a movement seeking to reject

23 On this issue, see Richard A. Horsley, ed., *In the Shadow of Empire: Reclaiming the Bible as a History of Faithful Resistance* (Louisville: Westminster John Knox, 2008). Also Richard A. Horsley, *Jesus and the Powers: Conflict, Covenant, and the Hope of the Poor* (Minneapolis: Fortress, 2010), section "You Shall Not Bow Down and Serve Them," pp. 1–16; and Reid, "Spirit Empowerment as Resistance Discourse: An Imperial-Critical Reading of Acts 2."

24 On the state-party endorsement of ancestor worship as a strategy to strengthen nationalism, see Kate Jellema, "Returning Home: Ancestor Veneration and the Nationalism of *Đổi Mới* Vietnam," in *Modernity and Re-Enchantment: Religion in Post-Revolutionary Vietnam*, ed. Philip Taylor (Singapore: Institute of Southeast Asian Studies, 2007), 57–89, esp. 65–70. For a detailed case study on posthumous veneration of past communist leader Tôn Đức Thắng, see Christoph Giebel, *Imagined Ancestries of Vietnamese Communism: Ton Duc Thang and the Politics of History and Memory* (Seattle: University of Washington Press, 2004). See also Giebel's "Museum-Shine: Revolution and Its Tutelary Spirit in the Village of My Hoa Hung," in *The Country of Memory: Remaking the Past in Late Socialist Vietnam*, ed. Hue-Tam Ho Tai (Berkeley: University of California Press, 2001), 77–108. For a Vietnamese evangelical criticism of the State's performance of ancestor worship to reinforce national unity and regime legitimacy, see Quynh-Hoa Nguyen, "Tin Lành: The Bible and the Construction of an Evangelical Vietnamese Christian Identity (1975–2007)" (Ph.D. diss., Claremont Graduate University, 2013), 192.

25 So argue Philip Taylor et al. in *Modernity and Re-Enchantment: Religion in Post-Revolutionary Vietnam* (Singapore: Institute of Southeast Asian Studies, 2007).

the broad claims of a state that fails to deliver societal betterment and, instead, *marginalizes* (by withdrawing or impeding social opportunity); *oppresses* (through the dispossession of personal property and the establishment of laws and social customs that institutionalize the marginalization of targeted groups); and *abuses* (through, for example, unfair compensation and public humiliation) the members of these ethnic minority groups.[26]

More importantly, pentecostal *worship* is conducive to imagining new social relationships and a reconfiguration of power in a context that considers the negative life experiences of marginalization, oppression, and abuse which the people bring with them to worship. Thinking of *worship* as being conducive to imagining proceeds from an understanding that *worship* is primarily a social activity, a time of formation that promotes human imagination and creates new meaning.[27] Imagination, in this case, is not the opposite of reason, for imagination is constructed within the web of meanings and the practiced values that people live in; thus imagination opens up space for conceiving new patterns of life and for giving life new meaning, even in the midst of oppression.[28] Imaginations, dreams, and visions are the incubators of new, victorious realities that will become concrete in the lives of the faithful through the power of the Spirit.[29] Here the rituals of *worship* give the activity physical form

26 Oscar Salemink, "Is Protestant Conversion a Form of Protest? Urban and Upland Protestants in Southeast Asia," in *Christianity and the State in Asia: Complicity and Conflict*, ed. Julius Bautista and Francis Khek Gee Lim (New York: Routledge, 2009), 36–58; James Lewis, "Christianity and Human Rights in Vietnam: The Case of the Ethnic Minorities, 1975–2007," in *Christianity and Human Rights: Christians and the Struggle for Global Justice*, ed. Frederick M. Shepherd (Lanham, MD: Lexington, 2009), 195–212.

27 On *worship* as promoting human imagination, see Philip Kenneson, "Gathering: Worship, Imagination, and Formation," in *The Blackwell Companion to Christian Ethics*, ed. Stanley Hauerwas and Samuel Wells (Malden, MA: Wiley-Blackwell, 2006), 55–69. On *worship* as creating new meaning, see the three chapters in "Part I: The Making of Meaning" of Graham Hughes's *Worship as Meaning: A Liturgical Theology for Late Modernity*, Cambridge Studies in Christian Doctrine (New York: Cambridge University Press, 2003), 11–111, esp. 30–42.

28 So argues Viktor Frankl in *Man's Search for Meaning* (1946. Boston: Beacon, 2006), and Sarah Coakley, "Kenosis and Subversion: On the Repression of 'Vulnerability' in Christian Feminist Writing," in *Swallowing a Fishbone?* ed. Daphne Hampson (London: SPCK, 1996), 82–111.

29 See, for example, Cho Yong-gi, *The Fourth Dimension* (Newberry, FL: Bridge Logos, 1979). On pentecostal imagination as having pragmatic concerns for the bodily, material, and social dimensions of life, see Amos Yong, *In the Days of Caesar: Pentecostalism and Political Theology*, Sacra Doctrina: Christian Theology for a Postmodern Age Series (Grand Rapids: Eerdmans, 2010), 329, 361–62. See also, on the pragmatic imagination of pentecostalism, Grant Wacker, *Heaven Below: Early Pentecostals and American Culture* (Cambridge: Harvard University Press, 2001). On the imagination as pneumatic activity, see

in a way that creates bodily habits, which, in turn, shape the worshiper's imagination and desire according to the Christian narrative presented in *worship*.[30] Through this cultivation of imagination, *worship* has the potential to contribute to cultural and social change.[31]

In pentecostal gatherings, liturgical performance allows individuals to participate in *worship* via personal rites and expressions of emotion that correspond to the existing individual and communal troubles they bring with them to such gatherings. In this context, imagination is formed in a particular way through focusing on the here and now and immediate issues; expecting *divine intervention*; gaining insights into the types of behaviors and attitudes considered best to show cooperation with the divine will; and encouragement, gained from the shared affections and solidarity of others in the same gathering, to believe in positive results. In pentecostal worship services, *testimonies* are also often given to provide examples of how believers experience goodness in life. These concrete examples further direct the pentecostal imagination toward a particular vision of an enhanced and better life.[32]

The simple lyrics of pentecostal songs—lyrics often viewed as impoverished of Christian theology—are, in fact, excellent conduits for the imagination. A simple lyric, such as "God will make a way," allows each participant in the worship service to "fill in the details" of what God can do, given the particular problems that person is facing.[33] One person might imagine

---

Amos Yong, *Spirit-Word-Community: Theological Hermeneutics in Trinitarian Perspective* (Eugene, OR: Wipf & Stock, 2002): 123–49.

30 See James K. A. Smith, *Imagining the Kingdom: How Worship Works* (Grand Rapids: Baker Academic, 2013), 92–100.

31 So argues Graham Ward in *Cultural Transformation and Religious Practice* (Cambridge: Cambridge University Press, 2005): 160–74.

32 For discussion on pentecostal testimony, see Scott A. Ellington, "History, Story, and Testimony: Locating Truth in a Pentecostal Hermeneutic," *Pneuma: The Journal of the Society for Pentecostal Studies* 23, no. 2 (September 2001): 245–63. Also, for a study of testimonies on pentecostal practices (including worship, tongues, and prayer for healing) by churchgoers, and theological reflection thereafter, see Mark J. Cartledge, *Testimony in the Spirit: Rescripting Ordinary Pentecostal Theology* (Burlington, VT: Ashgate, 2010).

33 Cf. Ryan R. Gladwin, "Charismatic Music and the Pentecostalization of Latin American Evangelicalism," in *The Spirit of Praise: Music and Worship in Global Pentecostal-Charismatic Christianity*, ed. Monique M. Ingalls and Amos Yong (University Park, PA: The Pennsylvania State University Press), 199–214. Gladwin argues, for instance, that Latin American pentecostal songs should go further in addressing social justice more explicitly. Similar criticism of contemporary worship songs (many of them penned by pentecostal-related Christians) as devoid of rich meaning can be found in Andrew Goodliff, " 'It's All about Jesus': A Critical Analysis of the Ways in Which the Songs of Four Contemporary Worship Songwriters Can Lead to an Impoverished Christology," *The Evangelical Quarterly* 81, no. 3 (July 2009): 254–68.

the restoration of dignity after having experienced wrongful social treatment. (A study by Charles Avila reports the desire of Filipino peasants for a refinement of their imagination on the belief that their low self-esteem is a result of their having internalized the colonizers' and ruling elites' thinking about peasants.[34]) Another person might envision new opportunities for a better livelihood after having experienced dispossession. Yet another person might imagine improved familial relationships after having experienced domestic violence, which has complex social, cultural, economic, and psychological aspects. In such cases, sublime Christian lyrics of the "high church" tradition, which provide lengthy theological expositions, may not, for disadvantaged grassroots individuals, be as conducive to the imagination as are the simple lyrics of pentecostal songs. In other words, new forms of consciousness are created through human gatherings (of expressive worshipers) and are facilitated through relevant means (singing songs with simple lyrics).

As is the case with conduciveness to the imagination, so also the provision of less theological detail may be more conducive to belief, as shown by comparing the discussions on the second and third persons of the Trinity in the Apostles' Creed:

> On the second person: *I believe in Jesus Christ, God's only Son, our Lord, who was conceived by the Holy Spirit, born of the Virgin Mary, suffered under Pontius Pilate, was crucified, died, and was buried; he descended into hell. On the third day he rose again; he ascended into heaven, he is seated at the right hand of the Father, and he will come to judge the living and the dead.*
>
> On the third person: *I believe in the Holy Spirit.*

The second article of the creed, on Jesus Christ, while having the value of elaborating the historicity of Jesus, has preframed a particular mode of thinking about Jesus; the third and simpler article, on the Holy Spirit, leaves room for imagination. Christians who possess a pentecostal sensibility, often dubbed "the people of the Spirit," benefit from such simplicity whenever it allows the faculty of imagination to prompt movement toward practical problem-solving, renewing of strength, and generating of hope.

34 Charles Avila, *Peasant Theology: Reflections by the Filipino Peasants on Their Process of Social Revolution*, WSCF Asia Book 1 (Bangkok: World Student Christian Federation Asia Region, 1976), 62–63.

For the underprivileged, the physical location of worship also functions in a manner conducive to imagining.[35] As the Vietnamese state seeks control of as much public space as possible, pentecostal worship gatherings, even in private houses, provide alternative communal areas. Thus the house-church worship venue represents a kind of grassroots gathering place that is not organized by any of the "big three": the State, the business sector, and the NGOs. Here the house-church gathering embodies an operational solution responding to restrictions on opening new church facilities; however, for Vietnamese believers it carries little theological significance (for example, the house church as a faithful image of the Early Church). The independent, local characteristic of pentecostal worship venues is also apparent in the fact that very often local participants, not denominational headquarters, decide for themselves on the venues for their worship. In remote areas of Vietnam, the pentecostal gathering itself and the physical place of pentecostal worship function together as a "built environment" (to use the language of British public theologian Timothy Gorringe), a human-made space that supports human recreation and directs human imagination in a particular manner by virtue of gathering at a given place.[36]

While the early C&MA missionaries introduced the belief *Jesus is Lord* as the first tenet in the Full Gospel pattern, this confession was to be understood chiefly in personal, spiritual, salvific terms, with a hint as well of a social dimension, namely, that Vietnamese society would improve if more people became evangelical Christians.[37] In pentecostalism's development within contemporary Vietnamese evangelicalism, the confession *Jesus is Lord* and the practice of *worship* have carried the additional political implication of subverting claims of the State to rule in ways that have negative impacts on the lives of underprivileged pentecostal evangelicals. Their confession and *worship* have done so by nurturing imagination, encouraging practical problem-solving,

35 On *places* as redeemable and anticipating the kingdom of God, see also Amos Yong, *In the Days of Caesar*, 331.

36 Timothy Gorringe, *A Theology of the Built Environment: Justice, Empowerment, Redemption* (Cambridge: Cambridge University Press, 2002). On the practice of worship in the open air as creating a public doxological space for an ethnic community, see the case study of Sarita D. Gallagher, "Worship among the Binandere of Papua New Guinea: An Illustration from Oceania," in *Scripting Pentecost: A Study of Pentecostal Worship, and Liturgy*, ed. Mark J. Cartledge and Aaron J. Swoboda (Burlington, VT: Ashgate, 2016), 200–14.

37 See "Soi tấm gương sáng" ["Following a Good Model"], *Thánh Kinh Báo* [*Bible Magazine*], no. 1 (January 1931): 1–2; "Gieo gì gặt nấy" ["Reap What You Sow"], *Thánh Kinh Báo* [*Bible Magazine*], no. 2 (February 1931): 1–2; "Kinh Thánh với xã hội" ["The Bible and the Society"], *Thánh Kinh Báo* [*Bible Magazine*], no. 3 (March 1931): 1–2.

renewing strength, and anchoring hope, accompanied by an expectation of divine help in the context of oppression, marginalization, and abuse.

5.3 Receiving Justice

In addition to *tongues-speaking* and *worship*, *prayer* is another prominent practice of Vietnamese pentecostal evangelicals. Pentecostal *prayer* has a pragmatic undertone in its focus on pleading for *divine intervention* for the healing of body and mind, deliverance from demonic oppression and evil influences, and the blessings of prosperity and well-being. Belief in the reality of the demonic realm and its evil influences in people's lives is not a new development among Vietnamese pentecostal evangelicals; pioneer C&MA missionaries to Vietnam as well as early native converts also practiced prayer for divine healing and exorcism in the early twentieth century.[38] While *tongues-speaking* was a defining practice of pentecostalism in the initial days of the movement in Vietnam, the practice has become less prominent among today's Vietnamese pentecostals, while *prayer* for *divine intervention* in the form of miraculous healing, deliverance, and blessings has become more central.

For Vietnamese pentecostal evangelicals, *prayer for deliverance* seeks *divine intervention* when believers face difficult issues. Such issues include but are not limited to: (1) physical, psychological, and spiritual problems that feed one another and cause sickness, trauma, stress, addiction, nightmares, mental illness, abnormal behaviors, etc.; (2) destruction of material goods and dispossession through such developments as worsening business, waning finances, damaging of crops, loss of livestock, usurpation of land, etc.; (3) social or political challenges, such as problems in relationships with governmental officials and people in one's social network—challenges ranging from successfully obtaining a passport and visa to travel abroad (often viewed by others as trivial) to receiving favors from those thought to hold executive power over situations affecting a believer's life; (4) physical, spiritual, and material challenges faced by one's family, clan, local congregation, or local community; and (5) consequences of environmental actualities, such as storms and floods, the soil fertility of the land, or water scarcity.[39]

38 For further information, see Phạm Văn Năm, ed., *Phép lạ rừng xanh* [*Miracles in the Jungle*] (Anaheim, CA: The Vietnamese District of the C&MA, 1998), and Gordon H. Smith (Mrs.), *Gongs in the Night: Reaching the Tribes of French Indo-China* (Grand Rapids: Zondervan, 1943).

39 For pentecostal ecological theology, see Aaron J. Swoboda, *Tongues and Trees: Toward a Pentecostal Ecological Theology* (Blandford Forum, UK: Deo, 2014).

Prayer for deliverance, because of its focus on *divine intervention* to make life better for the faithful, is subject to criticism on the charge of exceptionalism—the charge that pentecostal evangelicals consider themselves above all natural and social laws and deserving of special treatment by virtue of their being children of God. Revisiting the social context of Vietnamese pentecostal evangelicals, however, adds the insight that *prayer for deliverance* is often concerned for the overall well-being of a person or group when that state of well-being is threatened. Here *prayer for deliverance* often arises in the context of severely limited access to public assistance in the face of life-threatening problems. *Prayer for deliverance* is also popular among those having limited social and political capital. For example, prayers that might be regarded as trivial, such as petitioning God for favors from people in positions of power or influence, or asking that social transactions or the processing of paperwork may go smoothly, are important socially and psychologically, for grassroots pentecostal evangelicals often have less experience in dealing with political structures and are more easily intimidated and cast aside by local authorities.

Considering the above observations, *prayer for divine deliverance* exemplifies *justice* in an extraordinary manner: *divine intervention* provides for pentecostal evangelicals in their areas of need where the societal structures already in place fail to provide justly. Actual *prayers for divine deliverance* voiced by grassroots groups and individuals contain a plethora of concrete examples illustrating how these people feel they have been treated unjustly as they go about their daily business. The content of *prayers for divine deliverance* thus substantively details how, in grassroots thought, the serving of *justice* is viewed. This detailing at the grassroots level effectively deconstructs the equivocation of *justice* in the state-party's grandiloquent claims that Vietnamese society is well on the way toward being a just and democratic civilization. Concurrently, grassroots *prayer for divine deliverance* also embodies the rejection of evangelical theology's excessive rhetoric. For example, the theological argument that "the justice of God is also God's love" and, "if love spreads throughout humankind, it becomes justice"[40]—this argument may face criticism as creating confusion concerning what *justice* really is.

As a religious practice, *prayer for divine deliverance* is a set course for navigating between the material and the spiritual. In this navigation, material, social, and physical problems are attributed to a demonic spiritual legion led by a personified Satan. *Prayer for divine deliverance* thus joins in a spiritual war between a demonic force and an angelic, heavenly force. Belief in the existence

40 K. H. Ting, *God is Love*, new edition (Colorado Springs: David C. Cook, 2004), 317.

of demonic beings is supported both by biblical stories of Jesus' performance of exorcisms and by a Vietnamese folk culture that acknowledges an active, non-material world. The pentecostal evangelical view of *prayer for divine deliverance* as spiritual warfare against Satan has political implications: it unites pentecostals in a united front against a common spiritual enemy, thus potentially reducing disharmony in inter-church relationships; and it provides a language for speaking in spiritual terms about the pentecostal evangelical struggle for *justice*, thus avoiding the perception of pentecostals as confrontational toward earthly powers.[41]

Prayer for divine deliverance struggles with the issue of *theodicy*. The context of poverty, persecution, and oppression adds emphasis on the understanding that suffering is one way to join Jesus, the early apostles, and the early believers in the suffering of the cross.[42] *Prayer for divine deliverance* honestly acknowledges that suffering is inevitable, but also undesirable. Human prayer can result in *divine intervention*, thus suggesting some degree of openness on God's part—that God changes natural, social, and personal events in response to the prayers of the faithful.[43] Among Vietnamese pentecostal evangelicals, the fact that many prayers are not answered (that is, fulfilled) results in a number of creative explanations: God has answered in a way that people have not yet understood; God has not answered because the prayers are living in sin; the prayers articulated are not in line with God's will; and so forth. Although Vietnamese pentecostal evangelicals have not developed an adequately cogent, generally agreed-on argument regarding *theodicy*,[44] *prayer for divine deliverance* still

41 A similar argument can be found in Martin Lindhardt, "Why the Devil Is Satan so Important in Chilean Pentecostalism? Power, Resistance and Pentecostal Micro-Politics," in *Pentecostal Power: Expressions, Impact and Faith of Latin American Pentecostalism*, ed. Calvin L. Smith (Leiden: Brill, 2010), 227–48.

42 Thus the popular "Cross Theology" among the contemporary house churches in mainland China.

43 For an evangelical argument on the openness of God, see Clark H. Pinnock et al., *The Openness of God: A Biblical Challenge to the Traditional Understanding of God* (Downers Grove, IL: IVP Academic, 1994).

44 For an attempt to resist being stigmatized by unanswered prayers that points toward happiness and well-being as the integrating center of thought and toward alternative thinking categories for healing and deliverance, see Shane Clifton, "The Dark Side of Prayer for Healing: Toward a Theology of Well-Being," *Pneuma: The Journal of the Society for Pentecostal Studies* 36, no. 2 (2014): 204–25. See also Yong-gi Cho, *Suffering—Why Me?* (South Plainfield, NJ: Bridge, 1986); and Steven M. Fettke and Michael L. Dusing, "A Practical Pentecostal Theodicy? A Proposal," *Pneuma: The Journal of the Society for Pentecostal Studies* 38, no. 1–2 (2016): 160–79.

serves them as a valuable practice for enhancing life at the grassroots level, especially in cases when both natural and social resources are scarce.

Within the Full Gospel framework, belief that *Jesus is Coming King* can offer the understanding that Jesus will administer *justice* for the faithful through *divine deliverance*. *Jesus is Coming King* expects that Jesus will return to earth to rule as the one and only victorious king. The reign of Jesus, or more precisely, the reign of God through Jesus, benefits the created world because it entails peace and justice. As an eschatological concept, the belief that *Jesus is Coming King* includes an "already/not yet" tension. On the one hand, the actual coming of Jesus is thought of as a future event. On the other hand, the reign of God through Jesus is thought of as having already manifested itself whenever peace and justice are established in *the world*, thus providing glimpses into a future, full reign of God. The relationship between peace and justice is well summarized by Pope Paul VI in the words, *if you want peace, work for justice*.[45] Likewise for a peaceful reign, one important political dimension of the pentecostal evangelical belief that *Jesus is Coming King* is its connection with *justice*.

Functioning at the margins of society, and with less access to structural support, pentecostal evangelicals are attracted to the manifestation of care for humanity through *divine deliverance* administered by an all-powerful king. This deliverance is understood as a miraculous intervention of healing and restoration in the context of poverty, oppression, and marginalization.[46] Here the focus on care for the poorest, the most marginalized, and the most troubled by means of *divine deliverance* expresses grassroots pentecostal evangelicals' view that *justice is fulfilled through the experience of divine deliverance*.[47]

The idea that *justice is deliverance* receives textual support from reading the ministry of Jesus as one of caring for the poor and enacting the miraculous rescue of individuals according to their particular need. The ministry of Jesus is an example of the administration of *justice* from the standpoint that *justice* is

45 Pope Paul VI, "Message of His Holiness Pope Paul VI for the Celebration of the Day of Peace," January 1, 1972, accessed March 1, 2017, http://w2.vatican.va/content/paul-vi/en/messages/peace/documents/hf_p-vi_mes_19711208_v-world-day-for-peace.html.

46 On healing in particular as historically understood as a soteriological category, see also Kimberly Ervin Alexander, *Pentecostal Healing: Models in Theology and Practice* (Dorset, UK: Deo, 2006).

47 See also Grace Ji-Sun Kim, *Colonialism, Han, and the Transformative Spirit* (New York: Palgrave Macmillan, 2013). For a pentecostal theological argument on disposition toward the most troubled, such as drug addicts and prisoners, see Samuel Solivan, *Spirit, Pathos and Liberation: Toward an Hispanic Pentecostal Theology* (Sheffield, UK: Sheffield Academic Press, 1998); Robert Beckford, *God of the Rahtid: Redeeming Rage* (London: Darton, Longman & Todd, 2011).

made known in God's gracious action of delivering people. This understanding runs contrary to that which sees justice as retribution, the giving of due results according to one's action. Luke 4:18–19, which quotes Isaiah 61, informs the understanding of *justice is deliverance* in terms of caring for the poor, the captive, the blind, and the oppressed:

> The Spirit of the Lord is upon me, because he has anointed me to bring good news to the poor. He has sent me to proclaim release to the captives and recovery of sight to the blind, to let the oppressed go free, to proclaim the year of the Lord's favor. (NRSV)

The understanding of *justice* as an important aspect of Jesus' ministry can also be supported by recognizing that the term often rendered as *righteousness* in the New Testament can be better translated as *justice*.[48] *Righteousness*, as in "blessed are those who hunger and thirst for righteousness, for they will be filled" (Matthew 5:6, NRSV), is often thought of in relation to a person's performance of righteous deeds—in other words, as God's endowment of righteousness and blessing upon that person. At the semiotic level, however, *righteousness* also conveys the idea of rescuing and releasing the oppressed and powerless and restoring them to the community; thus *justice* is an acceptable alternative rendering of the term. Matthew 5:6, therefore, can be reread as, "blessed are those who hunger and thirst for a justice that delivers and restores to covenantal community, for God is a God who brings such justice."[49] Accordingly, *justice* made known through *divine deliverance* can be seen as a central theme in the teaching and work of Jesus.[50]

48 Glen Stassen and David P. Gushee, *Kingdom Ethics: Following Jesus in Contemporary Context* (Downers Grove, IL: IVP Academic, 2003), 41–42.

49 Ibid., 43. Note that the argument of Stassen and Gushee has the potential to contribute toward a Yoderian understanding of *justice* according to Jesus by offering a response to Jeffrey Stout's critique that Yoder's ethics is inadequate because it lacks a theory of justice. (See Jeffrey Stout, "The Spirit of Democracy and the Rhetoric of Excess," *Journal of Religious Ethics* 35, no. 1 [March 2007]: 3–21.) It is also noteworthy that Yoder thought *justice* was a synonym for *vengeance*, thus making justice incompatible with his commitment to nonviolence. On Yoder's thinking about *justice*, see his *The Politics of Jesus: Vicit Agnus Noster*, 2nd ed. (1972. Grand Rapids: Eerdmans, 1994), 210, where he calls for renouncing "participation in the interplay of egoisms which this world calls 'vengeance' or 'justice.' " Stassen and Gushee's thesis receives little scholarly attention, perhaps partly because the thesis is published as part of a textbook, and partly because others may find that its emphasis on the miraculous minimizes its contribution to an academic, philosophical discussion of *justice*.

50 Stassen and Gushee, *Kingdom Ethics*, 349.

Revisiting several passages in the Book of Isaiah in the light of accounts about the ministry of Jesus, Baptist theological ethicists Glen Stassen and David P. Gushee summarize *justice* as having four dimensions:

> (1) delivering of the poor and powerless from the injustice that they regularly experience; (2) lifting the foot of domineering power off the neck of the dominated and oppressed; (3) stopping the violence and establishing peace; and (4) restoring the outcasts, the excluded, the Gentiles, the exiles and the refugees to community.

This summary provides a convenient biblical framework for facilitating thinking about *justice* from the perspective of the underprivileged.[51]

The pentecostal perspective contributes in two ways to the discourse of *justice is deliverance* as it is developed by Stassen and Gushee. First, the pentecostal perspective is attentive to the ministry of the Spirit, thus adding a pneumatological dimension to the discourse, which otherwise runs predominantly in "Jesus" terms (though Stassen and Gushee do mention that Jesus works in the power of the Spirit).[52] Pentecostal scholarship, in its mining of Luke-Acts, supports the discourse of *justice is deliverance* further by providing textual exposition that substantiates the continuity of Jesus' ministry with that of the Spirit, thus also directing the discussion toward a fuller Trinitarian framework.[53] Second, and perhaps more significantly, pentecostals contribute to the debate by their actual, regular practice of *prayer for deliverance*.

The concept of *justice* as *deliverance* also helps to inform the Vietnamese scholarly evangelical understanding of *justice* as *love*. This understanding maintains that *love* is a force which propels Vietnamese evangelicals to join in a divine mission of caring for the whole world—caring that is translated into concrete actions as evangelism and social relief work.[54] The desire for specific acts of deliverance in moments of real need shapes their thinking about *love* in a particular direction, namely, that *grassroots pentecostal evangelicals*

51 Ibid.

52 Ibid., 30, 34.

53 See Martin William Mittelstadt, *Reading Luke-Acts in the Pentecostal Tradition* (Cleveland, TN: CPT Press, 2010), section "Social Justice/Ethics," 115–21; and the discussion on God's special love for the poor and marginalized in the work of Peruvian pentecostal scholar Darío López Rodriguez, *The Liberating Mission of Jesus: The Message of the Gospel of Luke*, trans. Stefanie E. Israel and Richard E. Waldrop (Eugene, OR: Wipf & Stock, 2012), 125–38.

54 Tu Truong, "Mệnh Trời: Toward a Vietnamese Theology of Mission" (Ph.D. diss., Graduate Theological Union, 2009), 131–40. Also Ting, *God is Love*, 317.

experience divine love when justice is manifested through concrete deliverance.[55] In short, for pentecostal evangelicals, *love is justice*. Here the scholarly proposal that *justice is love* and the grassroots understanding that *love is justice* provide an enhanced dialogical framework to further the Vietnamese evangelical social discourse.[56]

One anticipated challenge is that the pentecostal evangelical understanding of *justice* in terms of *divine deliverance* appears to lack a component of structural criticism. This lack reflects the pentecostal evangelical perspective's focus on grassroots issues, with (relatively) limited interest in structural change. The anticipated challenge and apparent lack, however, are lessened by viewing pentecostal evangelical practices as *tactics*. French Jesuit cultural critic (and psychoanalyst) Michel de Certeau suggests that the grassroots powerless function at the *tactical* level, while powerful institutional bodies operate at the *strategic* level.[57] As such, pentecostal evangelical practices and even thinking are defensive, limited, and governed by strategies established by the powerful—strategies of which pentecostal evangelicals may not be fully aware. For example, *prayer for divine deliverance* is a tactical, unconscious, pentecostal evangelical response to the national strategies and policies created by the state-party—strategies and policies that may enhance the privileges of those in power more than benefit the powerless. Criticism, therefore, that pentecostal evangelical beliefs and practices lack a structural dimension should consider their tactical nature. Here the argument of renowned political theorist James C. Scott is also worth mentioning: to effect change in a context of power asymmetry, it is the everyday, tactical action of the powerless that may "often be the most significant and the most effective over the long run."[58]

55 On healing practices as a form of benevolent action, see Mark J. Cartledge, "Pentecostal Healing as an Expression of Godly Love: An Empirical Study," *Mental Health, Religion & Culture* 16, no. 5 (2013): 501–22.

56 For an evangelical exposition of *love* and *justice*, see Bruce Ellis Benson, Malinda Elizabeth Berry, and Peter Goodwin Heltzel, "The Just and Peaceable Kingdom," in *Prophetic Evangelicals: Envisioning a Just and Peaceable Kingdom*, ed. Bruce Ellis Benson et al. (Grand Rapids: Eerdmans, 2012), 8–30, esp. 20–24. For a pentecostal theological exposition of *love*, see Amos Yong, *Spirit of Love: A Trinitarian Theology of Grace* (Waco, TX: Baylor University Press, 2012).

57 Michel de Certeau, *The Practice of Everyday Life*, trans. Steven F. Rendall (Berkeley: University of California Press, 1984), xviii–xx.

58 James C. Scott, *Weapons of the Weak: Everyday Forms of Peasant Resistance* (New Haven: Yale University Press, 1985), xvi. For a recent use of the theoretical work of Scott to study the rebellious acts of Vietnamese peasants after Vietnam's World Trade Organization accession, see Pamela Mcelwee, "From the Moral Economy to the World Economy: Revisiting Vietnamese Peasants in a Globalizing Era," *Journal of Vietnamese Studies* 2, no. 2 (August 1, 2007): 57–107. For an application of Scott's theory to the study

While, according to Scott, the peasant practices of everyday resistance consist in actions such as "foot-dragging, dissimulation, desertion, false compliance, pilfering, feigned ignorance, slander, arson, sabotage, and so on,"[59] the pentecostal practices of everyday resistance, such as religious *worship*, *prayer for divine deliverance*, and *tongues-speaking*, have greater potential for cultivating human dignity. The belief that *Jesus is Coming King*, with its connotation of ushering *justice* through *divine deliverance*, thus offers a logic for interpreting the pentecostal evangelical practice of *prayer for divine deliverance* as exemplifying a grassroots, tactical perspective on *justice* and for criticizing the political and theological ambivalence of existing discourses on *justice*.

5.4 Becoming Privileged

In addition to the practice of *prayer for divine deliverance*, *prayer for divine blessings* enjoys prominent status among Vietnamese pentecostal evangelicals today. Since most Vietnamese pentecostal evangelicals come from an underprivileged background, the idea of becoming privileged though *divine blessing* carries weight. While rooted in the Full Gospel framework's tenet that *Jesus is Healer* and that God, out of compassion, will privilege the faithful with healing from physical disease and sickness, the idea of *healing* as a *divine blessing* is expanded by adopting of the *threefold blessings* teachings of South Korean Assemblies of God minister David (formerly Paul) Cho Yong-gi.[60] These *threefold blessings* include salvation of the soul, healing for the body, and prosperity in all aspects of life—an idea derived from 3 John 1:2, which reads, "Beloved, I wish above all things that thou mayest prosper and be in health, even as thy soul prospereth" (KJV).

In this pentecostal evangelical understanding, *divine blessing* is thought of in ever-encompassing terms covering all aspects of life. Here salvation of the soul and healing of the body are the initial steps that enable a believer to begin the journey of experiencing holistic well-being through *divine blessings*.[61]

---

of Vietnamese peasants in North Vietnam from the 1950s to the 1980s, see Benedict J. Kerkvliet, *The Power of Everyday Politics: How Vietnamese Peasants Transformed National Policy* (Ithaca, NY: Cornell University Press, 2005).

59 James C. Scott, *Weapons of the Weak*, xvi.

60 See Cho Yong-gi, *Salvation, Health & Prosperity: Our Threefold Blessings in Christ* (Altamonte Springs, FL: Creation House, 1987).

61 For a recent use of *divine blessings* as a category for the analysis of (North American) *prosperity teaching*, see Kate Bowler, *Blessed: A History of the American Prosperity Gospel* (New York: Oxford University Press, 2013). For an example of the use of the language of *blessings* in pentecostalism, see Wen Reagan, "Blessed to Be a Blessing: The Prosperity

The onset of this journey focuses on physical, mental, psychological, spiritual, and material well-being.[62] But well-being can also be thought of in broader terms: the flourishing of the whole ecosystem surrounding a believer, for example, or a well-arranged built environment that supports overall human flourishing—an idea with overtones of positive psychology.[63] Here the popular *prosperity teaching* is not necessarily a promotion of overabundance, hoarding, and consumerism, but rather a mechanism for coping with poverty, sickness, and hopelessness.[64]

The ideas of *divine blessing* and *divine deliverance* are interrelated. *Divine deliverance* seeks miraculous intervention in emergency situations in response to the immediate need of the poor and oppressed, including healing from sickness. After *divine deliverance* occurs, *divine blessing* responds to pentecostal evangelicals' desire for and right to long-term well-being, happiness, and prosperity. While *divine deliverance* reveals divine *love* through *justice*, *divine blessing* reveals divine *grace* through *prosperity*, according to the belief that God grants the faithful health, wealth, and upward social mobility. It can thus be said that *divine deliverance* and *divine blessing* are intrinsically interconnected, as they are part and parcel of a larger phenomenon of *divine intervention* in the daily life of pentecostal evangelicals.

Although empirical testing and scientific investigation in general offer limited insights for understanding the mechanisms of receiving *divine healing* and *divine deliverance*, on the one hand, and the mechanisms of realizing *human*

Gospel of Worship Music Superstar Israel Houghton," in *The Spirit of Praise: Music and Worship in Global Pentecostal-Charismatic Christianity*, ed. Monique M. Ingalls and Amos Yong (University Park, PA: The Pennsylvania State University Press), 215–29.

62 Psychological healing has a complex social dimension, because in many cases it requires forgiveness and reconciliation after an experience of social injustice and wrongful treatment. On the one hand, there is a need to emphasize forgiveness so that victims of past wrongs can gain psychological healing. On the other hand, wrongdoers can also ask for forgiveness and reconciliation in order to avoid making proper restitution and to protect the social injustice that continues to benefit them.

63 See Martin E. P. Seligman, *Flourish: A Visionary New Understanding of Happiness and Well-being* (New York: Free Press, 2011). For a pentecostal theological discussion of *prosperity teaching* that leads to healing of the ecosystem, see Aaron J. Swoboda, "Posterity or Prosperity? Critiquing and Refiguring Prosperity Theologies in an Ecological Age," *Pneuma: The Journal of the Society for Pentecostal Studies* 37, no. 3 (January 1, 2015): 394–411. Providing a criticism of (Western) consumerism, Swoboda looks at *prosperity teaching* and the belief in abundance as harmful to the ecosystem. This chapter, in contrast, reviews the (Global South) grassroots' use of *prosperity teaching* in bringing about the restoration and improvement of human and natural life.

64 See also Paul Alexander, *Signs and Wonders: Why Pentecostalism is the World's Fastest-Growing Faith* (San Francisco: Jossey-Bass, 2009), 63–67.

prosperity, *well-being*, and *flourishing*, on the other hand, empirical testing is helpful, and it should be encouraged for investigating the connection of pentecostal practices and the general betterment of pentecostals' lives.[65] If such an association is demonstrated to exist and have positive effects, *divine healing* may well constitute an alternative "medicine" in a world that suffers from inadequate medical care, and *prosperity teaching* may, for better or worse, become a common religious response to a world rife with distributive injustice.[66]

Similarly to *prayer for divine deliverance*, *prayer for divine blessings* constitutes a *tactical*, everyday practice of the powerless that focuses on their personal, social, and environmental well-being; the practice, therefore, should not be subjected to criticism for lacking a structural concern. The *tactical* use of *prayer for divine blessings* is a grassroots response to the state-party's *strategic* use of national development to generate economic growth, for its use inadvertently creates inequality. While the strategies of the powerful appear to be comprehensive and inclusive, the involvement of interest groups, rent-seekers, and crony capitalists often leave people at the grassroots level with the short end of the stick; hence grassroots pentecostal evangelicals' attraction to *divine blessings* and their belief in *prosperity teaching*, while the powerful hoard wealth by manipulating for their own gain the implementation of *national development*.

On the downside, the ideas of *prosperity* and *blessing* run the risk of being caught up in materialism and following the direction of society by endorsing hedonism. Thus it is important to pair *divine blessing* and *human fasting*. While *divine blessing* represents a "theology of glory" in its promotion of a "better life," *human fasting* invokes a "theology of the cross" through one's experiencing the pain of hunger, thus reminding pentecostal evangelicals of the continuing existence of suffering, the death of Jesus, and the groaning of the Spirit for a creation that has not yet reached its full potential to flourish. In doing so, *human fasting* complements *divine blessing* by serving as a critical practice for resisting the co-opting of pentecostal evangelicals into a problematic built structure that may lead them to forget those who are left behind in the relentless social pursuit of economic development. *Human fasting* is thus viewed as a commitment not to turn a blind eye to the continued existence of surrounding suffering and injustice.

65 So suggests Candy Gunther Brown in *Testing Prayer: Science and Healing* (Cambridge, MA: Harvard University Press, 2012), 276–78.

66 See, for example, the development of prosperity teaching in Buddhism, traced in Rachelle M. Scott's *Nirvana for Sale?: Buddhism, Wealth, and the Dhammakaya Temple in Contemporary Thailand* (New York: State University of New York Press, 2009).

Contemporary pentecostal theology argues that *fasting* (alongside worship) is one of the optimal locations for spiritual formation.[67] Here *fasting* functions as a spiritual practice to reorient one's desires away from worldly things and toward godly things. In *The City of God*, Augustine suggests that the *Eucharist* orients human desires by way of a narrative of Christ: the *Eucharist* invites the faithful to participate in a pilgrimage toward the heavenly city of God, while leaving the city of humanity behind.[68] Notably, though several attempts have been made to use the *Eucharist* as an integrating center for pentecostal theology—attempts that focus on the practice's prominent status in the Christian tradition and its being conducive to Christian formation—the *Eucharist* is not widely used among grassroots Vietnamese pentecostal evangelicals to enhance their sensibilities toward the divine.[69] Although no Vietnamese pentecostal evangelicals would deny that the *Eucharist* represents a mystical dimension of faith, their Eucharistic performance is minimalistic, and the practice is viewed mainly as a communal act to "remember Jesus." Among grassroots Vietnamese pentecostal evangelicals, it is *fasting* that has the effect of reorienting human desires; it does so by way of inviting believers to deny themselves of a bodily craving in pursuit of godly things.

The spiritual-formation value of *fasting* also lies in the fact that it allows pain to be felt. In pentecostal spirituality, such pain includes two aspects: a reminder of how the current configuration of life has caused people's experience of pain, and travail, through which a believer is thought to share pain with the Spirit of God in the act of conceiving and bringing into existence new natural, cultural, and supernatural conditions for life; therefore, *fasting* is seen as both otherworldly and this-worldly. In giving up the consumption of food, a human kenotic act is performed—one that prepares new ground on which the natural and the supernatural may come together, that thus directs the pentecostal imagination concerning how life can be better configured, and which

67 On *fasting* as an integrating center for pentecostal theology, see Lee Roy Martin, *Fasting: A Centre for Pentecostal Theology* (Cleveland, TN: CPT Press, 2014), 150–60. Also see the discussion on *fasting* as a pentecostal spiritual practice in Daniel E. Albrecht and Evan B. Howard, "Pentecostal Spirituality," in *The Cambridge Companion to Pentecostalism*, ed. Cecil Robeck Jr. and Amos Yong (New York: Cambridge University Press, 2014), 235–53.

68 Augustine, *City of God* 19.24–26. See also James K. A. Smith, *Desiring the Kingdom: Worship, Worldview, and Cultural Formation* (Grand Rapids: Baker Academic, 2009), 133–15; and William T. Cavanaugh, *Being Consumed: Economics and Christian Desire* (Grand Rapids: Eerdmans, 2008), 1–2.

69 For example, Chris E. Green, *Toward a Pentecostal Theology of the Lord's Supper: Foretasting the Kingdom* (Cleveland, TN: CPT Press, 2012); also Simon Chan, *Pentecostal Ecclesiology: An Essay on the Development of Doctrine* (Blandford Forum, UK: Deo, 2010).

promotes the possibility that this imagined better life can indeed be realized through the power of the Spirit.[70]

At the grassroots level, the spiritual dimension of pentecostals' practice of *fasting* is complemented by a pragmatic dimension in that *fasting* embodies a human desire to expedite divine action. Here *fasting* is thought of as adding effectiveness to *prayer for divine deliverance* and *prayer for divine blessings*.[71] The account of Jesus' telling his disciples that "this type" of demon can only be cast out by *prayer* and *fasting* (Matthew 17:21) supports the grassroots pentecostal understanding of the importance of *fasting* for experiencing the supernatural in one's natural life.

The most explicit social dimension of *fasting* among Vietnamese pentecostal evangelicals is informed by 2 Chronicles 7:14 (NRSV), which reads, "If my people who are called by my name humble themselves, pray, seek my face, and turn from their wicked ways, then I will hear from heaven, and will forgive their sin and heal their land." This verse appears very frequently on the calendars printed by Vietnamese evangelicals and so is often displayed in the living rooms of their houses. Here *fasting* is believed to be the action that best shows humility and contrition, in acknowledgment of which God will forgive and will heal the land of Vietnam; thus life in general will become better for all.[72] Pentecostal evangelicals' voluntary adoption of *fasting*, therefore, implies their preexisting dissatisfaction with their life-experience in contemporary Vietnam and their dissatisfaction with the social conditions of Vietnam overall. As such, their *fasting* constitutes a social critique, though the language of *fasting* is thoroughly spiritual: *fasting* is considered a participation in spiritual warfare against spiritual strongholds that control the land and cause suffering, thus *fasting* prepares the way for a *divine intervention* that changes history and results in the betterment of life for all.[73] Nevertheless, pentecostal *fasting* does not necessarily constitute a practice of nonviolent political resistance seeking structural change,

---

70 On *fasting* as an act of emptying the self to make room for the gifts of God, see Joyce Ann Zimmerman, "Fasting as Feasting," *Liturgical Ministry* 19, no. 2 (2010): 72–77.

71 Derek Prince, *Fasting* (1986. New Kensington, PA: Whitaker House, 1993), 6–8. See also, from an Orthodox Christian perspective, Archimandrite Akakios, *Fasting in the Orthodox Church: Its Theological, Pastoral, and Social Implications*, 2nd ed. (Etna, CA: Center for Traditionalist Orthodox Studies, 1996), 93–94.

72 For an argument of *fasting* as a "grievous sacred moment," see Scot McKnight, *Fasting*, The Ancient Practices Series (Nashville: Thomas Nelson, 2009), 2. On *fasting* as bodily participation in lament, see David Lambert, "Fasting as a Penitential Rite: A Biblical Phenomenon?" *Harvard Theological Review* 96, no. 4 (October 2003): 477–512.

73 For a pentecostal argument on this point, see Derek Prince, *Shaping History through Prayer and Fasting* (1973. New Kensington, PA: Whitaker House, 2008).

as in the *fasting* of Mahatma Gandhi to protest caste separation in India. In a more generous interpretation, pentecostal *fasting* can be seen as a prophetic act of abstinence to express solidarity with those left behind economically and as an expression of goodwill seeking *blessings* and *prosperity* for all.

5.5 Conclusion

In retrospect, the pentecostal movement adds concern for the underprivileged at the top of Vietnamese evangelicalism's social agenda and constitutes a particular grassroots approach that seeks to enhance the life of the underprivileged in the face of the challenges of modernity in a communist society. A closer look at various pentecostal beliefs and practices has suggested they have a political dimension, demonstrated in the promotion of thinking, practices, and behaviors that seek to address several challenges in contemporary Vietnam. Among these challenges are the existing powers' ultimate claims to rule, the ambivalence of social justice, the cultural pressure for ideological hegemony, and the national pursuit of development that becomes an endorsement of hedonism. In this investigation, the pentecostal fourfold Full Gospel pattern is useful in organizing the multifaceted pentecostal emphasis on *divine intervention* as follows.

The proclamation that *Jesus is Lord* subverts inappropriate claims to rule, while the practice of *worship* promotes subversion of the *status quo* and is conducive to imagining a new life. The declaration that *Jesus is Coming King* seeks the bringing forth of *justice* as the grassroots pentecostal *prayers for deliverance* respond to the justice-equivocating rhetoric of the powers that be. The tenet that *Jesus is Spirit Baptizer* enables the practice of *tongues-speaking*, which exemplifies a plurivocality that challenges the use of univocality to establish cultural hegemony in a given society. The proposition that *Jesus is Healer* initiates belief in *divine blessings*—divine compensation for the *have-nots* in the midst of inequality—while the practice of *human fasting* expresses goodwill seeking the healing and prosperity of all.

When beliefs and practices are both considered, the Full Gospel framework offers a convenient structure for thinking that reciprocates the daily practices of pentecostal evangelicals and thus becomes helpful in facilitating an elaboration of how pentecostal spirituality has offered meaning to believers at the grassroots level.[74] For Vietnamese evangelicals, the Full Gospel framework also

74 On the potential of the Full Gospel's symbolism for developing pentecostal theology, see Veli-Matti Kärkkäinen, "David's Sling: The Promise and Problem of Pentecostal Theology

provides a useful global link between Vietnamese evangelicals and the wider trans-Pacific, evangelical-pentecostal body that has historically affiliated with this framework, mostly in its North American, South China, and South Korean constituencies.[75]

On further consideration, *subversion* and *imagination* appear to be what pentecostal beliefs and practices call for in contemporary Vietnamese society. The development of pentecostalism in Vietnam manifests the movement's holding as important the *subversion* of the political *status quo*, the rhetoric of ambivalent justice, cultural hegemony, and reckless economic pursuit. At the same time, this pentecostalism fosters the *imagination* of new configurations of power: a new, inclusive, plurivocal reality, and a new condition for life—a life characterized by *human prosperity* brought about through *divine deliverance* and *divine blessings*. Notably, the pentecostal imagination described here has not emerged in a vacuum; it has been preconditioned by the context of late-communist Vietnam's creating inequality while seeking economic growth, thus shaping the thinking of Vietnamese pentecostal evangelicals toward picturing the "good life" in terms of *prosperity* and *divine blessings*.

The emergence of *subversion* and *imagination* as political implications of the pentecostal movement among Vietnamese evangelicals is not a surprise. After all, *subversion* and *imagination* are the major themes in evangelical *apocalyptic* thinking about *the world*, specifically, its view that the undesirable current world must be subverted in anticipation of the unveiling of a new world—a new world beginning in the imagination of believers. Because *the world* functions as an overarching metaphysical category to refer to the overall reality in which evangelicals are engaging, the notions of *subversion* and *imagination* leave their imprints on evangelicals' thinking about other aspects of life, as becomes evident in several beliefs and practices at the grassroots level.[76]

Today: A Response to D. Lyle Dabney," *Pneuma: The Journal of the Society for Pentecostal Studies* 23, no. 1 (2001): 147–52; also Kenneth J. Archer, "The Fivefold Gospel and the Mission of the Church: Ecclesiastical Implications and Opportunities," in *Toward a Pentecostal Ecclesiology: The Church and the Fivefold Gospel*, ed. John Christopher Thomas (Cleveland, TN: CPT Press, 2010), 7–46. On the challenge of relating the symbolism of the Full Gospel to the symbolism of the Trinity, see Veli-Matti Kärkkäinen in the concluding remark of *Toward a Pentecostal Ecclesiology: The Church and the Fivefold Gospel*, ed. John Christopher Thomas, 261–71.

75 For the use of the Full Gospel framework as a common denominator between North American and East Asian evangelicalism, see Donald W. Dayton, "The Fourfold Gospel: Key to Trans-Pacific Continuities," in *From the Margins: A Celebration of the Theological Work of Donald W. Dayton*, ed. Christian T. Collins Winn (Eugene, OR: Pickwick, 2007), 359–66.

76 Regarding other pentecostal theologies, for an example of the use of *Spirit Baptism* as an integrative center, see Macchia, *Baptized in the Spirit*; on the use of *fasting*, see Martin,

The above beliefs and practices of grassroots pentecostal evangelicals can be treated as a *repertoire*, a collection of tools and devices that average evangelicals employ to tackle the challenges they face in *the world*.[77] Within the pentecostal *repertoire*, belief and practice are interrelated and mutually enrich one another. As a historical process, belief often shapes practice. But the everyday practice of faith also enriches belief, so that belief and practice are mutually informing. The continued experiences of *divine deliverance* and *divine blessings* in response to praying for them, for example, can influence believers' understanding of salvation and the lordship and kingship of Jesus. In turn, belief in the inclusivity of Spirit Baptism can result in practices and behaviors that promote ecclesial and social inclusivity.

Considering grassroots religious beliefs and practices as a *repertoire* is useful, for it allows for flexibility in a context that considers them notorious for being anything but clear-cut and well-organized.[78] Depending on the ways in which beliefs and practices are used, they both have the potential to effect, or to thwart, human liberation and flourishing. Doctrine has negative effects when turned into ideology—it then produces a people of the lie rather than a people of the truth.[79] Practice becomes problematic when it overemphasizes human agency in facilitating *divine deliverance* and *divine blessings*—it then creates an ecclesial hierarchy and ecclesial privilege based on levels of religious literacy and competency.[80] It remains to be seen whether pentecostal evangelicals, in different historical and global contexts, will adjust the current *repertoire* or drop it all together in favor of another model they may judge more useful.

Fasting, 150–60; on apocalyptic thinking as a motivating force in the rapid growth of pentecostalism, see David Faupel, *The Everlasting Gospel: The Significance of Eschatology in the Development of Pentecostal Thought* (Sheffield, UK: Sheffield Academic Press, 1996).

77 On pentecostalism as "a *repertoire* of religious explorations" and "a *repertoire* of a recognizable spiritual affinities," see David Martin, *Pentecostalism: The World Their Parish*, Religion & Modernity Series (Malden, MA: Blackwell, 2002), 6, 176.

78 On the challenge of correlating and organizing pentecostal beliefs and practices in constructing pentecostal theology, see John Christopher Thomas, ed., *Toward a Pentecostal Ecclesiology: The Church and the Fivefold Gospel.*

79 On lying and group evil, see M. Scott Peck, *People of the Lie: The Hope for Healing Human Evil* (Riverside, NJ: Simon & Schuster, 1983), 212–53.

80 Hence the suggestion that *discernment* is an important practice for keeping the pentecostal tongue in check. On the practice of *discernment*, see Nancy E. Bedford, "Little Moves against Destructiveness: Theology and the Practice of Discernment," in *Practicing Theology: Beliefs and Practices in Christian Life*, ed. Miroslav Volf and Dorothy C. Bass (Grand Rapids: Eerdmans, 2002), 157–81. Also Kathryn Tanner, "Theological Reflection and Christian Practices," in *Practicing Theology*, ed. Miroslav Volf and Dorothy C. Bass, 228–42: 232. On *discernment* (in relation to truth and pneumatological imagination) in developing pentecostal theology, see Amos Yong, *Spirit-Word-Community*, 151–84.

In the light of this observation, the pentecostal emphasis on *divine intervention*, embedded in pentecostal beliefs as well as practices, is not to be romanticized, even when it provides meaning and value to the poor, the powerless, and the outcasts, who feel inundated by *the world*. This emphasis on *divine intervention*, however, can be admired, as long as it struggles uneasily between the periphery and the center: on the one hand, the willingness to stay at the periphery, so to speak, by reaching out to the most troubled and pursuing an examined life via the invocation of faith-claims in problematic situations; on the other hand, the aspiration to claim a place at the center by being determined to pursue human prosperity and upward social mobility against all odds. In theological language, when the pentecostal movement refuses to settle at either the peripheral or at the center but instead continues to struggle "in-between," it represents a movement of the Spirit of God.

Conclusion

Living in today's Vietnam requires a careful analysis of the country's existing socio-political dynamics. The same careful analysis is precisely what is needed in Vietnamese evangelicalism—analysis of the complexity of the issues the tradition is facing in order to develop "an understanding of the times," to use the biblical language of 1 Chronicles 12:32. Under the tides of colonialism, warfare, and revolution, old evangelical adages such as "do not love the world" and "do not interfere in politics" lose most of their original meaning and relevance and offer little coherence with the contemporary Vietnamese evangelical manifesto. Neither does the quick importation of wisdom developed elsewhere help—wisdom such as the promotion of transformational development or the use of love as a guiding principle for the common good, for example—because the limited efforts spent on delineating the swift changes in both Vietnamese evangelicalism and its contemporary Vietnamese context are insufficient to allow a careful evaluation of new proposals.

At this juncture, it is crucial to examine the lives of contemporary Vietnamese evangelicals in at least four experiential dimensions: their *social* experience of marginalization and oppression based on religious and ethnic differences; their *political* experience of co-optation as the State strives to establish social consensus and ensure regime security; their *cultural* experience of stigmatization for "lacking" Vietnamese-ness and of pressure to become acquiescent to the cultural image promoted by the state-party; and their *economic* experience of the negative consequences of economic growth, such as dispossession, degradation of the health of the masses, and increased inequality.

Within this particular *Sitz im Leben*, global and local dynamics have led contemporary Vietnamese evangelical scholars to promote ideas such as *transformation, love, inculturation,* and *development*—ideas that have their own merit, yet have also been put to political use. Along the way in this discussion, grassroots ideas such as *apocalypse, deliverance, faith as a critique of culture,* and *prosperity* have been presented with the intention that they accompany, not contradict, existing ideas for the eliciting of creative tension and for moving the scholarly discussion forward. Here alternative ideas are presented not as neutral resolutions, but as notions rooted in a sensitivity to the overall underprivileged condition of Vietnamese evangelicals and in a research bias that seeks to ally with a grassroots perspective—thus its rather unapologetically selective use of theoretical arguments. As a result, the mode of advancing the

 | DOI:10.1163/9789004383838_008

philosophical argument lies less on the Platonic examination of abstract speculations, and more on the political investigation of thinking that is particular to a local situation. Understandably, such thinking requires multi-directional interaction that fuses the particular memory of the past and the boundless imagination of the future; links the natural world and the worlds beyond nature; and combines global interactions and local retrospections, to name a few. In the attempt to undertake theological reflection in today's Vietnam, this multi-directional interaction must occur in a single process through which the *novum* may emerge—a process representing what the postcolonial biblical scholar R. S. Sugirtharajah has called a "multi-directional swirl of cultural ideas."[1]

Reviewing the evolution of the major guiding social concepts and ideas within Vietnamese evangelicalism has resulted in a number of critical observations regarding Vietnamese evangelical thinking. Three of those observations are worthy of reiteration for advancing the Vietnamese evangelical theological discourse. First, in Vietnamese evangelical thinking it is the concept of *the world*, not *culture*, that is the overarching metaphysical category which refers to reality in its entirety. Modes of engaging *the world*, as expressed in the terms *transformation* and *apocalypse*, therefore serve as parameters that help guide Vietnamese evangelicals in their engagement of Vietnam. Second, the cultural agency of the Vietnamese evangelical tradition manifests more strongly in the intention to employ faith for the purposes of improving culture and promoting modernity for the betterment of life than in the development of cultural forms of the faith. Third, that Vietnamese evangelical thinking emerged first through Vietnam's encounters with Western powers and knowledge during colonial and postcolonial times certainly gives priority to theological inquiry vis-à-vis patterns of thought and practices that have colonial roots and contemporary manifestations.[2] Issues of power dynamics when Vietnamese meet Westerners, when ethnic highlanders meet *Việt* lowlanders, and when communist ideology meets evangelical faith are important for reenvisioning the Vietnamese evangelical manifesto.

The pentecostal emphasis on *divine intervention* is, to a great extent, a grassroots solution to the crisis that Vietnamese evangelicalism is facing in contemporary Vietnam. Embodied in simple beliefs and practices that aim at the

1 R. S. Sugirtharajah, *Postcolonial Reconfigurations: An Alternative Way of Reading the Bible and Doing Theology* (St. Louis: Chalice, 2003), 160.

2 For an exploration in the same direction in Africa, see Martin Lindhardt, ed., *Pentecostalism in Africa: Presence and Impact of Pneumatic Christianity in Postcolonial Societies* (Leiden: Brill, 2014).

betterment of life, the pentecostal movement in Vietnam rejects excessive rhetoric that does not immediately create meaning—excessive rhetoric in both the State's political discourse and evangelicals' theological discourse. Approaching *the world* with an apocalyptic understanding, grassroots pentecostal beliefs and practices promote both the subversion of the *status quo* and the imagination of a way of achieving human flourishing amid social conditions of oppression, marginalization, and abuse.

Yet despite its many positive elements, the pentecostal movement among Vietnamese evangelicals remains a mere pointer toward, more than a solution to, the unsolved crisis in Vietnamese evangelicalism. The tactical nature of pentecostal evangelicalism's engagement with structural evils, its imagination that is unconsciously preformed by what wider society regards as "a victorious life," and its denial of suffering are only a few examples of features that explain why the pentecostal movement has fallen short of embodying the exemplary evangelical way of life in contemporary Vietnam.

Yet another readily available example of shortcoming consists in the reality that the pentecostal movement among contemporary Vietnamese evangelicals has little contact with the postwar characteristics of current Vietnamese society. Here, several important issues need to be addressed in the near future: the existential struggle of people who experienced the Vietnam War; the post-traumatic psychology of winning and losing the war; the construction of collective memory; and the struggle to rebuild life both at home and in exile, to name a few.[3]

With the benefit of hindsight, this book and other historical reflections in Vietnam in recent years have viewed as a virtue the ability of Vietnamese intellectuals in colonial times (1920s–1930s) to entertain many perspectives on any given issue—a virtue that some scholarly circles view as lacking in contemporary Vietnam due to the State's efforts to assert cultural hegemony.[4]

3 Readers interested in engaging postwar Vietnam may consult Hue-Tam Ho Tai, ed., *The Country of Memory: Remaking the Past in Late Socialist Vietnam* (Berkeley: University of California Press, 2001). See also Scott Laderman and Edwin A. Martini, eds., *Four Decades On: Vietnam, the United States, and the Legacies of the Second Indochina War* (Durham, NC: Duke University Press, 2013); Vatthana Pholsena and Oliver Tappe, eds., *Interactions with a Violent Past: Reading Post-Conflict Landscapes in Cambodia, Laos, and Vietnam* (Chicago: University of Chicago Press, 2013); and Viet Thanh Nguyen, *Nothing Ever Dies: Vietnam and the Memory of War* (Cambridge: Harvard University Press, 2016). For an example of theological reflection on the Vietnam War that engages the experience of United States veterans of the Vietnam War from a Vietnamese-American perspective, see Jonathan Tran, *The Vietnam War and Theologies of Memory: Time and Eternity in the Far Country*, Challenges in Contemporary Theology Series (Malden, MA: Wiley-Blackwell, 2010).

4 As notable examples of thinking in the early 2010s, see Phan Châu Trinh Cultural Fund, *Tinh thần khai minh* [*Enlightenment Spirit*] (Hà Nội: Tri Thức, 2013).

Future studies that are rooted more deeply in the context of late-communist, economically booming Vietnam may be more critical of the practice of entertaining different perspectives. Scholars producing such studies may also find it imperative to develop a blueprint and clarify necessary praxis for adequately addressing the negative aspects of Vietnamese society on a large scale. Understandably, these future studies may find historical inspiration from works such as *Chính đề Việt Nam* [*Main Issues of Vietnam*], a major modern Vietnamese political treatise written in the 1945–1975 period.[5] Yet in today's world, the unsolved issues of the past are rendered even more complex by current upheavals: when prolonged hatred interlocks with hollow reconciliation in the midst of the (re)emergence of extremism and Social Darwinism on a global scale, the people groups inhabiting contemporary Vietnam may find it difficult to envision life in plain, humane terms.

In such a complex world as today's, the pentecostal movement intimates that solutions for our large-scale problems can be found only in the Spirit of God, that the energy and imagination needed to renew the Vietnamese evangelical tradition—or any Christian tradition, for that matter—will need to find its source in the pouring out of the Spirit.[6] May the Vietnamese evangelical tradition, and its pentecostal movement, continue to be renewed under the guidance of the Spirit of God and to offer meaning to those who may well need it most. In these ways will Vietnamese evangelicalism greatly contribute to the effectiveness of the various Christian traditions in promoting human liberation and flourishing—in Vietnam and beyond.

---

5 Tùng Phong, *Chính đề Việt Nam* [*Main Issues of Vietnam*] (Sài Gòn: Đồng Nai, 1965). See also Thế Uyên, *Nghĩ trong một xã hội tan rã* [*Reflection within a Disintegrated Society*] (Sài Gòn: Thái Độ, 1967).

6 See, for example, Grace Ji-Sun Kim, *The Holy Spirit, Chi, and the Other: A Model of Global and Intercultural Pneumatology* (New York: Palgrave MacMillan, 2011). For a theological methodology, consult Amos Yong, *The Spirit Poured Out on All Flesh: Pentecostalism and the Possibility of Global Theology* (Grand Rapids: Baker Academic, 2005), 28; and *Spirit-Word-Community: Theological Hermeneutics in Trinitarian Perspective* (Burlington, VT: Ashgate, 2002), part 2. Also, Office of Theological Concerns of the Federation of Asian Bishops' Conference (FABC), "The Spirit at Work in Asia Today: A Document of the Office of Theological Concerns," Paper no. 81 (May 1997), accessed March 1, 2017, http://www.fabc.org/fabc%20papers/fabc_paper_81.pdf.

Bibliography

"7culturalmountains.org." Accessed February 30, 2017. http://www.7culturalmountains.org/.

Ahmad, Aijaz. "The Politics of Literary Postcoloniality." *Race and Class* 36, no. 3 (1995): 1–20.

Aikman, David. *Jesus in Beijing: How Christianity is Transforming China and Changing the Global Balance of Power*. Washington, DC: Regnery, 2003.

Akakios, Archimandrite. *Fasting in the Orthodox Church: Its Theological, Pastoral, and Social Implications*. 2nd ed. Etna, CA: Center for Traditionalist Orthodox Studies, 1996.

Albrecht, Daniel E., and Evan B. Howard. "Pentecostal Spirituality." In *The Cambridge Companion to Pentecostalism*, edited by Cecil M. Robeck Jr. and Amos Yong, 235–53. New York: Cambridge University Press, 2014.

Alexander, Kimberly Ervin. *Pentecostal Healing: Models in Theology and Practice*. Dorset, UK: Deo, 2006.

Alexander, Paul. *Signs and Wonders: Why Pentecostalism is the World's Fastest-Growing Faith*. San Francisco: Jossey-Bass, 2009.

Alston, Philip, and Ryan Goodman, eds. *International Human Rights*. 2nd and revised edition. New York: Oxford University Press, 2012.

Ang, Claudine. "Regionalism in Southern Narratives of Vietnamese History: The Case of the 'Southern Advance' [*'Nam Tiến'*]." *Journal of Vietnamese Studies* 8, no. 3 (2013): 1–26.

Archer, Kenneth J. "The Fivefold Gospel and the Mission of the Church: Ecclesiastical Implications and Opportunities." In *Toward a Pentecostal Ecclesiology: The Church and the Fivefold Gospel*, edited by John Christopher Thomas, 7–46. Cleveland, TN: CPT Press, 2010.

Archer, Kenneth J., and Richard E. Waldrop. "Liberating Hermeneutics: Toward a Holistic Pentecostal Mission of Peace and Justice." *Journal of the European Pentecostal Theological Association* 31, no. 1 (2011): 65–80.

Arendt, Hannah. *Love and Saint Augustine*. Edited and with an interpretive essay by Joanna Vecchiarelli Scott and Judith Chelius Stark. Chicago: The University of Chicago Press, 1996.

Ashcroft, Bill, Gareth Griffiths, and Helen Tiffin. *Post-Colonial Studies: The Key Concepts*. 3rd edition. London: Routledge, 2013.

Asian Human Rights Commission. *Asian Human Rights Charter*. Hong Kong: Asian Legal Resource Centre, 1998.

Attanasi, Katherine, and Amos Yong, eds. *Pentecostalism and Prosperity: The Socioeconomics of the Global Charismatic Movement*. Christianities of the World 1. New York: Palgrave Macmillan, 2012.

Augustine. *The City of God*. Translated by Marcus Dods. In vol. 2 of *The Nicene and Post-Nicene Fathers*, edited by Philip Schaff. 14 vols. Grand Rapids: Eerdmans, 1956.

Austin, Denise. *"Kingdom-Minded" People: Christian Identity and the Contributions of Chinese Business Christians*. Leiden: Brill, 2011.

Avila, Charles. *Peasant Theology: Reflections by the Filipino Peasants on Their Process of Social Revolution*. WSCF Asia Book 1. Bangkok: World Student Christian Federation Asia Region, 1976.

Bakhtin, Mikhail. *Problems of Dostoevsky's Poetics*. Minneapolis: University of Minnesota Press, 1984.

Balcomb, Anthony. "What Theology? Whose Development?: Interrogating Theology and Development in the Secular Academy." *Journal of Theology for Southern Africa* 142 (March 2012): 6–20.

Banerjee, Abhijit, and Esther Duflo. *Poor Economics: A Radical Rethinking of the Way to Fight Global Poverty*. New York: PublicAffairs, 2011.

Bartleman, Frank. *Azusa Street*. Centennial edition. Gainesville, FL: Bridge-Logos, 2006.

Bays, Daniel H. *A New History of Christianity in China*. Malden, MA: Wiley-Blackwell, 2012.

Bebbington, David. *Evangelicalism in Modern Britain: A History from the 1730s to the 1980s*. London: Unwin Hyman, 1989.

Beckford, Robert. *God of the Rahtid: Redeeming Rage*. London: Darton, Longman & Todd, 2011.

Bedford, Nancy E. "Little Moves against Destructiveness: Theology and the Practice of Discernment." In *Practicing Theology: Beliefs and Practices in Christian Life*, edited by Miroslav Volf and Dorothy C. Bass, 157–81. Grand Rapids: Eerdmans, 2002.

Bell, Daniel M. *The Economy of Desire: Christianity and Capitalism in a Postmodern World*. Grand Rapids: Eerdmans, 2012.

Benson, Bruce Ellis, Malinda Elizabeth Berry, and Peter Goodwin Heltzel. "The Just and Peaceable Kingdom." In *Prophetic Evangelicals: Envisioning a Just and Peaceable Kingdom*, edited by Bruce Ellis Benson, Malinda Elizabeth Berry, and Peter Goodwin Heltzel, 8–30. Grand Rapids: Eerdmans, 2012.

Berger, Peter. "Max Weber is Alive and Well, and Living in Guatemala: The Protestant Ethic Today." *The Review of Faith and International Affairs* 8, no. 4 (2010): 3–9.

Bevans, Stephen B. *Models of Contextual Theology*. Maryknoll, NY: Orbis, 1992.

Bhabha, Homi K. *The Location of Culture*. New York: Routledge, 1994.

Bompani, Barbara. "Beyond Disciplinarity: Reflections on the Study of Religion in International Development." *Religion and Theology* 21, no. 3–4 (2014): 309–33.

Bourne, Richard. *Seek the Peace of the City: Christian Political Criticism as Public, Realist, and Transformative*. Eugene, OR: Cascade, 2009.

Bowler, Kate. *Blessed: A History of the American Prosperity Gospel*. New York: Oxford University Press, 2013.

Brett, Mark G. "Diaspora and Kenosis as Postcolonial Themes." In *Decolonizing the Body of Christ: Theology and Theory after Empire?*, edited by David Joy and Joseph Duggan, 127–40. New York: Palgrave Macmillan, 2012.

Brett, Mark G. *Decolonizing God: The Bible in the Tides of Empire*. Sheffield, UK: Sheffield Phoenix, 2009.

Brueggemann, Walter. *The Land: Place as Gift, Promise, and Challenge in Biblical Faith*. 2nd edition. Overtures to Biblical Theology. Minneapolis: Augsburg Fortress, 2003.

Brusco, Elizabeth. "Gender and Power." In *Studying Global Pentecostalism: Theories and Methods*, edited by Allan Anderson, Michael Bergunder, Andre F. Droogers, and Cornelis van der Laan, 74–92. Berkeley: University of California Press, 2010.

Bùi, Hải Thiêm. "Pluralism Unleashed: The Politics of Reforming the Vietnamese Constitution." *Journal of Vietnamese Studies* 9, no. 4 (December 1, 2014): 1–32.

Bùi, Trân Phượng. "Diễn từ nhận giải thưởng 'Vì sự nghiệp văn hoá giáo dục' của Quỹ Văn Hoá Phan Châu Trinh" ["Speech on Accepting the Honorary Award for Lifetime Achievement on Cultural and Educational Development by Phan Châu Trinh Cultural Fund"]. HCMC, March 29, 2013.

Burnell, Peter. *The Augustinian Person*. Washington, DC: The Catholic University of America Press, 2005.

Butler, Judith, and Athena Athanasiou. *Dispossession: The Performative in the Political*. Malden, MA: Polity, 2013.

"Các mục sư tại Hà Nội và những nhà cách mạng" ["The Pastors in Hà Nội and the Revolutionists"]. October 7, 2013. Accessed August 1, 2015. http://www.thuvientinlanh.org/cac-muc-su-tai-ha-noi-va-nhung-nha-cach-mang/.

Cadman, Grace Hazenberg. *Pen Pictures of Annam and Its People*. New York: The Christian Alliance Publishing, 1920.

Cadman, William. "Practical Piety." *Alliance Weekly*, June 26, 1926, 418.

Cao, Huy Thuần. *Thế giới quanh ta* [*The World around Us*]. Đà Nẵng: Đà Nẵng Publication, 2007.

Cao, Nanlai. *Constructing China's Jerusalem: Christians, Power, and Place in Contemporary Wenzhou*. Contemporary Issues in Asia and the Pacific. Stanford: Stanford University Press, 2011.

Carson, D. A. *Christ and Culture Revisited*. Grand Rapids: Eerdmans, 2008.

Cartledge, Mark J. *Encountering the Spirit: The Charismatic Tradition*. Traditions of Christian Spirituality. Maryknoll, NY: Orbis, 2007.

Cartledge, Mark J. "Family Socialization, Godly Love, and Pentecostal Spirituality: A Study among the Church of God (Cleveland, TN)." In *Research in the Social Scientific Study of Religion*, vol. 23, edited by Ralph L. Piedmont and Andrew Village, 1–27. Leiden: Brill, 2012.

Cartledge, Mark J. "Pentecostal Healing as an Expression of Godly Love: An Empirical Study." *Mental Health, Religion & Culture* 16, no. 5 (2013): 501–22.

Cartledge, Mark J. "The Socialization of *Glossolalia*." In *Sociology, Theology and the Curriculum*, edited by Leslie J. Francis, 125–34. London: Cassell, 1999.

Cartledge, Mark J. *Testimony in the Spirit: Rescripting Ordinary Pentecostal Theology*. Burlington, VT: Ashgate, 2010.

Cavanaugh, William T. *Being Consumed: Economics and Christian Desire*. Grand Rapids: Eerdmans, 2008.

Cavanaugh, William T. "What Constantine Has to Teach Us." In *Constantine Revisited: Leithart, Yoder, and the Constantinian Debate*, edited by John D. Roth, 83–99. Eugene, OR: Wipf & Stock, 2013.

Chan, Kin-Man. "Harmonious Society." In *International Encyclopedia of Civil Society*, edited by Helmut Anheier and Stefan Toepler, 821–25. New York: Springer, 2009.

Chan, Simon. *Pentecostal Ecclesiology: An Essay on the Development of Doctrine*. Blandford Forum, UK: Deo, 2010.

Chang, Ha-Joon. *Bad Samaritans: The Myth of Free Trade and the Secret History of Capitalism*. New York: Bloomsbury Press, 2008.

Chee, Pang Choong. "Studying Christianity and Doing Theology *Extra Ecclesiam* in China." In *Christian Theology in Asia*, edited by Sebastian Kim, 97–98. Cambridge: Cambridge University Press, 2008.

Chen, Kuan-Hsing. *Asia as Method: Toward Deimperialization*. Durham, NC: Duke University Press, 2010.

Chen, Martha Alter. "The Informal Economy: Definitions, Theories, and Policies." Women in Informal Employment Globalizing and Organizing Working Paper No. 1. August 2012. Accessed November 1, 2015. http://wiego.org/sites/wiego.org/files/publications/files/Chen_WIEGO_WP1.pdf.

Cherry, Haydon. "Digging up the Past: Prehistory and the Weight of the Present in Vietnam." *Journal of Vietnamese Studies* 4, no. 1 (February 1, 2009): 84–144.

Cherry, Haydon. "The State in Vietnam." *Journal of Vietnamese Studies* 11, no. 3–4 (Summer–Fall 2016): 1–16.

"Chinese Entrepreneurs to Become Ethical Leaders." *Globethics.net Newsletter*, no. 4 (2015). Accessed July 20, 2015. http://www.globethics.net/-/globethics-net-newsletter-no4-2015-april-2015-.

Cho, Yong-gi. *The Fourth Dimension*. Newberry, FL: Bridge Logos, 1979.

Cho, Yong-gi. *Salvation, Health & Prosperity: Our Threefold Blessings in Christ*. Altamonte Springs, FL: Creation House, 1987.

Cho, Yong-gi. *Suffering—Why Me?* (South Plainfield, NJ: Bridge, 1986).

Chow, Alexander. "Calvinist Public Theology in Urban China Today." *International Journal of Public Theology* 8, no. 2 (2014): 158–75.

Chow, Alexander. *Theosis, Sino-Christian Theology and the Second Chinese Enlightenment: Heaven and Humanity in Unity*. New York: Palgrave Macmillan, 2013.

Christian, Jayakumar. *God of the Empty-Handed: Poverty, Power, and the Kingdom of God*, 2nd edition. Victoria, Australia: Acorn Press, 2011.

Ci, Jiwei. *Dialectic of the Chinese Revolution: From Utopianism to Hedonism*. Stanford: Stanford University Press, 2004.

Cima, Ronald. "Vietnam: Historical Background." In *Vietnam: Current Issues and Historical Background*, edited by V. Largo, 73–190. New York: Nova Science Publishers, 2002.

Clifton, Shane. "The Dark Side of Prayer for Healing: Toward a Theology of Well-Being." *Pneuma: The Journal of the Society for Pentecostal Studies* 36, no. 2 (2014): 204–25.

Coakley, Sarah. "Kenosis and Subversion: On the Repression of 'Vulnerability' in Christian Feminist Writing." In *Swallowing a Fishbone?*, edited by Daphne Hampson, 82–111. London: SPCK, 1996.

The Communist Party of Vietnam. *Văn kiện đại hội đại biểu toàn quốc lần thứ XI* [*Documents of the 11th Congress of the Party*] (Hà Nội: Chính Trị Quốc Gia, 2011).

Cone, James H. *The Cross and the Lynching Tree*. Maryknoll, NY: Orbis, 2011.

Cook, Richard, and David Pao, eds. *After Imperialism: Christian Identity in China and the Global Evangelical Movement*. Studies in Chinese Christianity 1. Eugene, OR: Pickwick, 2011.

Courey, David J. *What Has Wittenberg to Do with Azusa?: Luther's Theology of the Cross and Pentecostal Triumphalism*. London: T&T Clark, 2015.

Cox, Harvey. *Fire from Heaven: The Rise of Pentecostal Spirituality & the Reshaping of Religion in the Twenty-First Century*. Reading, MA: Addison-Wesley, 1995.

Cramer, David, Jenny Howell, Jonathan Tran, and Paul Martens. "Scandalizing John Howard Yoder." *The Other Journal*, July 17, 2014. Accessed February 1, 2017. http://theotherjournal.com/2014/07/07/scandalizing-john-howard-yoder/.

Dayton, Donald W. "The Fourfold Gospel: Key to Trans-Pacific Continuities." In *From the Margins: A Celebration of the Theological Work of Donald W. Dayton*, edited by Christian T. Collins Winn, 359–66. Eugene, OR: Pickwick, 2007.

Dayton, Donald W. *Theological Roots of Pentecostalism*. Peabody, MA: Hendrickson, 1987.

de Certeau, Michel. *The Practice of Everyday Life*. Translated by Steven F. Rendall. Berkeley: University of California Press, 1984.

Deaton, Angus. *The Great Escape: Health, Wealth, and the Origins of Inequality*. Princeton: Princeton University Press, 2013.

DeBorst, Ruth Padilla. "An Integral Transformation Approach." In *The Mission of the Church: Five Views in Conversation*, edited by Craig Ott, 41–68. Grand Rapids: Baker Academic, 2016.

Drønen, Tomas Sundnes. "Weber, Prosperity and the Protestant Ethic: Some Reflections on Pentecostalism and Economic Development." *Svensk Missionstidskrift* 100, no. 3 (2012): 321–35.

Dutton, George E., Jayne S. Werner, and John K. Whitmore, eds. *Sources of Vietnamese Tradition*. Introduction to Asian Civilizations Series. New York: Columbia University Press, 2012.

Dwayne, Benjamin, Loren Brandt, and Brian McCaig. "Growth with Equity: Income Inequality in Vietnam, 2002–14." *The Journal of Economic Inequality* 15, no. 1 (March 2017): 25–46.

Đặng, Kim Sơn. *Công nghiệp hóa từ nông nghiệp* [*Industrialization through (the Industrialization of) Agriculture*]. Hà Nội: Nông Nghiệp, 2001.

Đặng, Ngọc Phúc. *Những người Tin Lành ở Việt Nam trước năm 1911* [*Protestants in Vietnam Prior to 1911*]. San Diego: Self-Published, 2011.

Đặng, Phong. *Tư duy kinh tế Việt Nam 1975–1989* [*Economic Thinkings in Vietnam 1975–1989*]. 2nd ed. HCMC: Tri Thức, 2014.

"Đầy đủ mọi nhu cầu" ["Fulfill All Your Needs"]. *Thánh Kinh Báo* [*Bible Magazine*], no. 412 (1974): 3–4.

Đỗ, Danh Huấn. "Làng Việt—đối tượng nghiên cứu của khu vực học" ["*Việt* Village—A Case Study in Area Studies"]. *Tạp Chí Khoa Học Xã Hội và Nhân Văn* [*Journal of Social Sciences and Humanities*] 26 (2010): 15–23.

Đỗ, Lai Thúy. "Phan Khôi và bước chuyển từ chính trị sang văn hóa" ["Phan Khôi and the Transition from Politics to Culture"]. *Văn Hóa Nghệ An* [*Culture of Nghệ An*], November 5, 2014. Accessed August 1, 2015. http://www.vanhoanghean.com.vn/chuyen-muc-goc-nhin-van-hoa/nhung-goc-nhin-van-hoa/phan-khoi-va-buoc-chuyen-tu-chinh-tri-sang-van-hoa.

Đỗ, Quang Chính, SJ. *Hòa mình vào xã hội Việt Nam* [*Blending into Vietnamese Society*]. Hà Nội: Tôn Giáo, 2008.

Đỗ, Quang Hưng. "Đạo Tin Lành ở Việt Nam và Hàn Quốc: Hai số phận văn hóa" ["Evangelicalism in Vietnam and South Korea: Two Cultural Destinations"]. *Tạp Chí Khoa Học Xã Hội Việt Nam* [*Journal of Vietnamese Social Sciences*], no. 9 (2013): 49–64.

Đỗ, Quang Hưng. "Hồ Chí Minh Và Đạo Tin Lành" ["Hồ Chí Minh and Evangelicalism"]. *Tạp Chí Khoa Học Xã Hội* [*Journal of Social Sciences*] 5 (2013), 1–12.

Đỗ, Quang Hưng. "Mấy vấn đề thần học Tin Lành ở Việt Nam hiện nay" ["Current Issues in Vietnamese Evangelical Theology"]. *Tạp Chí Khoa Học Xã Hội Việt Nam* [*Vietnamese Journal of Social Sciences*] 6 (2011). Accessed October 1, 2015. http://vssr.vass.gov.vn/noidung/tintuc/Lists/ngonnguvanhocvanhoa/View_Detail.aspx?ItemID=42.

Đỗ, Quang Hưng. "Người Tin Lành ở Hà Nội" ["The Evangelicals in Hà Nội"]. In *Đời Sống Tôn Giáo Tín Ngưỡng Thăng Long—Hà Nội* [*Religious Life of Thăng Long—Hà Nội*], edited by Đỗ Quang Hưng, 317–35. Hà Nội: Hà Nội Publishers, 2010.

Đỗ, Quang Hưng, and Trần Viết Nghĩa. *Tính hiện đại và chuyển biến của văn hóa Việt Nam thời cận đại* [*Modernity and the Changing of Vietnamese Culture in Modern Time*]. Hà Nội: Chính Trị Quốc Gia, 2013.

Đỗ, Thị Thoan, "Vị trí của kẻ bên lề: Thực hành thơ của nhóm *Mở Miệng* từ góc nhìn văn hóa" ["The Role of the Marginalized: Engaging the Group *Mở Miệng*'s Practices of Poetry from a Cultural Perspective"]. M.A. thesis, Vietnam National University, Hà Nội, 2010.

Ear, Sophal. *Aid Dependence in Cambodia: How Foreign Assistance Undermines Democracy*. New York: Columbia University Press, 2012.

Earl, Catherine. *Vietnam's New Middle Classes: Gender, Career, City*. Copenhagen: Nordic Institute of Asian Studies Press, 2014.

Easterly, William. *The Tyranny of Experts: Economists, Dictators, and the Forgotten Rights of the Poor*. New York: Basic Books, 2013.

Ellington, Scott A. "History, Story, and Testimony: Locating Truth in a Pentecostal Hermeneutic." *Pneuma: The Journal of the Society for Pentecostal Studies* 23, no. 2 (September 2001): 245–63.

Elliott, David W. P. *Changing Worlds: Vietnam's Transition from Cold War to Globalization*. New York: Oxford University Press, 2012.

Elshtain, Jean Bethke. "With or Against Culture?" *Books & Culture* 12, no. 5 (September-October 2006): 28–30.

Escobar, Arturo. *Encountering Development: The Making and Unmaking of the Third World*. Princeton: Princeton University Press, 1995.

Escobar, Arturo. " 'Post-Development' as Concept and Social Practice." In *Exploring Post-Development: Theory and Practice, Problems and Perspectives*, edited by Aram Ziai, 18–32. New York: Routledge, 2007.

Escobar, Samuel. *The New Global Mission: The Gospel from Everywhere to Everyone*. Downers Grove, IL: InterVarsity, 2003.

Esteva, Gustavo. "Development." In *The Development Dictionary*, edited by Wolfgang Sachs. 2nd edition. London and New York: Zed Books, 2010.

Eyben, Rosalind, Irene Guijt, Chris Roche, and Cathy Shutt. *The Politics of Evidence and Results in International Development: Playing the Game to Change the Rules?*. Warwickshire, UK: Practical Action Publishing, 2015.

Fällman, Fredrik. "Calvin, Culture, and Christ? Developments of Faith among Chinese Intellectuals." In *Christianity in Contemporary China: Socio-Cultural Perspectives*, edited by Francis Khek Gee Lim, 152–68. New York: Routledge, 2013.

Faupel, David. *The Everlasting Gospel: The Significance of Eschatology in the Development of Pentecostal Thought*. Sheffield, UK: Sheffield Academic Press, 1996.

Fettke, Steven M., and Michael L. Dusing. "A Practical Pentecostal Theodicy? A Proposal." *Pneuma: The Journal of the Society for Pentecostal Studies* 38, no. 1–2 (2016): 160–79.

Fikkert, Brian and Russell Mask. *From Dependence to Dignity: How to Alleviate Poverty through Church-Centered Microfinance*. Grand Rapids: Zondervan, 2015.

Fikkert, Brian, and Steve Corbett. *When Helping Hurts: Alleviating Poverty Without Hurting the Poor... and Yourself*. Chicago: Moody, 2009.

Forde, Adam. "Rethinking the Political Economy of Conservative Transition: The Case of Vietnam." *Journal of Communist Studies & Transition Politics* 26, no. 1 (March 2010): 126–46.

Foucault, Michel. *The Archaeology of Knowledge*. New York: Pantheon, 1972.

Fountain, Philip, Robin Bush, and R. Michael Feener, eds. *Religion and the Politics of Development: Critical Perspectives on Asia*. New York: Palgrave Macmillan, 2015.

Frankl, Viktor. *Man's Search for Meaning*. 1946. Boston: Beacon, 2006.

Freeman, Dena, ed. *Pentecostalism and Development: Churches, NGOs and Social Change in Africa*. New York: Palgrave Macmillan, 2012.

Fulton, Brent. *China's Urban Christians: A Light That Cannot Be Hidden*. Studies in Chinese Christianity series. Eugene, OR: Pickwick, 2015.

Gainsborough, Martin. *Vietnam: Rethinking the State*. London: Zed Books, 2010.

Gallagher, Sarita D. "Worship among the Binandere of Papua New Guinea: An Illustration from Oceania." In *Scripting Pentecost: A Study of Pentecostal Worship, and Liturgy*, edited by Mark J. Cartledge and Aaron J. Swoboda, 200–14. Burlington, VT: Ashgate, 2016.

Gallagher, Susan, ed. *Postcolonial Literature and the Biblical Call for Justice*. Jackson, MS: University Press of Mississippi, 1994.

Ge, Wen. "Engaging University Theologies with Church Theologies in China: A Postliberal Appraisal of the Emerging Sino-Christian Academic Theology." In *What Young Asian Theologians Are Thinking*, edited by Leow Theng Huat, 50–64. Singapore: Trinity Theological College, 2014.

Geertz, Clifford. *The Interpretation of Cultures: Selected Essays*. New York: Basic Books, 1973.

General Statistic Office of Vietnam. *1999 Vietnam Population and Housing Census*. Hà Nội: Tổng Cục Thống Kê, 1999.

General Statistic Office of Vietnam. *2009 Vietnam Population and Housing Census*. Hà Nội: Tổng Cục Thống Kê, 2009.

Giebel, Christoph. *Imagined Ancestries of Vietnamese Communism: Ton Duc Thang and the Politics of History and Memory*. Seattle: University of Washington Press, 2004.

Giebel, Christoph. "Museum-Shine: Revolution and Its Tutelary Spirit in the Village of My Hoa Hung." In *The Country of Memory: Remaking the Past in Late Socialist Vietnam*, edited by Hue-Tam Ho Tai, 77–108. Berkeley: University of California Press, 2001.

"Gieo gì gặt nấy" ["Reap What You Sow"]. *Thánh Kinh Báo* [*Bible Magazine*], no. 2 (February 1931): 1–2.

Gifford, Paul, and Trad Nogueira-Godsey. "The Protestant Ethic and African Pentecostalism: A Case Study." *Journal for the Study of Religion* 24, no. 1 (2011): 5–22.

Gilbert, Daniel. *Stumbling on Happiness*. New York: Alfred A. Knopf, 2006.

Gladwin, Ryan R. "Charismatic Music and the Pentecostalization of Latin American Evangelicalism." In *The Spirit of Praise: Music and Worship in Global*

Pentecostal-Charismatic Christianity, edited by Monique M. Ingalls and Amos Yong, 199–214. University Park, PA: The Pennsylvania State University Press.

Golf, Paul, and Pastor Lee. *The Coming Chinese Church: How Rising Faith in China Is Spilling Over Its Boundaries*. Oxford: Monarch, 2013.

Goodliff, Andrew. "'It's All about Jesus': A Critical Analysis of the Ways in Which the Songs of Four Contemporary Worship Songwriters Can Lead to an Impoverished Christology." *The Evangelical Quarterly* 81, no. 3 (July 2009): 254–68.

Gorringe, Timothy. *A Theology of the Built Environment: Justice, Empowerment, Redemption*. Cambridge: Cambridge University Press, 2002.

Goscha, Christopher. *Vietnam: A New History*. New York: Basic Books, 2016.

Gramsci, Antonio. *Selections from the Prison Notebooks*. New York: International Publishers, 1971.

Green, Chris E. *Toward a Pentecostal Theology of the Lord's Supper: Foretasting the Kingdom*. Cleveland, TN: CPT Press, 2012.

Goossen, Rachel Waltner. "'Defanging the Beast': Mennonite Responses to John Howard Yoder's Sexual Abuse." *Mennonite Quarterly Review* 89 (January 2015): 7–80.

Gunn, Geoffrey. *Rice Wars in Colonial Vietnam: The Great Famine and the Viet Minh Road to Power*. Lanham, MD: Rowman & Littlefield, 2014.

Gunther Brown, Candy. *Testing Prayer: Science and Healing*. Cambridge, MA: Harvard University Press, 2012.

Guo, Sujian, and Baogang Guo, eds. *China in Search of a Harmonious Society*. Lanham, MD: Lexington Books, 2008.

Gutierrez, Gustavo. *A Theology of Liberation: History, Politics, and Salvation*. Maryknoll, NY: Orbis, 1973.

Hagin, Kenneth E. *How God Taught Me About Prosperity*. Oklahoma City: Kenneth Hagin Ministries, 1985.

Hall, Stuart. "Cultural Identity and Diaspora." In *The Post-Colonial Studies Reader*, edited by Bill Ashcroft, Gareth Griffiths, and Helen Tiffin, 435–38. 2nd edition. New York: Routledge, 2006.

Harari, Yuval Noah. *Sapiens: A Brief History of Humankind*. London: Harvill Secker, 2014.

Harms, Erik. *Luxury and Rubble: Civility and Dispossession in the New Saigon*. Berkeley: University of California Press, 2016.

Harvey, Thomas Alan. *Acquainted with Grief: Wang Mingdao's Stand for the Persecuted Church in China*. Grand Rapids: Brazos, 2002.

Hauerwas, Stanley. *War and the American Difference: Theological Reflections on Violence and National Identity*. Grand Rapids: Baker Academic, 2011.

Haynes, Naomi. *Moving by the Spirit: Pentecostal Social Life on the Zambian Copperbelt*. Berkeley: University of California Press, 2017.

Hennayake, Nalani. *Culture, Politics, and Development in Postcolonial Sri Lanka*. Lanham: Lexington Books, 2006.

Hernández, Albert. *Subversive Fire: The Untold Story of Pentecost*. Lexington, KY: Emeth Press, 2010.

Hill, Johnny Bernard. *Prophetic Rage: A Postcolonial Theology of Liberation*. Grand Rapids: Eerdmans, 2013.

Hồ, Sĩ Quý. *Tiến bộ xã hội: Một số vấn đề về mô hình phát triển ở Đông Á và Đông Nam Á* [*Social Progress: Some Issues in East Asian's and Southeast Asian's Development Models*]. Hà Nội: Tri Thức, 2011.

Hồ, Tấn Sáng. "Đạo Tin Lành và ảnh hưởng của nó đối với một số lĩnh vực xã hội ở Tây Nguyên" ["Evangelicalism and Its Influence in Certain Aspects of Society in the Central Highlands"]. *Tạp Chí Nghiên Cứu Tôn Giáo* [*Journal of Religious Studies*], no. 4 (2008): 30–35.

Hoàng Đạo. "Mười điều tâm niệm của bạn trẻ: Điều thứ nhất—Theo mới" ["Ten Things for the Youth to Live By: The First Tenet—Embrace Newness"]. *Ngày Nay* [*Modern Times*], no. 25 (October 13, 1936).

Hoàng, Văn Đào. *Việt Nam Quốc Dân Đảng* [*Vietnamese Nationalist Party*]*: A Contemporary History of a National Struggle: 1927–1954*. Pittsburgh: RoseDog Books, 2008.

Hocken, Peter. *You He Made Alive: A Total Christian View of Prayer, Communal, Individual and with Special Reference to the Work of the Spirit in Prayer Groups*. London: Darton, Longman & Todd, 1974.

Horsley, Richard A. *Jesus and the Powers: Conflict, Covenant, and the Hope of the Poor*. Minneapolis: Fortress, 2010.

Horsley, Richard A., ed. *Hidden Transcripts and the Arts of Resistance: Applying the Work of James C. Scott to Jesus and Paul*. Atlanta: Society of Biblical Literature, 2004.

Horsley, Richard A., ed. *In the Shadow of Empire: Reclaiming the Bible as a History of Faithful Resistance*. Louisville: Westminster John Knox, 2008.

Howell, Brian. "Practical Belief and the Localization of Christianity: Pentecostal and Denominational Christianity in Global/Local Perspective." In *Religion and Globalization: Critical Concepts in Social Studies*, edited by Véronique Altglas, 2:210–29. New York and London: Routledge, 2011.

Howell, James C. *What Does the Lord Require?: Doing Justice, Loving Kindness, and Walking Humbly*. Louisville: Westminster John Knox, 2012.

Hughes, Graham. *Worship as Meaning: A Liturgical Theology for Late Modernity*. Cambridge Studies in Christian Doctrine. New York: Cambridge University Press, 2003.

Irwin, E. F. *With Christ in Indo-China*. Harrisburg, PA: Christian Publications, 1937.

Jaffray, R. A. "South China: Selections from the Annual Reports from the Southern Provinces of China." *Alliance Weekly*, August 1, 1908, 287–90.

Jaffray, R. A. " 'Speaking in Tongues'—Some Words of Kindly Counsel." *Alliance Weekly*, March 13, 1909, 395–96, 406.

Jeffrey, Ruth Goforth. *Amazing Grace: A Brief Account of My Life in China and Vietnam*. Stouffville, ON: D. I. Jeffrey, 1975.

Jellema, Kate. "Returning Home: Ancestor Veneration and the Nationalism of *Đổi Mới* Vietnam." In *Modernity and Re-Enchantment: Religion in Post-Revolutionary Vietnam*, edited by Philip Taylor, 57–89. Singapore: Institute of Southeast Asian Studies, 2007.

Jones, Ben. "Pentecostalism, Development NGOs and Meaning in Eastern Uganda." In *Pentecostalism and Development: Churches, NGOs and Social Change in Africa*, edited by Dena Freeman, 181–202. New York: Palgrave Macmillan, 2012.

Joshua (pseudonym). "Pentecostalism in Vietnam: A History of the Assemblies of God." *Asian Journal of Pentecostal Studies* 4, no. 2 (2001): 307–26.

Kao, Chen-yang. "Church as 'Women's Community': The Feminization of Protestantism in Contemporary China." *Journal of Archaeology and Anthropology* 78, no. 1 (2013): 107–40.

Kao, Chen-yang. "The Cultural Revolution and the Emergence of Pentecostal-style Protestantism in China." *Journal of Contemporary Religion* 24, no. 2 (2009): 171–88.

Kao, Chen-yang. "The House-church Identity and Preservation of Pentecostal-style Protestantism in China." In *Christianity in Contemporary China: Socio-Cultural Perspectives*, edited by Francis Khek Gee Lim, 207–19. New York: Routledge, 2013.

Kapoor, Ilan. *The Postcolonial Politics of Development*. New York: Routledge, 2008.

Kärkkäinen, Veli-Matti. "David's Sling: The Promise and Problem of Pentecostal Theology Today: A Response to D. Lyle Dabney." *Pneuma: The Journal of the Society for Pentecostal Studies* 23, no. 1 (2001): 147–52.

Kärkkäinen, Veli-Matti. " 'The Leaning Tower of Pentecostal Ecclesiology': Reflections on the Doctrine of the Church on the Way." In *Toward a Pentecostal Ecclesiology: The Church and the Fivefold Gospel*, edited by John Christopher Thomas, 261–71. Cleveland, TN: CPT Press, 2010.

Kay, William. "The Mind, Behaviour and Glossolalia—A Psychological Perspective." In *Speaking in Tongues*, edited by Mark J. Cartledge, 174–205. Milton Keynes, UK: Paternoster, 2006.

Keith, Charles. *Catholic Vietnam: A Church from Empire to Nation*. Berkeley: University of California Press, 2012.

Kelly, Liam. "Bản sắc văn hóa = Ideological Position" ["Cultural Identity = Ideological Position"], July 14, 2012. Accessed August 1, 2015. https://leminhkhai.wordpress.com/2012/07/14/ban-sac-van-hoa-ideological-position/.

Kelly, Liam. " 'Confucianism' in Vietnam: A State of the Field Essay." *Journal of Vietnamese Studies* 1, no. 1–2 (2006): 314–70.

Kennedy, Nell L. *Dream Your Way to Success: The Story of Dr. Yonggi Cho and Korea*. Plainfield, NJ: Logos International, 1980.

Kenneson, Philip. "Gathering: Worship, Imagination, and Formation." In *The Blackwell Companion to Christian Ethics*, edited by Stanley Hauerwas and Samuel Wells, 55–69. Malden, MA: Wiley-Blackwell, 2006.

Kerkvliet, Benedict J. *The Power of Everyday Politics: How Vietnamese Peasants Transformed National Policy*. Ithaca, NY: Cornell University Press, 2005.

Kerkvliet, Benedict J. "Workers' Protests in Contemporary Vietnam (with Some Comparisons to Those in the Pre-1975 South)." *Journal of Vietnamese Studies* 5, no. 1 (February 1, 2010): 162–204.

Kerr, Nathan. *Christ, History and Apocalyptic: The Politics of Christian Mission*. Eugene, OR: Cascade, 2008.

Kerr, Nathan. "*Communio Missionis*: Certeau, Yoder, and the Missionary Space of the Church." In *The New Yoder*, edited by Peter Dula and Chris K. Huebner, 317–35. Eugene, OR: Cascade, 2010.

Khang Lĩnh. "Một bông hồng cho quê hương" ["A Rose for My Country"]. *Thánh Kinh Báo* [*Bible Magazine*], no. 380 (November 1970): 8–12.

Khang Lĩnh. "Thế đứng của người thanh niên Cơ Đốc trong giai đoạn hiện tại" ["The Social Position of the Christian Youth at the Present Time"]. *Thánh Kinh Báo* [*Bible Magazine*], no. 374 (April 1970): 5–9.

Kim, Grace Ji-Sun. *Colonialism, Han, and the Transformative Spirit*. New York: Palgrave Macmillan, 2013.

Kim, Grace Ji-Sun. *The Holy Spirit, Chi, and the Other: A Model of Global and Intercultural Pneumatology*. New York: Palgrave MacMillan, 2011.

Kindoff, Jason. "Protestant Resilience under Chinese Communist Party Rule." In *God and Caesar in China: Policy Implications of Church-State Tensions*, edited by Jason Kindopp and Carol Lee Hamrin, 122–45. Washington, DC: The Brookings Institution, 2004.

King, David. "The New Internationalists: World Vision and the Revival of American Evangelical Humanitarianism, 1950–2010." *Religions* 3, no. 4 (October 2012): 922–49.

King, Paul. *Genuine Gold: The Cautiously Charismatic Story of the Early Christian and Missionary Alliance*. Tulsa: Word & Spirit, 2006.

"Kinh Thánh với xã hội" ["The Bible and the Society"]. *Thánh Kinh Báo* [*Bible Magazine*], no. 3 (March 1931): 1–2.

Kính Thiên. "Tín đồ có nên giữ Tết Nguyên Đán?" ["Should Believers Observe the Traditional New Year?"]. *Thánh Kinh Báo* [*Bible Magazine*], no. 10 (December 1931): 11–12.

Kobayashi, Yuka. "*Renquan*—Chinese Human Rights: An 'Import' from the West or a Chinese 'Export'?" In *Politics of the 'Other' in India and China: Western Concepts in Non-Western Contexts*, edited by Lion Koenig and Bidisha Chaudhuri, 179–92. New York: Routledge, 2016.

Kovacevic, Milorad. "Review of HDI Critiques and Potential Improvements." February 2011. Accessed October 25, 2015. http://hdr.undp.org/en/content/review-hdi-critiques-and-potential-improvements.

Kupfer, Kristen. "Saints, Secrets, and Salvation: Emergence of Spiritual-Religious Groups in China between 1978 and 1989." In *Christianity in Contemporary*

China: Socio-Cultural Perspectives, edited by Francis Khek Gee Lim, 183–203. New York: Routledge, 2013.

Kwok, Pui-lan. *Postcolonial Imagination and Feminist Theology*. Louisville: Westminster John Knox, 2005.

Laderman, Scott, and Edwin A. Martini, eds. *Four Decades On: Vietnam, the United States, and the Legacies of the Second Indochina War*. Durham, NC: Duke University Press, 2013.

Lagerkvist, Johan. *Tiananmen Redux: The Hard Truth About the Expanded Neoliberal World Order*. Bern: Peter Lang, 2016.

Lai, Pan Chiu, and Jason Lam, eds. *Sino-Christian Theology*. Frankfurt am Main: Peter Lang, 2010.

Lambert, David. "Fasting as a Penitential Rite: A Biblical Phenomenon?" *Harvard Theological Review* 96, no. 4 (October 2003): 477–512.

Land, Steven J. *Pentecostal Spirituality: A Passion for the Kingdom*. Sheffield, UK: Sheffield Academic Press, 1993.

Lausanne Committee for World Evangelization. "The Willowbank Report: Consultation on Gospel and Culture." Lausanne Occasional Paper 2, 1978. Accessed February 1, 2016, https://www.lausanne.org/content/lop/lop-2.

Le, Dung. "The Bamboo Cross: Toward a Vietnamese Theology and Christian Educational Ministry in Vietnam." D.Min. diss., Claremont School of Theology, 1994.

Le, Phu. "A Short History of the Evangelical Church of Viet Nam (1911–1965)." Ph.D. diss., New York University, 1972.

Le, Thu Huong, "Vietnam's Urban Middle Class: Rapidly Growing, Slowly Awakening." In *The Blooming Years: Kyoto Review of Southeast Asia*, edited by Pavin Chachavalpongpun, 528–31. Kyoto: Center for Southeast Asian Studies, 2017.

Le, Vince. "The Pentecostal Movement in Vietnam." In *Global Renewal Christianity: Spirit-Empowered Movements Past, Present, and Future*, vol. I: *Asia and Oceania*, edited by Vinson Synan and Amos Yong, 181–95. Lake Mary, FL: Charisma House, 2015.

Lê, Thị Giang. "Hệ phái Tin Lành Việt Nam (Miền Nam) ở Lâm Đồng" ["The Evangelical Church of Vietnam (South) in Lâm Đồng Province"]. M.A. thesis, Đà Lạt University, 2006.

Lê, Văn Thái. *Bốn mươi sáu năm trong chức vụ* [*Forty Six Years in Ministry*]. Sài Gòn: Tin Lành, 1970.

Lederle, Henry I. *Treasures Old and New: Interpretations of "Spirit-Baptism" in the Charismatic Renewal Movement*. Peabody, MA: Hendrickson, 1988.

Lee, Jung Young. *Marginality: The Key to Multicultural Theology*. Minneapolis: Fortress, 1995.

Lee, Young-hoon. *The Holy Spirit Movement in Korea: Its Historical and Theological Development*. Regnum Studies in Mission. Milton Keynes, UK: Regnum, 2009.

Leithart, Peter J. "Afterword." In *Constantine Revisited: Leithart, Yoder, and the Constantinian Debate*, edited by John D. Roth, 184–87. Eugene, OR: Wipf & Stock, 2013.

Leithart, Peter J. *Defending Constantine: The Twilight of an Empire and the Dawn of Christendom*. Downers Grove, IL: IVP Academic, 2010.

Leslie, Robert C. *Jesus and Logotherapy: The Ministry of Jesus as Interpreted through the Psychotherapy of Viktor Frankl*. New York: Abingdon, 1965.

Lewis, James. "Christianity and Human Rights in Vietnam: The Case of the Ethnic Minorities, 1975–2007." In *Christianity and Human Rights: Christians and the Struggle for Global Justice*, edited by Frederick M. Shepherd, 195–212. Lanham, MD: Lexington, 2009.

Lewis, James. "The Evangelical Religious Movement among the H'Mong of Northern Vietnam and the Government Response to It: 1989–2000." *Crossroad: An Interdisciplinary Journal of Southeast Asian Studies* 16, no. 2 (2002): 79–112.

Lindhardt, Martin. "Why the Devil Is Satan so Important in Chilean Pentecostalism? Power, Resistance and Pentecostal Micro-Politics." In *Pentecostal Power: Expressions, Impact and Faith of Latin American Pentecostalism*, edited by Calvin L. Smith, 227–48. Leiden: Brill, 2010.

Lindhardt, Martin, ed. *Pentecostalism in Africa: Presence and Impact of Pneumatic Christianity in Postcolonial Societies*. Leiden: Brill, 2014.

Ling, Samuel, and Stacey Bieler, eds. *Chinese Intellectuals and the Gospel*. San Gabriel, CA: China Horizon, 1999.

Lupton, Robert D. *Toxic Charity: How the Church Hurts Those They Help and How to Reverse It*. New York: HarperOne, 2011.

Lương, Thị Thoa, ed. *Nhân tố tôn giáo trong chủ nghĩa ly khai ở một số nước Đông Nam Á* [*The Religious Factor in Secessionism in Some Southeast Asian Countries*]. Hà Nội: Chính Trị Quốc Gia, 2013.

Lý, Xuân Chung. "Vai trò của đạo Tin Lành ở Hàn Quốc và nguyên nhân suy giảm tốc độ phát triển những năm gần đây" ["The Role of Evangelicalism in South Korea and Reasons of its Decreasing Growth Rate in Recent Years"]. *Tạp Chí Nghiên Cứu Đông Bắc Á* [*Journal of East Asian Studies*] no. 9 (2009). Accessed August 1, 2015. http://www.inas.gov.vn/590-vai-tro-cua-dao-tin-lanh-o-han-quoc-va-nguyen-nhan-suy-giam-toc-do-phat-trien-nhung-nam-gan-day.html.

Lyall, Leslie, ed. *Three of China's Mighty Men: Leaders of Chinese Church under Persecution*. Scotland: Christian Focus, 2006.

Ma, Wonsuk, William W. Menzies, and Hyeon-Sung Bae, eds. *David Yonggi Cho: A Close Look at His Theology and Ministry*. Baguio City, Philippines: APTS Press, 2004.

Macchia, Frank D. *Baptized in the Spirit: A Global Pentecostal Theology*. Grand Rapids: Zondervan, 2006.

MacIntyre, Alasdair. *After Virtue: A Study in Moral Theory*. South Bend, IN: University of Notre Dame Press, 1981.

Maggay, Melba Padilla. *Transforming Society*. Manila, Philippines: Institute for Studies in Asian Church and Culture, 1996.

Mandryk, Jason. *Operation World: The Definitive Prayer Guide to Every Nation*. 7th edition. Colorado Springs, CO: Biblica, 2010.

Marr, David G. *Vietnamese Tradition on Trial, 1920–1945*. Berkeley: University of California Press, 1984.

Martey, Emmanuel. *African Theology: Inculturation and Liberation*. Eugene, OR: Wipf & Stock, 2009.

Martin, Bernice. "The Pentecostal Gender Paradox: A Cautionary Tale for the Sociology of Religion." In *The Blackwell Companion to Sociology of Religion*, edited by Richard K. Fenn, 52–66. Malden, MA: Blackwell, 2001.

Martin, David. *Pentecostalism: The World Their Parish*. Religion & Modernity Series. Malden, MA: Blackwell, 2002.

Martin, Lee Roy. *Fasting: A Centre for Pentecostal Theology*. Cleveland, TN: CPT Press, 2014.

Masako, Ito. *Politics of Ethnic Classification in Vietnam*. Translated by Minako Sato. Kyoto Area Studies on Asia. Melbourne: Trans Pacific, 2013.

Masina, Pietro. *Vietnam's Development Strategies*. New York: Routledge, 2006.

Mathewes, Charles T. *The Republic of Grace: Augustinian Thoughts for Dark Times*. Grand Rapids: Eerdmans, 2010.

McCleary, Rachel M. *Global Compassion: Private Voluntary Organizations and U.S. Foreign Policy since 1939*. New York: Oxford University Press, 2009.

Mcelwee, Pamela. "From the Moral Economy to the World Economy: Revisiting Vietnamese Peasants in a Globalizing Era." *Journal of Vietnamese Studies* 2, no. 2 (August 1, 2007): 57–107.

McHale, Shawn Frederick. *Print and Power: Confucianism, Communism, and Buddhism in the Making of Modern Vietnam*. Honolulu: University of Hawaii Press, 2008.

McKnight, Scot. *Fasting*. The Ancient Practices Series. Nashville: Thomas Nelson, 2009.

McMichael, Philip. *Development and Social Change: A Global Perspective*. 5th edition. Thousand Oaks, CA: SAGE Publications, 2011.

Meagher, Kate. "Trading on Faith: Religious Movements and Informal Economic Governance in Nigeria." *Journal of Modern African Studies* 47, no. 3 (2009): 397–423.

Medina, Néstor. "Discerning the Spirit in Culture: Toward Pentecostal Interculturality." *Canadian Journal of Pentecostal-Charismatic Christianity*, no. 2 (2011): 131–65.

Medina, Néstor. *Mestizaje: (Re)mapping Race, Culture, and Faith in Latina/o Catholicism*. Maryknoll, NY: Orbis, 2009.

Michaud, Jean. "French Military Ethnography in Colonial Upper Tonkin (Northern Vietnam), 1897–1904." *Journal of Vietnamese Studies* 8, no. 4 (November 1, 2013): 1–46.

Michaud, Jean, and Tim Forsyth, eds. *Moving Mountains: Ethnicity and Livelihoods in Highland China, Vietnam, and Laos*. Seattle: University of Washington Press, 2011.

Miller, Donald E., and Tetsunao Yamamori. *Global Pentecostalism: The New Face of Christian Social Engagement*. Berkeley: University of California Press, 2007.

Miller, Donald E., Kimon H. Sargeant, and Richard Flory, eds. *Spirit and Power: The Growth and Global Impact of Pentecostalism*. New York: Oxford University Press, 2013.

Mitchell, Roger Haydon. *Church, Gospel, and Empire: How the Politics of Sovereignty Impregnated the West*. Eugene, OR: Wipf & Stock, 2011.

Mitchell, Roger Haydon. *The Fall of the Church*. Eugene, OR: Wipf & Stock, 2013.

Mitchell, Roger Haydon, and Julie Tomlin Arram, eds. *Discovering Kenarchy: Contemporary Resources for the Politics of Love*. Eugene, OR: Cascade, 2014.

Mittelstadt, Martin William. *Reading Luke-Acts in the Pentecostal Tradition*. Cleveland, TN: CPT Press, 2010.

Morse, Stephen. *Indices and Indicators in Development: An Unhealthy Obsession with Numbers*. New York: Routledge, 2013.

Myers, Bryant. "Progressive Pentecostalism, Development, and Christian Development NGOs: A Challenge and an Opportunity." *International Bulletin of Missionary Research* 39, no. 3 (2015): 115–20.

Myers, Bryant. "Relief and Development." In *Global Dictionary of Theology: A Resource for the Worldwide Church*, edited by William A. Dyrness and Veli-Matti Kärkkäinen, 739–45. Downers Grove, IL: IVP Academic, 2008.

Myers, Bryant. *Walking with the Poor: Principles and Practices of Transformational Development*. Revised and expanded edition. Maryknoll, NY: Orbis, 2011.

Myers, Bryant, Erin Dufault-Hunter, and Isaac B. Voss, eds. *Health, Healing, and Shalom: Frontiers and Challenges for Christian Health Missions*. Pasadena: William Carey Library, 2015.

National Assembly of Vietnam. "Constitution of the Socialist Republic of Vietnam." Accessed March 20, 2015. http://www.na.gov.vn/htx/English/C1479/default.asp?Newid=24766#gQNqmQstOBFE.

Nayar , Pramod K. *Postcolonial Literature: An Introduction*. New Delhi: Pearson, 2008.

Neubert, Mitchell J., Kevin D. Dougherty, Jerry Z. Park, and Jenna Griebel. "Beliefs about Faith and Work: Development and Validation of Honoring God and Prosperity Gospel Scales." *Review of Religious Research* 56, no. 1 (March 2014): 129–46.

Ngo, Tam T. T. *The New Way: Protestantism and the Hmong in Vietnam*. Seattle: University of Washington Press, 2016.

Ngo, Tam T. T. "Protestant Conversion and Social Conflict: The Case of the Hmong in Contemporary Vietnam." *Journal of Southeast Asian Studies* 46 (2015): 274–92.

Ngo, Tam T. T. " 'The Short-waved Faith': Christian Broadcastings and the Transformation of the Spiritual Landscape of the Hmong in Northern Vietnam." In *Mediated Piety: Technology and Religion in Contemporary Asia*, edited by Francis Khek Gee Lim, 139–59. Leiden: Brill, 2009.

Nguyen, Cuong. "The Growth of Certain Protestant Churches in Saigon under the Vietnamese Communist Government." D.Min. diss., San Francisco Theological Seminary, 1995.

Nguyen, KimSon. "The Catholic Church in Vietnam: An Example of Contextualization." *Asian Journal of Theology* 29, no. 1 (April 2015), 74–87.

Nguyen, Quynh-Hoa. "Tin Lành: The Bible and the Construction of an Evangelical Vietnamese Christian Identity (1975–2007)." Ph.D. diss., Claremont Graduate University, 2013.

Nguyen, Viet Thanh. *Nothing Ever Dies: Vietnam and the Memory of War*. Cambridge: Harvard University Press, 2016.

Nguyên Ngọc. "Chương trình vĩ đại bị dở dang của Phan Châu Trinh" ["The Great Unfinished Project of Phan Châu Trinh"]. University lecture. Hoa Sen University, HCMC, March 23, 2011.

Nguyễn, An Ninh. "The Ideal of Annamite Youth." In *Nguyễn An Ninh—tác phẩm* [*Nguyễn An Ninh—Collected Works*], edited by Mai Quốc Liên and Nguyễn Sơn, 57–78. HCMC: Văn Học, 2009.

Nguyễn, Cao Thanh. "Đạo Tin Lành ở Việt Nam từ 1975 đến nay, tư liệu và một số đánh giá ban đầu" [Evangelicalism in Vietnam, from 1975 to present: sources and initial comments]. The Government Committee for Religious Affairs, 2013. Accessed April 4, 2017. http://btgcp.gov.vn/Plus.aspx/vi/News/38/0/240/0/2737/.

Nguyễn, Đình Minh, ed. *Đoàn kết dân tộc ở Việt Nam* [*Solidarity among People Groups in Vietnam*]. Hà Nội: Chính Trị Quốc Gia—Sự Thật, 2016.

Nguyễn, Đức Lộc, ed. *Những người thiểu số ở đô thị: Lựa chọn, trở thành, khác biệt* [*Urban Minority Groups: Choosing, Becoming, Differentiating*]. Hà Nội: Tri Thức, 2016.

Nguyễn, Đức Lộc, ed. *Tình cảnh sống của người công nhân: Thân phận, rủi ro và chiến lược sống* [*Living Conditions of Workers: Life, Risk, and Coping Strategy*]. Hà Nội: Tri Thức, 2015.

Nguyễn, Hòa. "Nghiên cứu hậu thực dân ở Việt Nam: một nhu cầu thực tế hay một giả vấn đề?" ["Postcolonial Research in Vietnam: An Actual Need or a False Perception?"]. *Nhân Dân*, November 17–26, 2014. Accessed March 20, 2015. http://www.nhandan.com.vn/mobile/_mobile_vanhoa/_mobile_diendan/item/24937602.html.

Nguyễn, Ngọc Hà. "Đặc điểm tư duy và lối sống của con người Việt Nam hiện nay và những vấn đề đặt ra trước yêu cầu đổi mới và hội nhập quốc tế" ["Contemporary Thinking and Living Characteristics of the Vietnamese and Emerging Issues Due to Social Change and International Integration"]. Working paper of Viện Triết Học [Institute of Philosophy], 2010.

Nguyễn, Quang Hưng. "Chính sách tôn giáo so sánh với Hàn Quốc" ["Vietnam's Religious Policy in the Regional Context (In Comparison with the Republic of Korea)"]. *Tạp Chí Nghiên Cứu Tôn Giáo* [*Journal of Religious Studies*], no. 7 (2014): 21–35.

Nguyễn, Văn Dân. *Văn hóa và phát triển trong bối cảnh toàn cầu hóa* [*Culture and Development in the Context of Globalization*]. Hà Nội: Khoa Học Xã Hội, 2006.

Nguyễn, Văn Huyên. *Văn minh Việt Nam* [*The Civilization of Vietnam*]. Hà Nội: Thế Giới, 1995.

Nguyễn, Văn Minh. "Một số vấn đề về đạo Tin Lành trong cộng đồng người Hmông di cư tự do vào Tây Nguyên hiện nay" ["Some Issues Related to Evangelicalism in the H'Mong Community Migrating to the Central Highland at the Present"]. *Tạp Chí Dân Tộc Học* [*Journal of Ethnology*], no. 5 (2010): 38–47.

Nguyễn, Văn Năm. "Ảnh hưởng của Đạo Tin Lành với thiết chế xã hội truyền thống của đồng bào các dân tộc thiểu số ở Tây Nguyên" ["The Influence of Evangelicalism on Traditional Social Institutions of Ethnic Peoples in the Central Highlands"]. *Tạp Chí Nghiên Cứu Tôn Giáo* [*Journal of Religious Studies*], no. 4 (2008): 36–42.

Nguyễn, Văn Thắng, ed. *Giữ 'lý cũ' hay theo 'lý mới'? Bản chất của những cách phản ứng khác nhau của người H'Mong tại Việt Nam với ảnh hưởng của đạo Tin Lành* [*Keep 'Old Reason' or Follow 'New Reason'? Natures of the Responses of H'Mong people to Evangelicalism*]. Hà Nội: Khoa Học Xã Hội, 2009.

Nguyễn, Văn Thạo, and Nguyễn Viết Thông, eds. *Tìm hiểu một số thuật ngữ trong văn kiện Đại Hội XI của Đảng* [*Studying the Terminologies of the Documents of the Eleventh Congress of the Communist Party of Vietnam*]. Hà Nội: Chính Trị Quốc Gia, 2011.

Nguyễn, Xuân Hùng. "Relations Between Vietnamese Governments in History and the Evangelical Church." *Religious Studies Review* 1, no. 2 (May 2007): 38–50, accessed November 21, 2016, http://www.vjol.info/index.php/RSREV/article/viewFile/1324/1232.

Nhiều tác giả [Many authors]. *Tôn giáo và đời sống hiện đại ở Trung Quốc* [*Religion and Modern Life in China*]. Hà Nội: Khoa Học Xã Hội, 2014.

Niebuhr, Richard H. *Christ and Culture*. New York: Harper & Row, 1951.

Nienkirchen, Charles. *A. B. Simpson and the Pentecostal Movement*. Peabody, MA: Hendrickson, 1992.

Ninh, Kim. *A World Transformed: The Politics of Culture in Revolutionary Vietnam, 1945–1965*. Ann Arbor: University of Michigan Press, 2002.

Nordin, Astrid. *China's International Relations and Harmonious World: Time, Space and Multiplicity in World Politics*. New York: Routledge, 2016.

Office of the Prime Minister, The Republic of VietnamSocialist . "Approval of Strategy on Ethnic Minorities to the Year 2020," March 20, 2013. Accessed October 30, 2015. http://www.chinhphu.vn/portal/page/portal/chinhphu/noidungchienluocphattrienkinhtexahoi?_piref135_16002_135_15999_15999.strutsAction=ViewDetailAction.do&_piref135_16002_135_15999_15999.docid=1777&_piref135_16002_135_15999_15999.substract=.

Office of Theological Concerns of the Federation of Asian Bishops' Conference. "The Spirit at Work in Asia Today: A Document of the Office of Theological Concerns."

Paper no. 81, May 1997. Accessed March 1, 2017. http://www.fabc.org/fabc%20papers/fabc_paper_81.pdf.

Olsen, John D. *Thần đạo học* [*Theology*]. Sài Gòn: Tin Lành, 1958.

"Out of sight: Continuing grinding poverty in Vietnam's minority regions is a liability for the Communist Party." *The Economist*, April 4, 2015. Accessed April 30, 2015. http://www.economist.com/news/asia/21647653-continuing-grinding-poverty-vietnams-minority-regions-liability-communist-party-out.

Padilla, C. René. *Mission Between the Times: Essays on the Kingdom*. Revised and updated edition. Carlisle, UK: Langham Monographs, 2010.

Papice, David. "Choosing Success: The Lessons of East and Southeast Asia and Vietnam's Future—A Policy Framework for Vietnam's Socioeconomic Development 2011–2020." Accessed October 25, 2015. http://ash.harvard.edu/files/choosing_success.pdf.

Pears, Angie. *Doing Contextual Theology*. New York: Routledge, 2009.

Peck, M. Scott. *People of the Lie: The Hope for Healing Human Evil*. Riverside, NJ: Simon & Schuster, 1983.

Peet, Richard, and Elaine Hartwick. *Theories of Development: Contentions, Arguments, Alternatives*. 3rd edition. New York and London: The Guilford Press, 2015.

Pelley, Patricia M. "'Barbarians' and 'Younger Brothers': The Remaking of Race in Postcolonial Vietnam." *Journal of Southeast Asian Studies* 29, no. 2 (September 1998): 374–91.

Pelley, Patricia M. *Postcolonial Vietnam: New Histories of the National Past*. Durham, NC: Duke University Press, 2002.

Peycam, Philippe. *The Birth of Vietnamese Political Journalism: Saigon, 1916–1930*. New York: Columbia University Press, 2012.

The Pew Forum on Religion & Public Life. "Spirit and Power: A 10-Country Survey of Pentecostals." Washington, DC: Pew Research Center, 2006.

Phạm, Văn Đức, Phạm Hữu Toàn, and Nguyễn Đình Hòa, eds. *Vấn đề dân sinh và xã hội hài hòa* [*The Issue of Livelihood and Social Harmony*]. Hà Nội: Khoa Học Xã Hội, 2010.

Phạm, Văn Năm, ed. *Phép lạ rừng xanh* [*Miracles in the Jungle*]. Anaheim, CA: The Vietnamese District of the Christian and Missionary Alliance, 1998.

Phạm, Xuân Tín. "Lược sử Giáo Hội Tin Lành Việt Nam" ["A Short History of the Evangelical Church of Vietnam"]. Unpublished manuscript, 1991.

Phan, Bội Châu. *Overturned Chariot: The Autobiography of Phan Bội Châu*. Translated by Vĩnh Sính and Nicholas Wickenden. Honolulu: University of Hawaii Press, 1999.

Phan Châu Trinh Cultural Fund. *Tinh thần khai minh* [*Enlightenment Spirit*]. Hà Nội: Tri Thức, 2013.

Phan, Đình Liệu. "Lịch sử Hội Thánh Tin Lành Việt Nam" ["History of the Evangelical Church of Vietnam"]. Unpublished manuscript, 1966.

Phan, Khôi. "Giới thiệu và phê bình *Thánh Kinh Báo*" ["Introduction and Review of *The Bible Magazine*"]. *Phụ Nữ Tân Văn* [*Women's New Literature*], no. 74 (October 16, 1930).

Phan, Ngọc. *Một cách tiếp cận văn hóa* [*An Approach to Culture*]. Hà Nội: Thanh Niên, 1999.

Phan, Peter C. "Christianity in Vietnam Today (1975–2013): Contemporary Challenges and Opportunities." *International Journal of the Study of the Christian Church* 14, no. 1 (2014): 3–21.

Phan, Peter C. "Inculturation of Christianity and the Gospel." In *The Cambridge Dictionary of Christianity*, edited by Daniel Patte, 593–94. Cambridge: Cambridge University Press, 2010.

Phan, Peter C. *In Our Own Tongues: Perspectives from Asia on Mission and Inculturation*. Maryknoll, NY: Orbis, 2003.

Phan, Peter C. "The Socialist Republic of Vietnam." In *Christianities in Asia*, edited by Peter C. Phan, 130–140. Malden, MA: Wiley-Blackwell, 2010.

Pholsena, Vatthana, and Oliver Tappe, eds. *Interactions with a Violent Past: Reading Post-Conflict Landscapes in Cambodia, Laos, and Vietnam*. Chicago: University of Chicago Press, 2013.

Pieris, Aloysius. *An Asian Theology of Liberation*. Faith Meets Faith Series. Maryknoll, NY: Orbis, 1988.

Pinnock, Clark, Richard Rice, John Sanders, William Hasker, and David Basinger, *The Openness of God: A Biblical Challenge to the Traditional Understanding of God*. Downers Grove, IL: IVP Academic, 1994.

Politburo of Vietnam. "Nghị quyết của Bộ Chính Trị về văn học, nghệ thuật và văn hóa" ["Resolution of the Politburo about Literature, Arts, and Culture"], December 19, 1987. Accessed October 1, 2015. http://www.bvhttdl.gov.vn/vn/vb-qly-nn/4/592/index.html.

Pontifical Council for Justice and Peace. *Tóm lược học thuyết xã hội của Giáo Hội Công Giáo* [*Compendium of the Social Doctrine of the Church*]. Translated by Caritas Vietnam. Hà Nội: Tôn Giáo, 2007.

Pope Paul VI, "Message of His Holiness Pope Paul VI for the Celebration of the Day of Peace," January 1, 1972. Accessed November 18, 2015. http://w2.vatican.va/content/paul-vi/en/messages/peace/documents/hf_p-vi_mes_19711208_v-world-day-for-peace.html.

Prince, Derek. *Fasting*. 1986. New Kensington, PA: Whitaker House, 1993.

Prince, Derek. *Shaping History through Prayer and Fasting*. 1973. New Kensington, PA: Whitaker House, 2008.

Radio Free Asia. "Asia's Great Land Grab: A Special RFA Report," April 2015. Accessed April 30, 2015, http://www.rfa.org/english/news/special/landgrab/home.html.

Reagan, Wen. "Blessed to Be a Blessing: The Prosperity Gospel of Worship Music Superstar Israel Houghton." In *The Spirit of Praise: Music and Worship in Global Pentecostal-Charismatic Christianity*, edited by Monique M. Ingalls and Amos Yong, 215–29. University Park, PA: The Pennsylvania State University Press.

Reid, Robert G. "Spirit Empowerment as Resistance Discourse: An Imperial-Critical Reading of Acts 2." In *Trajectories in the Book of Acts: Essays in Honor of John Wesley Wyckoff*, edited by Paul Alexander, Jordan Daniel May, and Robert G. Reid, 21–45. Eugene, OR: Wipf & Stock, 2015.

Reimer, Reg. *Vietnam's Christians: A Century of Growth in Adversity*. Pasadena: William Carey Library, 2011.

Rist, Gilbert. *The History of Development: From Western Origins to Global Faith*. 4th edition. London and New York: Zed Books, 2014.

Robeck, Cecil M. Jr. *The Azusa Street Mission and Revival*. Nashville: Thomas Nelson, 2006.

Rodriguez, Darío López. *The Liberating Mission of Jesus: The Message of the Gospel of Luke*. Translated by Stefanie E. Israel and Richard E. Waldrop. Eugene, OR: Wipf & Stock, 2012.

Rodrik, Dani. *One Economics, Many Recipes: Globalization, Institutions, and Economic Growth*. Princeton: Princeton University Press, 2009.

Rumsby, Seb. "Vietnam Wrestles with Christianity: Why Hundreds of Thousands of Ethnic Hmong Have Converted to Christianity in Vietnam over the Past 30 Years." *The Diplomat*, November 13, 2017. Accessed November 22, 2017. https://thediplomat.com/2017/11/vietnam-wrestles-with-christianity/.

Said, Edward. *Culture and Imperialism*. New York: Vintage, 1994.

Said, Edward. *Đông phương luận* [*Orientalism*]. Translated by Lưu Đoàn Huynh, Phạm Xuân Ri, Trần Văn Tụy. Hà Nội: Tri Thức, 2014.

Said, Edward. *Orientalism*. New York: Vintage, 1979.

Said, Edward. *Power, Politics, and Culture*. New York: Vintage, 2002.

Said, Edward. *Representations of the Intellectual: The 1993 Reith Lectures*. New York: Pantheon, 1994.

Sakata, Shozo. "Rural Industries in Northern Vietnam: Strategies of Small-Scale Business Establishments in the Formation of Craft Villages." In *Vietnam's Economic Entities in Transition*, edited by Shozo Sakata, 204–26. New York: Palgrave Macmillan, 2013.

Salemink, Oscar. "Is Protestant Conversion a Form of Protest? Urban and Upland Protestants in Southeast Asia." In *Christianity and the State in Asia: Complicity and Conflict*, edited by Julius Bautista and Francis Khek Gee Lim, 36–58. New York: Routledge, 2009.

Satyavrata, Ivan. *Pentecostals and the Poor: Reflections from the Indian Context*. Baguio City, Philippines: Asia Pacific Theological Seminary Press, 2017.

Schirrmacher, Thomas, ed. "The Whole World." Special issue. *Evangelical Review of Theology* 34, no. 3 (2010).

Schlabach, Gerald. "Deuteronomic or Constantinian: What is the Most Basic Problem for Christian Social Ethics?" In *The Wisdom of the Cross: Essays in Honor of John*

Howard Yoder, edited by Stanley Hauerwas, Chris K. Huebner, Harry Huebner, and Mark Thiessen Nation, 449–71. Grand Rapids: Eerdmans, 1999.

Schlabach, Gerald. "The Christian Witness in the Earthly City: John H. Yoder as Augustinian Interlocutor." In *A Mind Patient and Untamed: Assessing John Howard Yoder's Contribution to Theology, Ethics, and Peacemaking*, edited by Ben C. Ollenburger and Gayle Gerber Koontz, 221–44. Telford, PA: Cascadia, 2004.

Schliesser, Christine. "On a Long Neglected Player: The Religious Factor in Poverty Alleviation." *Exchange (Online)* 43, no. 4 (2014): 339–59.

Scott, James C. *The Art of Not Being Governed: An Anarchist History of Upland Southeast Asia*. New Haven: Yale University Press, 2010.

Scott, James C. *Domination and the Arts of Resistance: Hidden Transcripts*. New Haven: Yale University Press, 1990.

Scott, James C. *Weapons of the Weak: Everyday Forms of Peasant Resistance*. New Haven: Yale University Press, 1985.

Scott, Peter, and William Cavanaugh, eds. *The Blackwell Companion to Political Theology*. Oxford: Blackwell, 2004.

Scott, Rachelle M. *Nirvana for Sale?: Buddhism, Wealth, and the Dhammakaya Temple in Contemporary Thailand*. New York: State University of New York Press, 2009.

Second Vatican Council. "Pastoral Constitution on the Church in the Modern World—*Gaudium et spes*," December 7, 1965. Vietnamese translation. Accessed October 25, 2015. https://www.catholic.org.tw/vntaiwan/vatican2/vatican2.htm, and http://www.simonhoadalat.com/HOCHOI/NamThanh/DucTin/47TongHopGiaoHuanVat2.htm.

Segundo, Juan Luis. *The Liberation of Theology*. Maryknoll, NY: Orbis, 1976.

Seligman, Martin E. P. *Flourish: A Visionary New Understanding of Happiness and Wellbeing*. New York: Free Press, 2011.

Sen, Amartya. *Development as Freedom*. New York: Oxford University Press, 1999.

Sen, Amartya. *The Idea of Justice*. 2009. Reprint, Cambridge: Harvard University Press, 2011.

Sen, Amartya. "Human Development Report 2010," November 2010. Accessed October 25, 2015. http://hdr.undp.org/en/content/human-development-report-2010.

Sen, Amartya. *Human Rights and Asian Values*. New York: Carnegie Council on Ethics and International Affairs, 1997.

Sidaway, James D. "Spaces of Postdevelopment." *Progress in Human Geography* 31, no. 3 (June 2007): 345–61.

Sider, J. Alexander. "Constantinianism before and after Nicea: Issues in Restitutionist Historiography." In *A Mind Patient and Untamed: Assessing John Howard Yoder's Contributions to Theology, Ethics, and Peacemaking*, edited by Ben C. Ollenburger and Gayle Gerber Koontz, 126–44. Telford, PA: Cascadia, 2004.

Sider, Ronald J. *Nonviolent Action: What Christian Ethics Demands but Most Christians Have Never Really Tried*. Grand Rapids: Brazos, 2015.

Simpson, A. B. *The Fourfold Gospel*. 1890. Reprint, Harrisburg, PA: Christian Publications, 1984.

Singhal, Saurabh, and Ulrik Beck. "Ethnic Disadvantage: Evidence Using Panel Data." In *Growth, Structural Transformation, and Rural Change in Viet Nam: A Rising Dragon on the Move*, edited by Finn Tarp, 256–75. New York: Oxford University Press, 2017.

Smith, Gordon H. (Mrs.). *Gongs in the Night: Reaching the Tribes of French Indo-China*. Grand Rapids: Zondervan, 1943.

Smith, James K. A. *Desiring the Kingdom: Worship, Worldview, and Cultural Formation*. Grand Rapids: Baker Academic, 2009.

Smith, James K. A. *Imagining the Kingdom: How Worship Works*. Grand Rapids: Baker Academic, 2013.

Smith, James K. A. *Thinking in Tongues: Pentecostal Contributions to Christian Philosophy*. Grand Rapids: Eerdmans, 2010.

Smith, James K. A. "Tongues as 'Resistance Discourse'—A Philosophical Perspective." In *Speaking in Tongues*, edited by Mark J. Cartledge, 81–110. Milton Keynes, UK: Paternoster, 2006.

Smith, Kay Higuera, Jayachitra Lalitha, and L. Daniel Hawk, eds. *Evangelical Postcolonial Conversations: Global Awakenings in Theology and Praxis*. Downers Grove, IL: IVP Academic, 2014.

Socio-Medical Committee, Evangelical Church of Vietnam (South). "Giới thiệu" ["About Us"]. Accessed October 25, 2015. http://httlvn.org/ubytxh/index.php?do=page&id=146.

Socio-Medical Committee, Evangelical Church of Vietnam (South). "Những quan điểm về công tác xã hội" ["Perspective on Social Work"]. Accessed October 25, 2015. http://somedco.blogspot.com.

"Soi tấm gương sáng" ["Following a Good Model"]. *Thánh Kinh Báo* [*Bible Magazine*], no. 1 (January 1931): 1–2.

Solivan, Samuel. *Spirit, Pathos and Liberation: Toward an Hispanic Pentecostal Theology*. Sheffield, UK: Sheffield Academic Press, 1998.

Song, C. S. *Theology from the Womb of Asia*. Maryknoll, NY: Orbis, 1986.

Song, Hong-xia. "Christ and Culture in Contemporary China: Exploring Theological Options." Ph.D. diss., Fuller Theological Seminary, 2011.

Spittler, Russell P. "Spirituality, Pentecostal and Charismatic." In *The New International Dictionary of Pentecostal and Charismatic Movements*, edited by Stanley M. Burgess and Eduard M. van der Maas, 1109–12. Revised and expanded edition. Grand Rapids: Zondervan, 2002.

Spivak, Gayatri Chakravorty. "Can the Subaltern Speak?" In *The Post-Colonial Studies Reader*, edited by Bill Ashcroft, Gareth Griffiths, and Helen Tiffin, 28–38. 2nd edition. New York: Routledge, 2006.

Stark, Rodney, and Xiuhua Wang. *A Star in the East: The Rise of Christianity in China*. West Conshohocken, PA: Templeton, 2015.

Stassen, Glen. "Concrete Christological Norms for Transformation." In *Authentic Transformation: A New Vision of Christ and Culture; with a Previously Unpublished Essay by H. Richard Niebuhr*, by Glen Stassen, D. M. Yeager, and John Howard Yoder, 127–90. Nashville: Abingdon, 1996.

Stassen, Glen. *Just Peacemaking: Transforming Initiatives for Justice and Peace*. Louisville: Westminster John Knox, 1992.

Stassen, Glen. *A Thicker Jesus*. Louisville: Westminster John Knox, 2012.

Stassen, Glen and David P. Gushee. *Kingdom Ethics: Following Jesus in Contemporary Context*. Downers Grove, IL: IVP Academic, 2003.

Stebbins, I. R. *41 năm hầu việc Chúa với Hội Thánh Tin Lành Việt Nam (1920–1961)* [*41 Years Serving God with the Evangelical Church of Vietnam (1920–1961)*]. Akron, OH: Spiritual Light Magazine, 2004.

Steinkamp, Orrel. *The Holy Spirit in Vietnam*. Carol Stream, IL: Creation House, 1973.

Stiglitz, Joseph. *Globalization and Its Discontents*. New York: Penguin Books, 2002.

Stout, Jeffrey. "The Spirit of Democracy and the Rhetoric of Excess." *Journal of Religious Ethics* 35, no. 1 (March 2007): 3–21.

Sugirtharajah, R. S. *The Bible and the Third World: Precolonial, Colonial and Postcolonial Encounters*. New York: Cambridge University Press, 2001.

Sugirtharajah, R. S. *Postcolonial Reconfigurations: An Alternative Way of Reading the Bible and Doing Theology*. St. Louis: Chalice, 2003.

Swoboda, Aaron J. "Posterity or Prosperity? Critiquing and Refiguring Prosperity Theologies in an Ecological Age." *Pneuma: The Journal of the Society for Pentecostal Studies* 37, no. 3 (January 1, 2015): 394–411.

Swoboda, Aaron J. *Tongues and Trees: Toward a Pentecostal Ecological Theology*. Blandford Forum, UK: Deo, 2014.

Sylvester, Christine. "Development Studies and Postcolonial Studies: Disparate Tales of the 'Third World.' " *Third World Quarterly* 20, no. 4 (1999): 703–21.

Synan, Vinson. *The Holiness-Pentecostal Tradition: Charismatic Movements in the Twentieth Century*. 2nd edition. Grand Rapids: Eerdmans, 1997.

Tai, Benny. "Public Theology, Justice and Law: A Preliminary Note." *Chinese Graduate School of Theology Journal* 54 (January 2013): 73–96.

Tai, Hue-Tam Ho. *Millenarianism and Peasant Politics in Vietnam*. Cambridge: Harvard University Press, 1983.

Tai, Hue-Tam Ho. *Radicalism and the Origins of the Vietnamese Revolution*. Cambridge: Harvard University Press, 1996.

Tai, Hue-Tam Ho, ed. *The Country of Memory: Remaking the Past in Late Socialist Vietnam*. Berkeley: University of California Press, 2001.

Tai, Hue-Tam Ho, and Mark Sidel, eds. *State, Society and the Market in Contemporary Vietnam: Property, Power and Values*. New York: Routledge, 2013.

Tang, Edmond. "'Yellers' and Healers: Pentecostalism and the Study of Grassroots Christianity in China." In *Asian and Pentecostal: The Charismatic Face of Christianity in Asia*, edited by Allan Anderson and Edmond Tang, 379–94. 2nd ed. Milton Keynes, UK: Regnum, 2011.

Tanner, Kathryn. "Theological Reflection and Christian Practices." In *Practicing Theology: Beliefs and Practices in Christian Life*, edited by Miroslav Volf and Dorothy C. Bass, 228–42. Grand Rapids: Eerdmans, 2002.

Tanner, Kathryn. *Theories of Culture: A New Agenda for Theology*. Minneapolis: Fortress, 1997.

Tarango, Angela. *Choosing the Jesus Way: American Indian Pentecostals and the Fight for the Indigenous Principle*. Chapel Hill, NC: The University of North Carolina Press, 2014.

Taylor, K. W. *A History of the Vietnamese*. Cambridge: Cambridge University Press, 2013.

Taylor, K. W. "Nguyễn Hoàng và bước mở đầu Nam tiến của người Việt" ["Nguyễn Hoàng and the Beginning of Viet Nam's Southward Expansion"]. In *Những vấn đề lịch sử Việt Nam* [*Vietnamese Historical Problems*], by Nhiều tác giả [Many authors], 161–84. HCMC: Trẻ, 2001.

Taylor, Philip. "Minorities at Large: New Approaches to Minority Ethnicity in Vietnam." *Journal of Vietnamese Studies* 3, no. 3 (October 1, 2008): 3–43.

Taylor, Philip. "Poor Policies, Wealthy Peasants: Alternative Trajectories of Rural Development in Vietnam." *Journal of Vietnamese Studies* 2, no. 2 (August 1, 2007): 3–56.

Taylor, Philip, ed. *Modernity and Re-Enchantment: Religion in Post-Revolutionary Vietnam*. Singapore: Institute of Southeast Asian Studies, 2007.

Thái, Phước Trường. *Hội Thánh Tin Lành Việt Nam: 100 năm hình thành và phát triển* [*The Evangelical Church of Vietnam: 100 Years of Forming and Development*]. HCMC: Hội Thánh Tin Lành Việt Nam Miền Nam, 2011.

The Theological Education Fund. *Ministry in Context: The Third Mandate Programme of the Theological Education Fund*. London: Theological Education Fund, World Council of Churches, 1972.

The Third Lausanne Congress. *The Cape Town Commitment: A Confession of Faith and a Call to Action*. Peabody, MA: Hendrickson, 2011.

Thế Uyên. *Nghĩ trong một xã hội tan rã* [*Reflection within a Disintegrated Society*]. Sài Gòn: Thái Độ, 1967.

Ting, K. H. *God is Love*. New edition. Colorado Springs: David C. Cook, 2004.

Tinker, George E. *American Indian Liberation: A Theology of Sovereignty*. Maryknoll, NY: Orbis, 2008.

Tong, Joy K. C. "Christian Ethics and Business Life: An Ethnographic Account of Overseas Chinese Christian Entrepreneurs in China's Economic Transition." In

Christianity in Contemporary China: Socio-Cultural Perspectives, edited by Francis Khek Gee Lim, 169–82. New York: Routledge, 2013.

Tong, Joy K. C., and Fenggang Yang. "The Femininity of Chinese Christianity: A Study of a Chinese Charismatic Church and Its Female Leadership." In *Global Chinese Pentecostal and Charismatic Christianity*, edited by Fenggang Yang, Joy K. C. Tong and Allan Anderson, 329–44. Leiden: Brill, 2017.

Tran, Jonathan. *The Vietnam War and Theologies of Memory: Time, Eternity, and Redemption in the Far Country*. Challenges in Contemporary Theology Series. Malden, MA: Wiley-Blackwell, 2010.

Tran, Thi Phuong Hoa. "Franco-Vietnamese Schools and the Transition from Confucian to a New Kind of Intellectual in the Colonial Context of Tonkin." Harvard-Yenching Institute Working Paper Series, 2009. Accessed August 15, 2015. http://www.harvard-yenching.org/sites/harvard-yenching.org/files/featurefiles/TRAN%20Thi%20Phuong%20Hoa_Franco%20Vietnamese%20schools2.pdf.

Tran, Van Doan. "Harmony as a Category of Asian Ethics and Theology." *Sino-Christian Studies* 7 (June 2009): 43–65.

Trần, Hữu Dũng. "Dân chủ và phát triển: Lý thuyết và chứng cớ" ["Democracy and Development: Theory and Evidence"]. *Thời Đại Mới* [*Vietnamese Review of Studies and Discussions*] 10, March 2007. Accessed October 25, 2015. http://www.tapchithoidai.org/ThoiDai10/200710_THDung.htm.

Trần, Ngọc Thêm. *Những vấn đề văn hóa học: Lý luận và ứng dụng* [*Issues in Cultural Studies: Theory and Application*]. HCMC: Văn Hóa Văn Nghệ, 2014.

Trần, Quốc Vượng. *Văn hóa Việt Nam: Tìm tòi và suy gẫm* [*Vietnamese Culture: Search and Reflection*]. Hà Nội: Văn Hóa Dân Tộc, 2000.

Trần, Thái Sơn. "Sau hai mươi năm" ["After Twenty Years"]. Unpublished manuscript, 1995.

Trần, Văn Giàu. *Giá trị tinh thần truyền thống của dân tộc Việt Nam* [*Traditional Values of the Vietnamese People*]. Hà Nội: Khoa Học Xã Hội, 1980.

Trịnh, Văn Thảo. *Ba thế hệ tri thức người Việt (1862–1954)* [*Three Generations of Vietnamese Intellectuals (1862–1954)*]. Hà Nội: Thế Giới, 2013.

Truitt, Allison. *Dreaming of Money in Ho Chi Minh City*. Critical Dialogues in Southeast Asian Studies. Seattle: University of Washington Press, 2013.

Truong, Buu Lam. *Colonialism Experienced: Vietnamese Writings on Colonialism, 1900–1931*. Ann Arbor: University of Michigan Press, 2000.

Truong, Tu. "Mệnh Trời: Toward a Vietnamese Theology of Mission." Ph.D. diss., Graduate Theological Union, 2009.

Tse, Justin K. H., and Jonathan Y. Tan, eds. *Theological Reflections on the Hong Kong Umbrella Movement*. Asian Christianity in the Diaspora. New York: Palgrave Macmillan, 2016.

Tùng Phong. *Chính đề Việt Nam* [*Main Issues of Vietnam*]. Sài Gòn: Đồng Nai, 1965.

Tường Vi. "7 năm truyền Tin Lành và hoạt động xã hội trên toàn cõi Việt Nam" ["Seven Years of Evangelism and Social Action in Vietnam"]. *Thánh Kinh Báo [Bible Magazine]* no. 391 (December 1971): I–VIII.

Turner, Sarah, Christine Bonnin, and Jean Michaud. *Frontier Livelihoods: Hmong in the Sino-Vietnamese Borderlands*. Seattle: University of Washington Press, 2015.

United Nations World Commission on Environment and Development. *Our Common Future (Brundtland Report)*. Oxford: Oxford University Press, 1987.

Van De Walle, Bernie. *The Heart of the Gospel: A. B. Simpson, the Fourfold Gospel, and Late Nineteenth-Century Evangelical Theology*. Eugene, OR: Pickwick, 2009.

Vassal, Gabrielle M. *Ba năm ở An Nam [Three Years in Annam]*. Translated into Vietnamese by Nguyễn Nam Huân. 1910. HCMC: Hội Nhà Văn, 2015.

Văn Tạo, and Furuta Moto. *Nạn đói năm 1945 ở Việt Nam: Những chứng tích lịch sử [The 1945 Famine in Vietnam: Historical Evidences]*. Hà Nội: Tri Thức, 2011.

Ver Beek, Kurt Alan. "The Impact of Short-Term Missions: A Case Study of House Construction in Honduras after Hurricane Mitch." *Missiology* 34, no. 4 (October 2006): 477–95.

Ver Beek, Kurt Alan. "Lessons from the Sapling: Review of Quantitative Research on Short-Term Missions." In *Effective Engagement in Short-Term Missions: Doing It Right!,* edited by Robert J. Priest, 474–502. Pasadena: William Carey Library, 2008.

Villafañe, Eldin. *The Liberating Spirit: Toward an Hispanic American Pentecostal Social Ethic*. Grand Rapids: Eerdmans, 1993.

Vĩnh, Sính, ed. *Phan Châu Trinh and His Political Writings*. Ithaca, NY: Cornell University Press, 2009.

von Sinner, Rudolf. "Pentecostalism and Citizenship in Brazil: Between Escapism and Dominance." *International Journal of Public Theology* 6, no. 1 (2012): 99–117.

Vondey, Wolfgang. *Pentecostalism: A Guide for the Perplexed*. New York: T&T Clark, 2013.

Võ, Hữu Đức. "Lược sử Hội Thánh Tin Lành Việt Nam (1975–1991)" ["A Brief History of the Evangelical Church of Vietnam (1975–1991)"]. Unpublished manuscript, 1991.

Vu, Tuong. "The Party v. the People." *Journal of Vietnamese Studies* 9, no. 4 (December 1, 2014): 33–66.

Vu, Tuong. *Paths to Development in Asia: South Korea, Vietnam, China, and Indonesia*. Cambridge: Cambridge University Press, 2010.

Vu, Tuong. " 'To Be Patriotic is to Build Socialism': Communist Ideology in Vietnam's Civil War." In *Dynamics of the Cold War in Asia: Ideology, Identity, and Culture*, edited by Tuong Vu and Wasana Wongsurawat, 33–52. New York: Palgrave, 2009.

Vũ, Khiêu. *Người tri thức Việt Nam qua các chặng đường lịch sử [The Vietnamese Intellectuals in History]*. HCMC: HCMC Publishing House, 1987.

Vũ, Hữu Ngoạn. "Giải quyết tốt mối quan hệ giữa đổi mới, ổn định và phát triển" ["Solving Well the Relationship of Reform, Sustainability, and Development"]. *Tạp Chí Cộng Sản [Journal of Communism]* 826 (August 2011): 47–50.

Vũ, Thị Thu Hà. "Lực lượng truyền giáo của đạo Tin Lành ở Trung Quốc trước Cách Mạng Văn Hóa" ["Evangelist Manpower of Evangelicalism in China before the Chinese Cultural Revolution"]. *Tạp Chí Nghiên Cứu Tôn Giáo* [*Journal of Religious Studies*], no. 5 (2012): 55–62; no. 6 (2012): 58–71.

Vũ, Thị Thu Hà. "Những đóng góp của đạo Tin Lành trong qua trình truyền giáo vào Trung quốc cuối thế kỉ XIX đầu thế kỉ XX" ["The (Social) Contribution of Protestantism During Its Coming to China in the Late Nineteenth Century and the Early Twentieth Century"]. *Tạp Chí Nghiên Cứu Tôn Giáo* [*Journal of Religious Studies*], no. 6 (2009): 47–55; no. 7–8 (2009): 95–102.

Vũ, Văn Hà. "Kết hợp hài hòa chính sách kinh tế với chính sách xã hội" ["Harmonious Integration of Economic Policy with Social Policy"]. *Tạp chí Cộng Sản* [*Journal of Communism*] 861 (July 2014): 70–75.

Vương, Thị Kim Oanh. "Các yếu tố tâm lý—xã hội ảnh hưởng tới sự phục hồi và phát triển đạo Tin Lành tại tỉnh Kon Tum trong giai đoạn hiện nay" ["Social-Psychological Factors that Influence the Resurgence and Development of Evangelicalism in Kon Tum Province in the Present Time"]. *Tạp Chí Tâm Lý Học* [*Journal of Psychology*], no. 3 (2001): 60–62.

Vuving, Alexander L. "Vietnam in 2012: A Rent-Seeking State on the Verge of a Crisis." In *Southeast Asian Affairs 2013*, edited by Daljit Singh, 325–47. Singapore: Institute of Southeast Asian Studies, 2013.

Wacker, Grant. *Heaven Below: Early Pentecostals and American Culture*. Cambridge: Harvard University Press, 2001.

Wagner, C. Peter. *Dominion!: How Kingdom Action Can Change the World*. Grand Rapids: Chosen Books, 2008.

Wang, Ming-dao. *A Stone Made Smooth*. Southampton, UK: OMF Books, 1982.

Wang, Stephen. *The Long Road to Freedom: The Story of Wang Mingdao*. Translated by Ma Min. Kent, TN: Sovereign World, 2002.

Ward, Graham. *Cultural Transformation and Religious Practice*. Cambridge: Cambridge University Press, 2005.

Ward, Graham. *Unbelievable: Why We Believe and Why We Don't*. London: I. B. Tauris, 2014.

Wariboko, Nimi. *Economics in Spirit and Truth: A Moral Philosophy of Finance*. New York: Palgrave, 2014.

Wariboko, Nimi. *The Pentecostal Principle: Ethical Methodology in New Spirit*. The Pentecostal Manifestos Series. Grand Rapids: Eerdmans, 2011.

Watts, Fraser. "Psychology and Theology." In *The Cambridge Companion to Science and Religion*, edited by Peter Harrison, 190–206. New York: Cambridge University Press, 2010.

Weaver, Alain Epp. *Mapping Exile and Return: Palestinian Dispossession and a Political Theology for a Shared Future*. Minneapolis: Fortress, 2014.

Weaver, Alain Epp. *States of Exile: Visions of Diaspora, Witness, and Return*. Scottdale, PA: Herald Press, 2008.

Wells-Dang, Andrew. *Civil Society Networks in China and Vietnam: Informal Pathbreakers in Health and the Environment*. New York: Palgrave Macmillan, 2012.

Werner, Jayne S. *Peasant Politics and Religious Sectarianism: Peasant and Priest in the Cao Dai in Viet Nam*. New Haven: Yale University Press, 1981.

Whitehead, Raymond L., ed. *No Longer Strangers: Selected Writings of Bishop K. H. Ting*. Maryknoll, NY: Orbis, 1989.

Wickeri, Janice, ed. *Love Never Ends: Papers by K. H. Ting*. Nanjing: Nanjing Amity, 2000.

Wickeri, Philip L. *Reconstructing Christianity in China: K. H. Ting and the Chinese Church*. Maryknoll, NY: Orbis, 2007.

Wickeri, Philip L., and Janice Wickeri, eds. *A Chinese Contribution to Ecumenical Theology: Selected Writings of Bishop K. H. Ting*. Geneva: WCC Publications, 2002.

Wielander, Gerda. *Christian Values in Communist China*. New York: Routledge, 2015.

Wilcox, Wynn. *Allegories of the Vietnamese Past: Unification and the Production of a Modern Historical Identity*. New Haven: Yale University Press, 2011.

Wolterstorff, Nicholas. *Justice: Rights and Wrongs*. Princeton: Princeton University Press, 2008.

Womack, Brantly. *China among Unequals: Asymmetric Foreign Relations in Asia*. Singapore: World Scientific, 2010.

Womack, Brantly. *China and Vietnam: The Politics of Asymmetry*. New York: Cambridge University Press, 2006.

Woodhead, Linda. “Feminism and the Sociology of Religion: From Gender-blindness to Gendered Difference.” In *The Blackwell Companion to Sociology of Religion*, edited by Richard K. Fenn, 67–84. Malden, MA: Blackwell, 2001.

Woodside, Alexander. *Lost Modernities: China, Vietnam, Korea, and the Hazards of World History*. Cambridge: Harvard University Press, 2006.

World Bank. “mapVIETNAM.” Accessed April 4, 2017. http://www.worldbank.org/mapvietnam/.

Yang, Huilin. *China, Christianity, and the Question of Culture*. Translated by Zhang Jing. Waco, TX: Baylor University Press, 2014.

Yang, Huilin. “ ‘Ethicized’ Chinese-Language Christianity and the Meaning of Christianity.” *Contemporary Chinese Thought* 35, no. 4 (2004): 68–84.

Yang, Huilin, and Daniel H. N. Yeung, eds. *Sino-Christian Studies in China*. Cambridge: Cambridge Scholars Publishing, 2006.

Yoder, John Howard. *Body Politics: Five Practices of the Christian Community before the Watching World*. 1992. Reprint, Scottdale, PA: Herald Press, 2001.

Yoder, John Howard. *For the Nations: Essays Evangelical and Public*. Grand Rapids: Eerdmans, 1997.

Yoder, John Howard. "How H. Richard Niebuhr Reasoned: A Critique of Christ and Culture." In *Authentic Transformation: A New Vision of Christ and Culture; with a Previously Unpublished Essay by H. Richard Niebuhr*, by Glen Stassen, D. M. Yeager, and John Howard Yoder, 31–89. Nashville: Abingdon, 1996.

Yoder, John Howard. *The Politics of Jesus: Vicit Agnus Noster*. 2nd edition. Grand Rapids: Eerdmans, 1994.

Yoder, John Howard. *The Priestly Kingdom: Social Ethics as Gospel*. Notre Dame: University of Notre Dame Press, 1985.

Yong, Amos. *In the Days of Caesar: Pentecostalism and Political Theology*. Sacra Doctrina: Christian Theology for a Postmodern Age Series. Grand Rapids: Eerdmans, 2010.

Yong, Amos. *Spirit-Word-Community: Theological Hermeneutics in Trinitarian Perspective*. Burlington, VT: Ashgate, 2002.

Yong, Amos. *Spirit of Love: A Trinitarian Theology of Grace*. Waco, TX: Baylor University Press, 2012.

Yong, Amos. *The Spirit of Creation: Modern Science and Divine Action in the Pentecostal-Charismatic Imagination*. Grand Rapids: Eerdmans, 2011.

Yong, Amos. *The Spirit Poured Out on All Flesh: Pentecostalism and the Possibility of Global Theology*. Grand Rapids: Baker Academic, 2005.

Young San Theological Institute, ed. *Dr. Yonggi Cho's Ministry & Theology: A Commemorative Collection for the 50th Anniversary of Dr. Yonggi Cho's Ministry*. 2 vols. Seoul: Hansei University Logos, 2008.

Yunus, Muhammad. *Banker to the Poor: Micro-Lending and the Battle against World Poverty*. New York: PublicAffairs, 2007.

Zhang, Shaoying, and Derek McGhee. *China's Ethical Revolution and Regaining Legitimacy: Politics and Development of Contemporary China*. New York: Palgrave Macmillan, 2017.

Ziebertz, Hans-Georg, and Friedrich Schweitzer, eds. *Dreaming the Land: Theologies of Resistance and Hope*. International Practical Theology. Berlin: Lit-Verlag, 2007.

Zimmerman, Joyce Ann. "Fasting as Feasting." *Liturgical Ministry* 19, no. 2 (2010): 72–77.

Zink, Eren. *Hot Science, High Water Assembling Nature, Society and Environmental Policy in Contemporary Vietnam*. Copenhagen: Nordic Institute of Asian Studies Press, 2013.

Index

Printed in the United States
By Bookmasters